# THE RACING MAN'S BEDSIDE BOOK

## Classic Racing Stories

# THE RACING MAN'S BEDSIDE BOOK

## Classic Racing Stories

Compiled by
Julian Bedford

First published by Colt Books in 1997

This edition published in 2001
by Raceform Ltd,
Compton, Newbury, Berkshire, RG20 6NL

Selection and linking passages copyright © Julian Bedford 1997, 2001
Volume copyright © Colt Books Ltd 1997, 2001

The Acknowledgements on pages 222 and 223 constitute an extension of this
copyright page

ISBN 1-901100-78-2

British Library Cataloguing-in-Publication Data
A catalogue record for this book is available from the British Library

Printed and bound in Great Britain
by Omnia, Glasgow


Cover picture
'The Life of a Thoroughbred'
by John Alfred Wheeler (1821-1877)
© National Horseracing Museum

# CONTENTS

# INTRODUCTION

The racing of horses is the oldest of sports, its reportage only a little younger. To choose from more than twenty centuries of prose and verse in which man has hymned horse is an invidious task. But like the sport itself, it is so much fun. The pleasure is in no way lessened by the knowledge that only a fraction can be included or that others have been this way before. 'Other men's flowers' was the title Arthur Waverley bestowed on his collection of Chinese verse and all anthologies are indeed that: a walk through the garden of literature, snipping a bloom here and cutting some greenery there. There are favourites that reappear in most of these flower arrangements but the art, if there is one, is presenting the old afresh.

Many readers will have enjoyed the bumptious amateurism of Siegfried Sassoon's captain but in placing him next to Dick Francis's determined pro, hopefully I can provoke some reflection on how the sport has changed; or stayed the same, if one believes Sir John Astley's advice on gambling to hold good over a century after it was written. How much has changed in Newmarket since the days of Duke Cosmo, John Macky and Daniel Defoe? Are racecourse crowds of Dio Chrysostom much altered from those of David Ashforth? And the perennial questions, who was the best? The best horse, jockey, or trainer.

I have not sought to answer these questions but laid out others' thoughts in six fillets, one for each section of the racing community and one for the stage on which it is all enacted. I make little apology for drawing on the pens of Jeffrey Bernard and Damon Runyon on several occasions – both write charmingly – or for reprinting Ernest Hemingway's classic short story My Old Man.

Of the lesser known selections, I urge the racing man to read Nana, not just the racing extract reproduced here – one of the best all-round descriptions of a day's racing I have come across, but one too long to be printed in full – but the whole book, a wonderfully seedy tale of the demi monde in nineteenth-century Paris. With luck other extracts will also take the racing man's fancy and send him to sleep, dreaming of winners past and winners yet to come.

Julian Bedford, 1997

For
my godson Xavi, my most devoted reader,
and my long-suffering parents

# HORSES

'The credit of a racehorse, a gambler and a
whore lasteth but a short time.'
*Torriano*

*In the beginning was the horse*

Aleppo
Ye 21st December, 1703

DEAR Brother,
Your obliging favour of the 7 Aprill came to my hands the
16th October, by our convoy, and by whom I assygne these,
with hope will have better success in arriving safe than the
many letters wrote   you, besydes I have never been favoured
with any letters from you but that I immediately answered ye
first conveyance that succeeded after receipt thereof, being very
desirous of maintaining a punctuall correspondence, for nothing is more gratefull to me than to hear the welfare of my Rela-
tions and friends, and more particularly your good Self. I take
no notice what discourse you have had with my Father, and its
very true he has ordered my returning, wch I should gladly
obey would my affaires permit, therefore hope he will be
pleased to excuse my delay untill a more propper season, for I
assure I am not in Love with this place to stay an hour longer
than is absolutely necessary.

Since my Father expects I should send him a stallion, I esteem
myself happy in a colt I bought about a year and a half agoe, with
a desygne indeed to send him ye first good opportunity. He comes
four the latter end of March or the beginning of Aprill next; his

colour is Bay, and his near foot before with both his hind feet have white upon them, he has a blaze downe his face, something of the largest. He is about 15 hands high, of the most esteemed race among the Arabs, both by Syre and Dam, and the name of the said race is called Mannicka.

The only fear I have about him at present is that I shall not be able to get him aboard this war time, though I have the promise of a very good and intimate friend, the Honble and Revnd Henry Bridges, son of Lord Chandoes, who embarks in the Ipswich. Captain William Waklin, who presume will not refuse taking in a horse for him since his brother is one of ye Lords of ye Admiralty; besides I desygne to go to Scandn to assist in getting him off. Wch, if I call accomplish, and he arrives in safety, I believe he will not be disliked, for he is esteemed here, where I could have sold him at considerable price if I had not desygned him for England.

I have desired Bridges to deliver him to my brother John or Cozen Charles, who he can find first, and they are to follow my Father's orders in sending him into ye country. For ye ffreight and all charges to his landing I will order payment of, though am not certain wht it may amount to. Am told by a friend, who sent home a horse last year, it cost him inclusive 100£ Stg. When you see Coz Peirson, pray tender him my humble salutes, and since his Daughter is ready, I shall endeavour, with all speed, to prepare myself. ... I have given my friend, Mr Bridges, 2 chequuens to drink with you (in case you are in towne), and Brother John and Coz Charles, which I wd call to mind is a present worth yr notice.

I heartily wish you health and prosperity (and as the season invites) a merry Xmas with many succeeding.

I respectfully remain, dear brother,

Your most affec Brother,
THOMAS DARLEY.

*Darley's stallion completed the journey to stand at the family's Aldby Park stud for over twenty years, mingling his hot-blooded genes with the native English stock. The result: the thoroughbred, a horse bred for speed and strength. The Darley Arabian, as the stallion has come to be known, is the forefather of most of today's racehorses. One tail-male descendant was St Paddy, whose 1960 season is next assessed by Timeform.*

# St Paddy

THE JOURNALIST whose duty is to pass judgement on the status of a new arrival in his field of criticism is bedevilled by contradictory motives: the tendency, common at some time to all of us, to denigrate the present breed, and sigh for the past; and the need to exaggerate merit, even in unsuspected places, on the principle that the bigger the celebrity, the better the news value. These factors make comparison between past and present difficult enough, without detailed research into the conditions under which former giants revealed their prowess, and the result is that attempts in this direction are usually shrugged off with the observation that comparisons are invidious, if not odious. Yet, since the quality of greatness knows no absolutes, comparisons of this kind are essential in any serious estimate of an individual's real merit.

Commentators on horse-racing are fortunate in this respect. Not only do men have far more facets to their character than horses, but there is a wealth of information available about the history and performances of racehorses since the sport began. The bare result of a race may not tell the whole story, but it is frequently more reliable than an event seen through the subjective eye of some long-dead critic. With human beings the problem is much more difficult. Which was the better batsman, Trumper or Bradman? There are many other factors to be taken into consideration, besides the obvious ones of the number of runs each scored, the strength of the bowling opposed to them, and the difficulty or ease of the wickets on which they performed. No final answer to the question is possible, since these were batsmen of completely different style, function and temperament. The same applies to any comparison between Irving and Gielgud, or Bernhardt and Duse. Any actor who possessed in combination the salient qualities of Gielgud, Olivier, Guinness and Richardson might be a candidate for absolute greatness, but fortunately for the critics, perfection to this degree is unattainable.

Statesmen on the other hand can at least be judged by their policies, their motives and their failings, and it seems true to say that politically we live nowadays in the shallows, and only on occasion scale the rare heights of the mediocre. It is not of course a new thing for political life to become the breeding-ground of incompetence and platitudinising, and it is true that in other fields of human endeavour there are lean years and good. In politics the lean appear to last longer. To return to racing, we are told year after year that our current crop of two-year-olds is a poor lot, yet year after year they maintain much the same general level of merit. It is in particular cases that differences are apparent, and there may for instance be a vast gulf in ability between the best Derby winner and the worst, but it is unwise, without scrupulous examination of all the evidence, to conclude that this year's is necessarily worse than last.

This digression is occasioned by the nature of the publicity accorded to St Paddy since his Derby victory. First a victim of downright disparagement, he became the subject of exaggerated plaudits after his performance in a St Leger hardly worth the name of classic race. Neither of these reactions, general though they were, was fair to St Paddy. In extenuation it may be said that no horse that ran in the Derby managed to win a race subsequently, until St Paddy himself beat Apostle in the Great Voltigeur Stakes in August, and before that race St Paddy had failed at Goodwood. On the other hand evidence was available, particularly after the King George VI and Queen Elizabeth Stakes running of Kythnos, to establish the merit of St Paddy's Derby performance. It is also true that St Paddy was a most impressive winner of the St Leger, but to win that race with some ease did not even require a horse up to average classic-winning standard, let alone a world-beater. St Paddy's status must stand or fall by his performance in the Derby, and to some extent perhaps by his victory over Apostle in the Great Voltigeur Stakes. On a line through the running of Kythnos in the Derby and the King George VI and Queen Elizabeth Stakes, St Paddy does not after all compare unfavourably with Aggressor, who, when all is said, humbled the invincible Petite Etoile.

St Paddy's two-year-old career had made it plain that he was handled from the outset with the classics in view. He had only two outings, and the first merely provided him with experience, but he was a most impressive winner of the Royal Lodge Stakes. Convincing as this victory was, it did not provide proof that St Paddy was right up to top classic standard, and no such proof was forthcoming before the Two Thousand Guineas, since the opportunity of running him in the Column Produce Stakes at the Newmarket Craven meeting was declined. So as it had been for Crepello, the Guineas was St Paddy's first race of the season, and what doubts there were about him as a Guineas prospect were the same as those that had applied to Crepello, who had won the Two Thousand despite the too short trip and despite the firmish ground. St Paddy's chance of doing the same was sufficiently recognised for him to start second favourite. His performance in the race was disappointing, but it must not be overlooked that his training had probably been designed with the Derby as his main objective. Racing over on the far side, just behind the leading group, he made a forward move two furlongs out, but lacked the pace to deal with speedy horses like Martial and Venture VII over a mile on firm going. When it was evident that he was not going to be placed, he was not pressed, and finished sixth, some six lengths behind the winner.

Three weeks later St Paddy looked a different horse in the Dante Stakes at York. At no part of the race did it seem likely that he would be beaten. Settling in third place early on, and always travelling freely and well, he drew up into second place over three furlongs out, pulling over everything, with his jockey looking round for potential danger. Shortly afterwards St Paddy went up on the bit to beat the leader, without having to be let down, and he won easing up, by three lengths. St Paddy's performance was impressive, even taking into account that second and third were the relatively unfit Ancient Lights and the green and inexperienced Balaji. There were some useful horses behind, and they were beaten a long way too. One cause for slight alarm did present itself at York. St Paddy wore a Kineton noseband to help steady him on the way down, though this was dispensed with, by permission of the stewards, in the race itself. St Paddy had previously shown that he was inclined to race a bit too freely, and although he had been perfectly tractable in the Dante Stakes, the possibility could not be ignored that he might run himself out in the Derby. In other respects St Paddy seemed a very live Derby prospect, and emphatically the best of the runners trained in England.

The betting on the race confirmed that this was the general opinion. Favourite was a French horse, Angers, and second favourite an Irish colt, Die Hard. St Paddy was one of the joint third favourites, the other two being Irish. Never had Ireland held so strong a hand at Epsom. How far the result of the race was affected by the tragic accident to the favourite, Angers, will never be known, but St Paddy put up a smooth and convincing performance. He was sweating a little in the parade-ring, but looked extremely well, and moved beautifully on the way to the post, though he was keen, and had to be held under strong restraint. For most of the way to the top of the hill Tudor Period and Die Hard disputed the lead, with St Paddy just behind them. Coming to Tattenham Corner the front line was made up of Die Hard, Auroy and Tulyartos, with Kythnos, Marengo and St Paddy right on their heels. As soon as they turned into the straight, it was evident that, barring accidents, St Paddy was going to win. Die Hard was first round the corner, but shortly afterwards Tulyartos began to drop out, and Kythnos and St Paddy moved up closer. Die Hard was passed by Auroy, but the latter had no answer when St Paddy was sent about his business two furlongs out. St Paddy went ahead below the distance, and quickly drew clear to win decisively, his rider having only to keep him going with hands and heels. The winning margin over Alcaeus, who had been badly interfered with coming down the hill, was three lengths, and Kythnos was a further half-length behind in third place.

Clear-cut as was St Paddy's victory, it did not satisfy the critics for long. Before Goodwood Auroy, fourth in the Derby, could not reach the first six in the King Edward VII Stakes, won by Atrax; Alcaeus was decisively beaten by Chamour in the Irish Derby, and Proud Chieftain, fifth at Epsom, finished eighth of the nine runners for the Eclipse Stakes. When on top of all these reverses St Paddy himself was beaten in the Gordon Stakes at Goodwood, the most that anyone could find to say for him was that he was the best of a very bad lot of three-year-olds. There was, however, good reason for his failure. He had to be let right down after jarring himself at Epsom, and when he was being gradually brought back with routine work, he was again held up, this time completely, by coughing. It was not much more than a fortnight before the Gordon Stakes that he was able to resume work at all. In the race St Paddy settled down third of the eight runners, and drew to the front on the bit two furlongs out. At that point, with High Hat shut in behind Proud Chieftain, it looked as if St Paddy was going to trot up. Not until Kipling, who was receiving 5 lb, ranged into view did St Paddy's rider move on him. When St Paddy was shaken up, he ran on, but was unable to hold off his challenger, who won by a neck. With both eyes firmly fixed on the St Leger, it would have been folly in the circumstances for St Paddy's jockey to give his mount a severe race.

The opinion, by now generally voiced, that St Paddy was a Derby winner below average, did not prevent his starting at very short odds to beat Apostle in the Great Voltigeur Stakes at York. In the parade-ring St Paddy looked particularly hard and fit. Every muscle stood out, and he could not have been turned out in better trim. St Paddy put up a completely satisfactory performance. After settling down a couple of lengths behind Oak Ridge, he fell a little further behind, when the latter kicked on just before turning into the straight. Once in line for home St Paddy soon overhauled Oak Ridge, and went to the front, still racing on the bit, about three furlongs out. Apostle, who had been tracking St Paddy all the way, followed him, and when pulled to the leader's outside, gradually drew up on him, until at the distance there was nothing between the two horses. Apostle seemed to be going quite as well as St Paddy, and it looked as though he might win, but when his jockey got down to brass tacks, and really set about riding him, St Paddy produced the necessary extra, and gradually drew away in the last furlong to win by three-quarters of a length. It is to be doubted whether in any circumstances St Paddy could have beaten Apostle by more than a couple of lengths, but Apostle is a good horse, and St Paddy's performance at York confirmed that he had the ability to win the St Leger. In view of the composition of the field for the last classic, confirmation hardly seemed necessary.

If there was any doubt at all about St Paddy's taking the St Leger, once Alcaeus was withdrawn from the race, it could only be on the grounds of his stamina, or lack of it. Admittedly his dam won only over five furlongs, and his sire's stamina failed him in the St Leger, but that was probably because he was a headstrong customer, who refused to settle down. On the other hand St Paddy had proved that he stayed a mile and a half really well, and there was enough stamina in his pedigree to encourage the belief that another couple of furlongs or so would not be beyond him, particularly since he had learned to race less freely than he did earlier in the season. In view of the speculation about St Paddy's stamina, the news that he was to be provided with a pacemaker at Doncaster was received with considerable interest. But his connections knew what they were about, even if the riders of those St Leger runners endowed more with stamina than with speed did not. It was never intended that the pace should be fast, and Off Key was allowed to do an admirable job of dictating a very easy gallop for St Paddy. For the first half-mile Off Key fought for his head, but Spartan Green still ran obediently at his quarters, with St Paddy racing easily in third place on his stable-companion's heels. Three furlongs out St Paddy drew to the front, and still on the bit, soon went ahead. At the distance, with his rider looking round for danger, he raced clear in style, and was eased off near the post, or would have won by five lengths instead of the three that separated him and Die Hard.

|  |  | Hyperion | Gainsborough |
|  | Aureole | (ch 1930) | Selene |
|  | (ch 1950) | Angelola | Donatello II |
| St Paddy |  | (b 1945) | Feola |
| (b.c. 1957) |  | Bois Roussel | Vatout |
|  | Edie Kelly | (br 1935) | Plucky Liege |
|  | (br 1950) | Caerlissa | Caerleon |
|  |  | (b 1935) | Sister Sarah |

Before the Derby there were critics who discounted St Paddy's prospects on the grounds that his relatives on the dam's side were a long way removed from classic quality. It is true that the best his dam could do in nine races as a three-year-old was to win a £100 apprentice race, and that her two foals before St Paddy were the selling handicapper Ben Beoch, and a mean, sweaty, jady filly, Fighting Edie, who failed to win a race in two seasons. So St Paddy can hardly brag about his family connections. But even before the Derby he had shown emphatically that he was a good racehorse, and once a horse has proved himself on the racecourse, it is nonsense to take much notice of his tail-female line in assessing his chance in a classic. It is legitimate to attach importance to this sort of thing, when speculating whether a horse is likely to be a high-class performer, but once the proof is there, a horse's prospects in a particular race must be assessed entirely upon his racecourse performances, and not upon his ancestry, except of course that one may be compelled, in the absence of racecourse evidence, to fall back on a pedigree for an estimate of stamina.

St Paddy is a handsome, powerful individual, and a strong resolute galloper, with a fine, fluent action. He has learned to settle down remarkably well, and it is a tribute to his trainer and his jockey that a horse who might well have been headstrong should have been so transformed into one of sober temperament. It has been frequently asserted that St Paddy is no Crepello. In one respect at least he is the latter's superior. But for one setback in midsummer he has remained sound throughout his three-year-old season, and there seems no reason why he should not continue to do so. He has not had a strenuous career, he has proved himself well up to average classic standard, and there is every likelihood that he will develop into a really top-class four-year-old. His programme for 1961 is said to include the Ormonde Stakes at Chester, the Coronation Cup and the King George VI and Queen Elizabeth Stakes. St Paddy, who incidentally is his owner's fourth Derby winner in seven years, has never raced on soft going, but judging by his action, he should not be put to any serious inconvenience when he does.

RACEHORSES OF 1960, *Timeform Annual*

*A characteristically perceptive essay out of Halifax where, for over fifty years, the organisation founded by the late Phil Bull has been running the rule on the season's racecourse performances. Its collected wisdom, Racehorses of the Year, has mixed the chronometer and the muse to engaging and profitable effect. How Bull would have assessed Brien Boru is anyone's guess.*

# *The Kellys and the O'Kellys*

THE PEOPLE about the stables always made a great fuss with Lord Ballindine, partly because he was one of the stewards, and partly because he was going to run a crack horse for the

Derby in England; and though, generally speaking, he did not care much for personal complimentary respect, he usually got chattered and flattered into good humour at Igoe's.

'Well, my lord,' said a sort of foreman, or partner, or managing man, who usually presided over the yard, 'I think we'll be apt to get justice to Ireland on the downs this year. That is, they'll give us nothing but what we takes from 'em by hard fighting, or running, as the case may be.'

'How's Brien looking this morning, Grady?'

'As fresh as a primrose, my lord, and as clear as crystal: he's ready, this moment, to run through any set of three-year-olds as could be put on the Curragh, anyway.'

'I'm afraid you're putting him on too forward.'

'Too forrard, is it, my lord? Not a bit. He's a hoss as naturally don't pick up flesh; though he feeds free, too. He's this moment all wind and bottom, though, as one may say, he's got no training. He's niver been sthretched yet. Faith it's thrue I'm telling you, my lord.'

'I know Scott doesn't like getting horses, early in the season, that are too fine – too much drawn up; he thinks they lose power by it, and so they do; it's the distance that kills them, at the Derby. It's so hard to get a young horse to stay the distance.'

'That's thrue, shure enough, my lord; and there isn't a gentleman this side the wather, anyway, undherstands thim things betther than your lordship.'

'Well, Grady, let's have a look at the young chieftain: he's all right about the lungs, anyway.'

'And feet too, my lord; niver saw a set of claner feet with plates on: and legs too! If you were to canter him down the road, I don't think he'd feel it; not that I'd like to thry, though.'

'Why, he's not yet had much to try them.'

'Faix, he has, my lord: didn't he win the Autumn Produce Stakes?'

'The only thing he ever ran for.'

'Ah, but I tell you, as your lordship knows very well – no one betther – that it's a ticklish thing to bring a two-year-old to the post, in anything like condition – with any running in him at all, and not hurt his legs.'

'But I think he's all right – eh, Grady?'

'Right? – your lordship knows he's right. I wish he may be made righter at John Scott's, that's all. But that's unpossible.'

'Of course, Grady, you think he might be trained here, as well as at the other side of the water?'

'No, I don't, my lord: quite different. I've none of thim ideas at all, and never had, thank God. I knows what we can do, and I knows what they can do: breed a hoss in Ireland, train him in the North of England, and run him in the South; and he'll do your work for you, and win your money, steady and shure.'

'And why not run in the North, too?'

'They're too 'cute, my lord: they like to pick up the crumbs themselves – small blame to thim in that matther. No; a bright Irish nag, with lots of heart, like Brien Boru, is the hoss to stand on for the Derby; where all run fair and fair alike, the best wins; but I won't say but he'll be the bethter for a little polishing at Johnny Scott's.'

'Besides, Grady, no horse could run immediately after a sea voyage. Do you remember what a show we made of Peter Simple at Kilrue?'

'To be shure I does, my lord: besides, they've proper gallops there, which we haven't – and they've bethter manes of measuring horses: why, they can measure a horse to half a pound, and tell his rale pace on a two-mile course, to a couple of seconds. Take the sheets off, Larry, and let his lordship run his hand over him. He's as bright as a star, isn't he?'

'I think you're betting him too fine. I'm sure Scott'll say so.'

'Don't mind him, my lord. He's not like one of those English cats, with jist a dash of speed about 'em, and nothing more – brutes that they put in training half a dozen times in as many months. Thim animals pick up a lot of loose, flabby flesh in no time, and loses it in less; and, in course, av' they gets a sweat too much, there's nothin left in 'em; not a hapoth. Brien's a different guess sort of animal from that.'

'Were you going to have him out, Grady?'

'Why, we was not – that is, only just for walking exercise, with his sheets on: but a canter down the half-mile slope, and up again by the bushes won't go agin him.'

'Well, saddle him then, and let Pat get up.'

'Yes, my lord'; and Brien was saddled by the two men together, with much care and ceremony, and Pat was put up – 'and now,

Pat,' continued Grady, 'keep him well in hand down the slope – don't let him out at all at all, till you come to the turn: when you're fairly round the corner, just shake your reins the laste in life, and when you're halfway up the rise, when the lad begins to short a bit, let him just see the end of the switch – just raise it till it catches his eye; and av' he don't show that he's disposed for running, I'm mistaken. We'll step across to the bushes, my lord, and see him come round.'

Lord Ballindine and the managing man walked across to the bushes accordingly, and Pat did exactly as he was desired. It was a pretty thing to see the beautiful young animal, with his sleek brown coat shining like a lady's curls, arching his neck, and throwing down his head, in his impatience to start. He was the very picture of health and symmetry; when he flung up his head you'd think the blood was running from his nose, his nostrils were so ruddy bright. He cantered off in great impatience, and fretted and fumed because the little fellow on his back would be the master, and not let him have his play – down the slope, and round the corner by the trees. It was beautiful to watch him, his motions were so easy, so graceful. At the turn he answered to the boy's encouragement, and mended his pace, till again he felt the bridle, and then as the jock barely moved his right arm, he bounded up the rising ground, past the spot where Lord Ballindine and the trainer were standing, and shot away till he was beyond the place where he knew his gallop ordinarily ended. As Grady said, he hadn't yet been stretched; he had never yet tried his own pace, and he had that look so beautiful in a horse when running, of working at his ease, and much within his power.

'He's a beautiful creature,' said Lord Ballindine, as he mournfully reflected that he was about to give up to Dot Blake half the possession of his favourite, and the whole of the nominal title. It was such a pity he should be so hampered; the mere éclat of possessing such a horse was so great a pleasure; 'He is a fine creature,' said he, 'and, I am sure, will do well.'

'Your lordship may say that: he'll go precious nigh to astonish the Saxons, I think. I suppose the pick-up at the Derby'll be nigh four thousand this year.'

'I suppose it will – something like that.'

'Well; I would like a nag out of our stables to do the trick on the downs, and av' we does it iver, it'll be now. Mr Igoe's standing a deal of cash on him. I wonder is Mr Blake standing much on him, my lord?'

'You'd be precious deep, Grady, if you could find what he's doing in that way.'

'That's thrue for you, my lord; but av' he, or your lordship, wants to get more on, now's the time. I'll lay twenty thousand pounds this moment, that afther he's been a fortnight at Johny Scott's the odds agin him won't be more than ten to one, from that day till the morning he comes out on the downs.'

'I dare say not.'

'I wondher who your lordship'll put up?'

'That must depend on Scott, and what sort of a siring he has running. He's nothing, as yet, high in the betting, except Hardicanute.'

'Nothing, my lord; and, take my word for it, that horse is ownly jist run up for the sake of the betting; that's not his nathural position. Well, Pat, you may take the saddle off.'

ANTHONY TROLLOPE, *The Kellys and the O'Kellys*

# *He Could Have Been a Contender*

*The Classics are the Grail of the Turf. St Paddy won his Derby and Leger. Brien Boru just the Derby, his racing career curtailed by the book's happy ending. For most horses, however, talk of Epsom, Newmarket, Longchamp and Louisville is idle fancy, a dream. Damon Runyon, who could have given Jung a few pounds and a beating when it came to the interpretation of dreams and their dreamers, tells the tale of Little Alfie, owner and trainer of Last Hope, who hocked his fiancée's engagement ring to pay the entry fee for the Kentucky Derby, a transaction the fiancée, the ever-loving Miss Beulah Beauregard, took very much amiss. As she saw it, 'a babe in arms will know Last Hope cannot walk a mile and a quarter, which is the Derby distance, let alone run so far, and that even if Last Hope can run a mile and a quarter, he cannot run it fast enough to get up a sweat'.*

*Such words cut a racing man deep and the engagement was broken off, Miss Beauregard taking off with a New York banker, Mr Paul D. Veere, a gentleman under-endowed with horses and over-endowed with* coconuts. Little Alfie pursued his Derby dream by walking Last Hope and his one other horse, Governor Hicks, from Miami towards Louisville. Half-way there, and mighty pleased with the way Last Hope was shaping up, he ran into a now jilted Miss Beauregard in a field, struggling with a mule and a plough. The Derby was still a few weeks away, Governor Hicks showed greater promise on the plough than on the track and Miss Beauregard was ready to forgive the hocking of the engagement ring so he stayed.

N OW, it comes a Sunday, and all day long there is a very large storm with rain and wind that takes to knocking over big trees, and one thing and another, and no one is able to go outdoors much. So late in the evening Little Alfie and Miss Beulah Beauregard and all the Bensons are gathered about the stove in the kitchen drinking skimmin's, and Little Alfie is telling them all over again about how Last Hope will win the Kentucky Derby, especially if it comes up mud, when they hear a hammering at the door.

When the door is opened, who comes in but Mr Paul D. Veere, sopping wet from head to foot, including his little moustache, and limping so he can scarcely walk, and naturally his appearance nonplusses Miss Beulah Beauregard and Little Alfie, who can never forget that Mr Paul D. Veere is largely responsible for the saddle galls he gets riding up from Miami.

In fact, several times since he stops at Miss Beulah Beauregard's ancestral home, Little Alfie thinks of Mr Paul D. Veere, and every time he thinks of him he is in favour of going over to Mr Paul D. Veere's shooting-lodge on the Altamaha and speaking to him severely.

But Miss Beulah Beauregard always stops him, stating that the proud old Southern families in this vicinity are somewhat partial to the bankers and other rich guys from the North who have shooting lodges around and about in the piny woods, and especially on the Altamaha, because these guys furnish a market to the local citizens for hunting guides, and corn liquor, and one thing and another.

Miss Beulah Beauregard says if a guest of the Bensons speaks to Mr Paul D. Veere severely, it may be held against the family, and it seems that the Benson family cannot stand any more beefs against it just at this particular time. So Little Alfie never goes, and here all of a sudden is Mr Paul D. Veere right in his lap.

Naturally, Little Alfie steps forward and starts winding up a large right hand with the idea of parking it on Mr Paul D. Veere's chin, but Mr Paul D. Veere seems to see that there is hostility afoot, and he backs up against the wall, and raises his hand, and speaks as follows:

'Folks,' Mr Paul D. Veere says, 'I just go into a ditch in my automobile half a mile up the road. My car is a wreck,' he says, 'and my right leg seems so badly hurt I am just barely able to drag myself here. Now, folks,' he says, 'it is almost a matter of life and death with me to get to the station at Tillinghast in time to flag the Orange Blossom Special. It is the last train tonight to Jacksonville, and I must be in Jacksonville before midnight so I can hire an aeroplane and get to New York by the time my bank opens at ten o'-clock in the morning. It is about ten hours by plane from Jacksonville to New York,' Mr Paul D. Veere says, 'so if I can catch the Orange Blossom, I will be able to just about make it!'

Then he goes on speaking in a low voice and states that he receives a telephone message from New York an hour or so before at his lodge telling him he must hurry home, and right away afterward, while he is trying to telephone the station at Tillinghast to make sure they will hold the Orange Blossom until he gets there no matter what, all the telephone and telegraph wires around and about go down in the storm.

So he starts for the station in his car, and just as it looks as if he may make it, his car runs smack-dab into a ditch and Mr Paul D. Veere's leg is hurt so there is no chance he can walk the rest of the way to the station, and there Mr Paul D. Veere is.

'It is a very desperate case, folks,' Mr Paul D. Veere says. 'Let me take your automobile, and I will reward you liberally.'

Well, at this Miss Beulah Beauregard's papa looks at a clock on the kitchen wall and states as follows:

'We do not keep an automobile, neighbour,' he says, 'and any way,' he says, 'it is quite a piece from here to Tillinghast and the Orange Blossom is due in ten minutes, so I do not see how you can possibly make it. Rest your hat, neighbour,' Miss Beulah Beauregard's papa says, 'and have some skimmin's, and take things easy, and I will look at your leg and see how bad you are bunged up.'

Well, Mr Paul D. Veere seems to turn as pale as a pillow as he hears this about the time, and then he says:

'Lend me a horse and buggy,' he says. 'I must be in New York in person in the morning. No one else will do but me,' he says, and as he speaks these words he looks at Miss Beulah Beauregard and then at Little Alfie as if he is speaking to them personally, although up to this time he does not look at either of them after he comes into the kitchen.

'Why, neighbour,' Miss Beulah Beauregard's papa says, 'we do not keep a buggy, and even if we do keep a buggy we do not have time to hitch up anything to a buggy. Neighbour,' he says, 'you are certainly on a bust if you think you can catch the Orange Blossom now.'

'Well, then,' Mr Paul D. Veere says, very sorrowful, 'I will have to go to jail.'

Then he flops himself down in a chair and covers his face with his hands, and he is a spectacle such as is bound to touch almost any heart, and when she sees him in this state Miss Beulah Beauregard begins crying because she hates to see anybody as sorrowed up as Mr Paul D. Veere, and between sobs she asks Little Alfie to think of something to do about the situation.

'Let Mr Paul D. Veere ride Governor Hicks to the station,' Miss Beauregard says. 'After all,' she says, 'I cannot forget his courtesy in sending me half-way here in his car from his shooting-lodge after I pop him with the pot of cold cream, instead of making me walk as those Yale guys do the time they red-light me.'

'Why,' Little Alfie says, 'it is a mile and a quarter from the gate out here to the station. I know,' he says, 'because I get a guy in an automobile to clock it on his meter one day last week, figuring to give Last Hope a workout over the full Derby route pretty soon. The road must be fetlock deep in mud at this time, and,' Little Alfie says, 'Governor Hicks cannot as much as stand up in the mud. The only horse in the world that can run fast enough through this mud to make the Orange Blossom is Last Hope, but,' Little Alfie says, 'of course I'm not letting anybody ride a horse as valuable as Last Hope to catch trains.'

Well, at this Mr Paul D. Veere lifts his head and looks at Little Alfie with great interest and speaks as follows:

'How much is this valuable horse worth?' Mr Paul D. Veere says.

'Why,' Little Alfie says, 'he is worth anyway fifty G's to me, because,' he says, 'this is the sum Colonel Winn is giving to the winner of the Kentucky Derby, and there is no doubt whatever that Last Hope will be this winner, especially,' Little Alfie says, 'if it comes up mud.'

'I do not carry any such large sum of money as you mention on my person,' Mr Paul D. Veere says, 'but,' he says, 'if you are willing to trust me, I will give you my IOU for same, just to let me ride your horse to the station. I am once the best amateur steeplechase rider in the Hunts Club,' Mr Paul D. Veere says, 'and if your horse can run at all there is still a chance for me to keep out of jail.'

Well, the chances are Little Alfie will by no means consider extending a lone of credit for fifty G's to Mr Paul D. Veere or other banker, and especially a banker who is once an amateur steeplechase jock, because if there is one thing Little Alfie does not trust it is an amateur steeplechase jock, and furthermore Alfie is somewhat offended because Mr Paul D. Veere seems to think he is running a livery stable.

But Miss Beulah Beauregard is now crying so loud nobody can scarcely hear themselves think, and Little Alfie gets to figuring what she may say to him if he does not rent Last Hope to Mr Paul D. Veere at this time and it comes out later that Last Hope does not happen to win the Kentucky Derby after all. So he finally says all right, and Mr Paul D. Veere at once outs with a little gold pencil and a notebook, and scribbles off a marker for fifty G's to Little Alfie.

And the next thing anybody knows, Little Alfie is leading Last Hope out of the barn and up to the gate with nothing on him but a bridle as Little Alfie does not wish to waste time saddling, and as he is boosting Mr. Paul D. Veere on to Last Hope Little Alfie speaks as follows:

'You have three minutes left,' Little Alfie says. 'It is almost a straight course, except for a long turn going into the last quarter. Let this fellow run,' he says. 'You will find plenty of mud all the way, but,' Little Alfie says, 'this is a mud-running fool. In fact,' Little Alfie says, 'you are pretty lucky it comes up mud.'

Then he gives Last Hope a smack on the hip and away goes Last Hope lickity-split through the mud and anybody can see from the way Mr Paul D. Veere is sitting on him that Mr Paul D. Veere knows what time it is when it comes to riding. In fact, Little Alfie himself says he never seen. a better seat anywhere in his life, especially for a guy who is riding bareback.

Well, Little Alfie watches them go down the road in a gob of mud, and it will always be one of the large regrets of Little Alfie's life that he leaves his split-second super in hock in Miami, because he says he is sure Last Hope runs the first quarter through the mud faster than any quarter is ever run before in this world. But of course Little Alfie is more excited than somewhat at this moment, and the chances are he exaggerates Last Hope's speed.

However, there is no doubt that Last Hope goes over the road very rapidly, indeed, as a coloured party who is out squirrel hunting comes along a few minutes afterward and tells Little Alfie that something goes past him on the road so fast he cannot tell exactly what it is, but he states that he is pretty sure it is old Henry Devil himself, because he smells smoke as it passes him, and hears a voice yelling hi-yah. But of course the chances are this voice is nothing but the voice of Mr Paul D. Veere yelling words of encouragement to Last Hope.

It is not until the station-master at Tillinghast, a guy by the name of Asbury Potts, drives over to Miss Beulah Beauregard's ancestral home an hour later that Little Alfie hears that as Last Hope pulls up at the station and Mr Paul D. Veere dismounts with so much mud on him that nobody can tell if he is a plaster cast or what, the horse is gimping as bad as Mr Paul D. Veere himself, and Asbury Potts says there is no doubt Last Hope bows a tendon, or some such, and that if they are able to get him to the races again he will eat his old wool hat.

'But, personally,' Asbury Potts says as he mentions this sad news, 'I do not see what Mr Paul D. Veere's hurry is, at that, to be pushing a horse so hard. He has fifty-seven seconds left by my watch when the Orange Blossom pulls in right on time to the dot,' Asbury Potts says.

Well, at this Little Alfie sits down and starts figuring, and finally he figures that Last Hope runs the mile and a quarter in around 2.03 in the mud, with maybe one hundred and sixty pounds up, for Mr Paul D. Veere is no feather duster, and no horse ever runs a mile and a quarter in the mud in the Kentucky Derby as fast as this, or anywhere else as far as anybody knows, so Little Alfie claims that this is practically flying.

But of course few citizens ever accept Little Alfie's figures as strictly official; because they do not know if Asbury Potts's watch is properly regulated for timing race horses, even though Asbury Potts is 100 per cent right when he says they will never be able to get Last Hope to the races again.

Well, I meet up with Little Alfie one night this summer in Mindy's Restaurant on Broadway, and it is the first time he is observed in these parts in some time, and he seems to be looking very prosperous, indeed, and after we get to cutting up old touches he tells me the reason for this prosperity.

It seems that after Mr Paul D. Veere returns to New York and puts back in his bank whatever it is that it is advisable for him to put back, or takes out whatever it is that seems best to take out, and gets himself all rounded up so there is no chance of his going to jail, he remembers that there is a slight difference between him and Little Alfie, so what does Mr Paul D. Veere do but sit down and write out a cheque for fifty G's to Little Alfie to take up his IOU, so Little Alfie is nothing out on account of losing the Kentucky Derby, and, in fact, he is stone rich, and I am glad to hear of it, because I always sympathize deeply with him in his bereavement over the loss of Last Hope. Then I ask Little Alfie what he is doing in New York at this time, and he states to me as follows:

'Well,' Little Alfie says, 'I will tell you. The other day,' he says, 'I get to thinking things over, and among other things I get to thinking that after Last Hope wins the Kentucky Derby, he is a sure thing to go on and also win the Maryland Preakness, because,' Little Alfie says, 'the Preakness is a sixteenth of a mile shorter than the Derby, and a horse that can run a mile and a quarter in the mud in around 2.03 with a brick house on his back is bound to make anything that wears hair look silly at a mile and three-sixteenths, especially,' Little Alfie says, 'if it comes up mud.'

DAMON RUNYON, *It Comes Up Mud*

# Tulyar

*Little Alfie's training methods would not meet with universal approval.
Most horses reside in a stable under the care of their trainers (see
below), consuming vast quantities of food and being cosseted by their
lads, vets and farriers. This should make them run fast. Sometimes it
works. The trainer Marcus Marsh described the regime at Fitzroy
Stables as he prepared the Aga Khan's Tulyar for the Derby of 1952.*

ALY PERCHED precariously on the edge of my desk, swinging
a twill-clad leg and studying his polished toe with seemingly spell-bound fascination.

'So we haven't anything for the Guineas, but how about the
rest of the season? What can we hope to win?'

'Frankly nothing big,' I said, 'with the possible exception of Tulyar, we haven't any real classic horses.'

All the normal charm of Aly was suddenly washed away.

'It's not good,' he said, 'not good at all. We'll have to do
better than that.'

'Well, that's the way it is, Aly,' I said, 'it's just one of those things.
You either have the horses or you haven't . . . and this year we
haven't.'

He left Fitzroy House, no way pleased, and I put it all down
to the natural disappointment of an owner. But it was a little more
than that, as I would soon discover. Unbeknown to me, Aly had
already made arrangements to have the bulk of the horses transferred to Noel Murless at the end of the season. And already too,
the eyes of the Aga were beginning to turn more and more towards the Continent where the financial grass was that much greener. We'd had our first hint of things to come when Nearque, a big
colt considered by many to have been our best two-year-old in
1951, was transferred from Fitzroy to France. Aly wanted to aim
him at some of the more lucrative prizes over there such as the
Grand Prix de Paris.

In the light of later knowledge, all this of course appears a little ironic. For we were on the brink of a record-breaking season,
but I agree that it would have been hard to foresee.

Our potential classic animals such as Mehmandar and Norooz

had done little to impress as two-year-olds. And I was still very puzzled by Tulyar's disappointing run in the Horris Hill. So too was Charlie [Smirke].

One morning over breakfast at Fitzroy he said, 'I'm pretty convinced now, Marcus, that if I'd sat back and waited, I would have won easily enough. I think he may be the kind who'll run for ever, but only has this one brilliant burst of speed . . . one that he can produce just once in a race.'

I was always prepared to listen to Charlie and this opinion made even more sense when, riding Tulyar that way in his first outing of the season at Hurst Park, he got home by a length from Trim Curry with the odds-on favourite, King's Bench, third.

As King's Bench had won the previous season's Middle Park, it was very tempting to make encouraging sounds, but not very practical. At Hurst Park, King's Bench had looked like a horse in need of a race.

I didn't run Tulyar in the Two Thousand Guineas, as I considered him more of a Derby or a Leger horse. But a week after this first classic, he won the Ormonde Stakes over a mile and six furlongs at Chester. He was due that day to carry 7 st 9 lb, a weight beyond Charlie's wildest dreams, and so Doug Smith rode him.

'Well, you've got to hand it to him,' said Doug afterwards. ' He's the kind who'll stay for ever and he'll certainly get the trip at Epsom.'

He made no reference to the fact that Tulyar had just scraped home by half-a-length in a very moderate time, but then I wouldn't have expected him to say anything about it. Doug always tries very hard to say something good about every horse he rides.

He reminds me a little of the story about the funeral of the man nobody liked. Afterwards the handful of mourners stood around the grave, desperately trying to think of something nice they could say about the deceased. Finally one of them spoke up.

'He was,' he said, 'a very good speller at school.'

Now that, you can be sure, would have been Doug.

I was using Tulyar at this time as a yardstick for my other classic animals and he certainly wasn't the most reliable one I'd ever had. He was so lazy that, on his off days, anything was liable to beat him out on the gallops.

He really was an extraordinary horse, medium-sized, brown

and filled with a vast, oceanic indifference to the world around him. He would stand for hours gazing patiently out into space, often balanced on three legs, and I haven't seen many horses do that. It would have been very difficult for anyone to dislike Tulyar. He was gentle, courageous and without any real vices, unless one regards laziness as such.

Every once in a while, watching him, I would get a tantalising glimpse of greatness, then it would go as quickly as it had come. Next day, he would be his normal lackadaisical self and I'd wonder whether I had really seen anything at all. For such a little fellow, he did have the most incredible stride and his front feet would go out way beyond his nose.

Meantime, life at Fitzroy had become a little worrying. There was a continual undercurrent. I knew something was wrong, but I couldn't quite place it. Aly was pleasant enough on the surface, but not quite so willing to confide as he had been before. Of course, if I had known that my contract had already been terminated there would have been no mystery at all. And I still find it difficult to understand why he didn't tell me, because this really wasn't his style. Possibly he found this a particularly difficult thing to say. Possibly he was already regretting his decision. But this is something now that I will never know.

One day when riding out at exercise together, he nodded towards the string.

'Are they beginning to look any better to you now?' he asked.

'No,' I said, 'they still look a very moderate bunch of animals to me. I have an open mind about Tulyar, but I can't see any of the others winning a classic race this year.'

He shook his head sadly, saying, 'You know we'll have to think very seriously about having them transferred to France. Training over there is becoming so much cheaper and the prize money so much bigger.'

'Well, Aly,' I said, 'that's obviously up to you. But I'm very much afraid that wherever you train, the result will be the same . . . that you won't achieve any really permanent success until you first improve the breed.'

Gar who read the signs far better than I did was mildly amused by all this. 'Well, old boy,' he'd say, 'we're in the three guinea seats today' . . . meaning that our stock was high. On the bad days, it would be, 'the two-and-nines, end of the row'.

It had already become crystal clear to me that my only chance of achieving anything with Tulyar was to give him a great deal of racing and so accordingly, eight days after the Ormonde, I ran him in the Lingfield Derby Trial.

Charlie let him lay well back in the early stages and he was only seventh with a furlong-and-a-half to run. Then Charlie asked and Tulyar answered the way the good ones do. He went past the others as though they were standing still, making hacks of them all and watching him, my last doubts were washed away. This was no paper tiger. This was a racehorse good enough to give us the right to dream.

As the Derby drew near, we ran into a heatwave and each day, I listened to the weather reports and prayed for rain. For all of Tulyar's best performances had come when the going was soft and I wasn't at all sure how he would act on top of the ground.

Charlie shared these doubts and was, in fact toying with the idea of switching to Indian Hemp, a colt that Sir Humphrey de Trafford had sold to the Canadian Max Bell at the start of the season.

Five days before the race, we gave Tulyar his final gallop and Charlie was supposed to bring him up the peat moss strip which always provides a certain amount of 'give'. I hacked down to the far end and waited for them. They were coming pretty fast with Tulyar in the lead and then, to my horror, I realised that Charlie had picked the wrong gallop. Instead of the peat moss, he was coming down the parallel strip which was rocklike.

It's moments such as this that give trainers their grey hairs, turn young men old and old ones older. Any second, I expected to see Tulyar break down and, as they pulled up, I cantered over, still fearing the worst.

'You bloody fool,' I said to Charlie. 'What are you trying to do, ruin him?'

But Charlie was looking far from penitent. 'It's all right, Marcus,' he said, 'don't worry. This one will do for me at Epsom. He's even better on top of the ground.'

And once I had simmered down, I began to realise the full implications. Rain or shine, Tulyar was now a very hot tip indeed.

I went to the Derby luncheon with Aly.

'I think you can have a pretty big eachway bet on him now,' I said.

'Are you sure?' he asked.

'I have been in racing too long, Aly,' I said, 'to be sure of anything. But put it this way, it will take a very good horse to beat him and I haven't seen any yet.'

Aly's eyes began to glitter, the way they always did when he believed himself to be on the brink of a big coup. Tulyar's odds were at that moment 100–7.

They will tell you that, for a trainer, big-race tension diminishes steadily, year by year, and there is only one thing wrong with that statement. It isn't true. Any Derby in which you have a fancied runner becomes a pretty tense affair and it doesn't get any easier with the passing years. It gets worse. But the emotions I experienced this time were very different from those I'd had in 1934.

With Windsor Lad, it had been a much more personal thing. I had bought him and tutored him and believed in him when very few others did. At Epsom, he had been the sole representative of a very small stable pitted against the emperors.

With Tulyar, I was very conscious of the fact that my reputation was at stake. I was fronting for the most powerful and the most demanding stable in Europe and the only vehicle I had with which to satisfy that demand was this eccentric, little chap called Tulyar. I was very anxious to prove to both the Aga and Aly that, given the right horse, I could follow through and reap the harvest.

Tulyar was his normal sleepy-time self on the morning of the race. Even the most placid animals are apt to get up on their toes during that long parade past the stands, but not my fellow. He sauntered along as if he had all day before him and, if he had been a man, I'm sure his hands would have been in his pockets and his feet shuffling the dust. He didn't quite yawn, but he somehow contrived to look terribly bored and when he sighted the distant tapes, you could almost hear him say, 'You don't mean to tell me I've got to canter all that way just to get down to the gate!'

For weeks, it had been assumed that the French would be the ones to fear. But now there was a sudden, late swing Tulyar's way and, by the time they reached the start, the bookmakers were asking 11–2. The main danger seemed likely to come from Lord

Rosebery's Bob Major, Bill Rickaby up . . . Mrs Pat Rank's Gay Time, ridden by the youthful Lester Piggott . . . and, the French challengers such as Silnet, Argur and Worden II.

Tulyar had been drawn number sixteen and I thought he looked terribly small and fragile. Charlie's main task lay in keeping him clear of trouble and yet in touch with the leaders by the time they reached Tattenham Corner, so that he would be in a position to make the late challenge a furlong or so from home.

The first part of this plan worked like a charm. After a furlong, Charlie had Tulyar bobbing along in that carefree way of his and clear of all interference. Coming down the hill, the whips were out and French oaths sounding across the downs, but Tulyar was still in a world of his own, unconcerned by the foibles of others.

Gordon [Richards] on Monarch More was leading as they rounded Tattenham Corner. Bob Major was just behind and being tracked by Tulyar, for us the perfect position and then, suddenly, dramatically, everything changed. Monarch More stopped rapidly and Bob Major began to falter. And so again in a big race, Charlie encountered that moment of swift decision when riding orders perchance be tossed into the balmy, summer air.

He could either hook back or go on and, feeling that if he hooked back there could be no guarantee that Tulyar would come again, he slipped him through on to the rails and made the long run for home. His first brilliant burst of speed took him clear of the field, but there was still almost three furlongs to run. I don't know whether Charlie or I suffered the most, as Tulyar came galloping down the straight with half-a-dozen challengers hammering at his heels. Inside the final furlong Lester, on Gay Time, was definitely beginning to gain ground on the wide outside and once again I had cause to be glad that I had Charlie up. Sensing the danger, he switched his whip to the left hand and went over to join Gay Time, performing what I have always regarded as the most brilliant of all race-riding manoeuvres, stealing another horse's ground. He came just close enough to make Gay Time break his stride and yet not close enough to be accused of interference in any way . . . and there is a perilously narrow dividing line between the two.

They crossed the line still in close company with Tulyar the winner by half-a-length. Lester wanted to lodge an objection, but was dissuaded from doing so by Pat Rank. I can quite see how Lester, being very young and probably meeting this tactic for the first time, might have considered himself hard done by.

That night, Aly threw a celebration dinner and dance in London's West End and, like all Aly's parties, there was the usual bounteous supply of beautiful girls, champagne and laughter. Aly had good cause for celebration, having taken my advice and clipped the bookmakers for £40,000.

But if I expected him to be fully satisfied, I was clearly wrong. For two days later, at Epsom, he said in a puzzled sort of way, 'I still don't understand, Marcus, why you didn't recognise Tulyar's quality before.'

I could have reminded Aly that some six months earlier he had been trying very hard to sell Tulyar for £7,000. I could have pointed out that five days before the Derby, Charlie, a fair judge of a racehorse, had been in no great hurry to climb aboard. But I said none of these things. I believed that in a quieter moment, Aly would reason all this out for himself.

I had, of course, long since come to realise that I wasn't Aly's kind of trainer. He really wanted a big, bold gambler and I was never that. I have always felt that as a trainer, one should resist the temptation of being bold with other people's money. It's true I didn't give him all that many tips, but it's equally true that the ones I gave him nearly always came up. I wouldn't have given them, unless I had been pretty sure about that.

Aly lived in a world that, I am afraid, was never very real. There were no ogres in Aly's world, no heartbreaks, no despair before the dawn, no sad stories. If there was something he found unpleasant to contemplate, he just forgot about it, until it went away. And knowing this, I would perhaps have been wiser to praise his horses more, to continually raise his hopes. But I have never built castles of sand for Aly or any of my owners, because I don't believe it's right. You can sometimes keep an owner by saying such and such an animal is a bit below par, but we can maybe get him placed in a few second-class races. Still racing is such an expensive business that I think it's usually kinder to advise them to either sell him or take him home as a family pet. You don't get very rich that way, but at least you can look yourself in the shaving mirror the following morning.

Tulyar continued to move along the primrose path. Six weeks

after the Derby, he gobbled up the Eclipse and a week after that took the King George VI and Queen Elizabeth Stakes, again edging out Gay Time.

It would be rather begging the truth to suggest that, in those days, Gordon and Charlie were in any way blood brothers. And with Charlie bound to be overweight for the big race at Ascot, Gordon was naturally hoping to get the ride on Tulyar. This fact alone was enough to whip Charlie into a frenzy of self-denial, severe enough to make the average Tibetan monk look pretty second rate. The turkish baths in Jermyn Street, Piccadilly, had always been, for him, a sort of spiritual home, but now they became a little more than that. In between racing, he practically lived there, emerging from time to time to sniff the night air, before disappearing once more into the jungle heat. He finally arrived at Ascot, wan but triumphant, a mere two pounds overweight . . . and no one was going to quibble about that.

I was feeling guilty about Tulyar. I normally make it a rule never to give a horse a hard race between Epsom and Ascot. I made an exception in Tulyar's case because he was such an idle chap at home that I felt he probably needed the run. To save him too much travelling, I took him direct from Sandown to Ascot, but he didn't eat up for two long days and would have been far better at Fitzroy in his own surroundings. As he won, it turned out all right from that point of view, but I don't think it was fair really and I would never do it again. With this in mind, I withdrew him from all his prior engagements to the St Leger.

I went to Goodwood in a contented frame of mind and found Nesbit Waddington, Aly's stud manager who had been a very good friend to me, in the paddock. We were talking about this and that when he suddenly said how sorry he was that the horses were leaving me at the end of the year.

'Well,' I said, 'it's the first I've heard about it.'

He was visibly shaken.

'I can't understand that,' he said. 'Aly made the arrangement right at the start of the season. I can't imagine why he hasn't told you.'

Nor could I and this was, of course, the feature about the whole affair that hurt. My three-year contract was due for renewal at the end of the 1952 season and Aly had every right in the world to end it, if he wished. But it is normal to give prior warning. If I was going to lose the Aga's horses, I would obviously soon need to find some others to fill the boxes at Fitzroy and I had, in fact, recently been forced to turn down requests from owners whose horses I would love to have taken.

I felt that I was entitled to an explanation and so rang the Aga.

'I can assure you,' he said, 'I have only just heard about this myself. Aly made the deal entirely without my knowledge and I can only say I'm deeply sorry. Unfortunately, it's too late to change it now, but I have no wish to lose you. I am going to give you £50,000 annually to buy yearlings for me which can be trained at Fitzroy.'

It would have been hard to find a nicer man with whom to deal than the Aga. But although I appreciated the gesture tremendously, it did pose a problem. For the Aga always marked his trainer's catalogue before a sale, putting a tick against the yearlings which appealed to him and so one's hands were largely tied. This wouldn't have mattered all that much if he had been an infallible judge, but unfortunately he wasn't. On the question of pedigree, there was probably no more knowledgeable man alive, but he showed no interest at all in the conformation of a horse. And you just can't base your buying on books alone. Frankly, I would gladly have given back £40,000 of that annual sum in exchange for the benefit of a free choice. But how can you say a thing like that to a demi-god?

I was told by a confrère that the Aga subsequently laid down the law to Aly.

'You just can't do this to Marsh,' he said. 'In two seasons out of three he has trained the top prize winner, first Palestine and now Tulyar. So why do you want to lose him?'

'I don't,' said Aly simply, 'he's my friend.'

I can't pretend to understand the ramifications of Aly's mind at that moment. But anyway it was agreed that I should keep all the horses I currently had in training, including of course Tulyar, and that Noel Murless would receive the bulk of the yearlings from the Aga's own studs.

Just before the Leger, Tulyar gave me a bad moment when going down by ten lengths to Mehmandar in a final gallop, but he was presumably just having his eccentric fun with us all. For on the day itself, he made the winning of a classic look a very easy business indeed when showing Kingsfold and Alcinus the way home. He won in a virtual canter, ears pricked and looking like a horse that had barely begun to run.

That ended Tulyar's season. He had won all his seven races and prizes to the value of £75,173, a record for a three-year-old colt in this country. He could doubtless have won the Two Thousand Guineas and the Arc de Triomphe as well. But the Guineas, being far too short for him, could have dented his chances in the other classics, while the Arc might well have hampered his four-year-old career.

So Tulyar came home to a well-deserved rest and the life of leisure which he so enjoyed. And with the coming of autumn, I too began to count my blessings.

Despite all the alarums and excursions, I had wound up as top trainer for 1952. And, with that sleepy-time little fellow called Tulyar training on, the beacons of hope loomed big and bright.

MARCUS MARSH, *Racing with the Gods*

# Who's the Best

*What can be better than a good horse? Two or more competing against each other. The anticipation that accompanies a big race showdown is inspirational. Supporters of either camp make ever more extravagant claims of the fleetness of their fancy until one would believe ancient Greece's Pegasus had returned and was matched at level weights against Shibdiz, the legendary horse of Arabia. Then the day dawns, the talking's over – save for 'Bruff' Scott and John McCririck – and only the sward lies between victory and defeat. When a good crop of horses vie for the top honours, no season can be long enough for the equine hedonist. The Honourable George Lambton describes one such year.*

ST SIMON did not run after 1884. He had educated the public as to what a high-class racehorse should be, and the two-year-olds of 1885 nobly lived up to that standard – Ormonde, Minting, The Bard.

I doubt if there were ever three such good horses of one year. Besides these three there were Saraband, Mephisto, Gay Hermit, St Mirin, Loved One, Fullerton, Oberon, The Cob, Carlton, Miss

Jummy, Modwena. Nearly all these horses made Turf history at some period of their career by winning great races.

The flying little Modwena, the property of the Duke of Portland, won nine good races as a two-year-old, but this was not surprising seeing how she was bred, by Galopin out of Mowerina. I remember so well the mare starting at six to five on for the Post Sweepstakes at the Second October Meeting at Newmarket.

There was a rumour that John Porter was running a good horse belonging to the Duke of Westminster, and everyone was on the qui vive in the paddock. The general verdict was that Porter's youngster was a great, fine horse, but had not the best of shoulders, and was not likely to beat such a filly as Modwena.

In the race, ridden by Fred Archer, the big colt won without an effort, although the verdict was only a length. This two-year-old was the redoubtable Ormonde, who never suffered defeat.

Ten days later Ormonde came out for the Criterion Stakes at the Houghton Meeting, which he won in a canter by three lengths. On the following Wednesday he started at six to four on for the Dewhurst Plate, and again won easily by four lengths. That completed his labours for the year 1885.

Ormonde as a two-year-old, and even as a three-year-old, was very low in front of the saddle, and in his slow paces was not a taking mover. Archer told me himself that until the horse was extended he always felt himself to be sitting on his neck. This no doubt gave rise to the idea that Ormonde had not the best of shoulders. He retired into winter quarters, in the opinion of many people the probable Derby winner of the following year.

Now The Bard, the joint property of General Owen Williams and Mr Robert Peck, and trained by Martin Gurry, was an exactly opposite type of racehorse. He was a beautifully made little chestnut horse, ticked with white, in shape and conformation impossible to fault.

He made his first appearance in the Brocklesby Stakes at Lincoln, which he won easily by two lengths. He won sixteen races without knowing defeat, a wonderful record for a two-year-old, and he was never properly extended in any of these races. His last race that year was for the Tattersall Sale Stakes at Doncaster, and he then retired for the season, his half-owner, General Williams, declaring that he would not run again before the Derby, and that no horse in the world would ever beat him, and there were many people who agreed with him.

Minting, owned by Mr R. C. Vyner, like Ormonde, was a great big colt of enormous power and substance, but in spite of that Matthew Dawson managed to bring him out in June for the Seaton Delaval Plate at Newcastle, when, ridden by Jack Watts, and starting favourite, he won in a canter by six lengths.

He followed this up by a victory in the Prince of Wales Stakes at Goodwood, again ridden by Watts and winning by five lengths, Jacobite, a nice colt belonging to Mr Bowes, being second on each occasion. He then won the Champagne Stakes, this time his jockey being Archer, and he beat Gay Hermit and others easily by a length and a half. After that he beat two bad horses in a Triennial Stakes at Newmarket, and then came the Middle Park Plate, a race which gave rise to an immense amount of discussion both before and after.

Robert Peck had at this time retired from active training, and had put Humphreys in charge of his own horses and stable, but he still held the reins and kept the closest supervision over the establishment.

Minting's chief opponent was Saraband, a beautiful chestnut colt belonging to Sir John Blundell Maple (who then raced under the name of Mr Childwick) and trained by Humphreys. He had won six races out of seven, and it was known that his trainer entertained the highest opinion of him.

Even in those days rumour was busy with the names of the leading jockeys, though, thank heaven, not to the same extent as it is at the present moment, and there was no doubt that Archer, Minting's jockey, and Robert Peck were great friends.

Archer rode for Peck whenever he could, he dined with him, he hunted with him, and that was quite sufficient to make the suspicious and 'know all' brigade say that Archer was in Peck's pocket. Therefore, previous to the Middle Park Plate, there was a prevalent 'canard' that Saraband would win the race and not Minting.

I remember the race vividly. It was run in very heavy going, and, coming down Bushes Hill, Braw Lass, trained by John Dawson and ridden by a 'pillar to post' jockey called Giles, held a useful lead from Wood on Saraband, Archer on Minting waiting on the pair.

Everyone expected Braw Lass to stop as she breasted the hill, but instead of this, slipping through the mud, she increased her lead. There was a roar from the ring as Archer and Wood were seen to call seriously on their horses. Minting rolled badly as he came into the Dip. In a desperate race home it was always doubtful if Saraband would catch Braw Lass. Two hundred yards from the post Archer, having balanced Minting, put in one of those superhuman efforts which had gained him the name of 'The Demon', and got up in the last twenty strides to win a neck from the mare, amid immense excitement, Saraband being beaten a neck for second place.

After the race gossip was rife, the aforesaid 'clever brigade' saying, 'What did we tell you? If Saraband had been good enough to win, Archer would never have got up on Minting.' A story went round the clubs that Mat Dawson had said, 'If it had not been for me brother John coming down like an angel from Heaven wi' his Braw Lass, Minting would not have won the Middle Park Plate.'

I very much doubt if the old gentleman ever made this remark, as I am convinced he never for one moment questioned the integrity of his jockey.

At that time, and always, I had a great admiration for Matthew Dawson, and many are the pleasant afternoons I have spent in his company, listening to his words of wisdom on horses, men and jockeys. Knowing my love of racing, and being a great raconteur, he never seemed tired of imparting his great store of knowledge to me.

At Exning, a fortnight after the Middle Park Plate, I was having a cup of tea with Mat while he partook of whisky, when in strolled Archer. They began talking about the race: 'You nearly threw that race away, Fred,' said the old man.

Archer admitted that he had held Braw Lass too cheaply, thinking he had only one horse to beat in Saraband, and that he had called on his horse too suddenly coming into the Dip, with the result that Minting was completely unbalanced, and it was a hundred yards before he could get him going again. 'But,' said he, 'the horse does not act well downhill, and he will not suit the Epsom course.'

After Archer had left I asked Mat what he thought about this with reference to the following year's Derby. The old man scratched his head and said, in his usual broad Scotch, 'I'm no saying he's not right; I've had doubts meself, and the young divil, when he's ridden a horse, seems to know more about him than I do.'

Thus at the end of the season 1885 we have three unbeaten two-year-olds, all engaged in the Derby of the following year, owned by great sportsmen, trained by three of the best trainers of the day, and sure to be ridden by high-class jockeys. The Bard was not engaged in the Two Thousand Guineas.

During the winter and spring of 1885–86, I was more interested in hunting and steeplechasing, and I had not been flat-racing except at Liverpool before the Two Thousand week. But up to that time none of the crack three-year-olds had been seen in public.

Reports as to their progress were most flattering. John Porter was supposed to have said that Ormonde was the best horse he had ever trained; Mat Dawson vowed Minting was a smasher; and Peck averred that The Bard was better than ever under the skilful training of Gurry, and also that he would give the two cracks a dusting-up with Saraband in the Two Thousand, as he was very forward and greatly improved.

The week before the First Spring Meeting I was staying at Exning and went to see Mat Dawson. He showed me Minting, who was looking a picture, having gone through one of Mat's severe preparations with every satisfaction; and there was no mistake about it, a horse had to work for his living when Mat set about him. Often three canters before a gallop, and out nearly three hours every morning.

I wonder how the horses of these days would stand it? Perhaps they would do better on it than we think. But at the same time Mat liked his horse to go out for a race full of confidence, and, as he put it, 'thinking he could lick creation'.

Before going away I asked him what he thought about Ormonde. He replied, 'When John Porter says he has a good horse, you may be certain that he has a d——d good one, but he does not know what I have got,' adding, 'when it comes to a matter of talking, Ormonde wins the Two Thousand, but, when it comes to a matter of racing, Minting will win.'

On the day of the race confidence in Minting was unbounded. Ridden by Watts, he started at eleven to ten, Saraband, with Archer, three to one, and Ormonde, George Barrett up, seven to two, any

**41**

price the rest. George Barrett was a dashing young jockey just coming to the front, much like Archer in style, but inclined to be in a hurry.

The race was disappointing to watch. From the fall of the flag Ormonde and Minting raced right away from the field, both jockeys trying to cut the other down. Half-way up the hill it was all over, and Ormonde won cleverly, if not easily, by two lengths, nothing else near.

As I saw Minting again roll and change his legs coming into the Dip, I remembered Archer's words to Mat Dawson after the Middle Park Plate, but unfortunately for my pocket I had forgotten them before the race.

Naturally the disappointment of Mr Vyner and Mat Dawson was great, and old Mat retired from view for two days, but never again from that moment did he have any illusions as to which was the better horse.

Archer's view of the Two Thousand is interesting. I was much disappointed at what I thought rather a tame display on the part of Minting, arguing that he must be quite 10 lb behind Ormonde. Archer would not have this, saying that when you get two smashing good horses trying to cut each other down over the Rowley Mile the pressure is so great that one or the other is sure to crack some way from home; it may be just a toss up which gives way first, but the one who does has no struggle left. He said, 'Minting will never beat Ormonde, but Ormonde will never again beat Minting two lengths in a properly run race.'

I have experienced the truth of this theory many times in my racing career, and there is no better illustration than when Diadem, the best mare that I have ever trained, and that great sprinter, Tetratema, met at Goodwood over six furlongs. They raced together for five furlongs at terrific speed, Tetratema eventually winning a length and a half. Carslake, who rode Tetratema, told me afterwards that he did not have an ounce in hand at the moment when the mare cracked.

Ormonde and Minting never met again till Ascot of the following year, when Minting was again beaten, this time by a neck, with the great Bendigo three lengths off.

It was decided soon after the Two Thousand, that if Ormonde kept well, Minting should not run in the Derby, but should be kept for the Grand Prix. So Ormonde had nothing to beat but The Bard, who had not yet run that year, although he had satisfied Peck in his home work that he was good enough to win ninety-nine Derbies out of a hundred.

But the public would have nothing but Ormonde, and with Archer up, the Duke of Westminster's horse started at nine to four on, and The Bard (Wood) nine to two against. As in the Two Thousand, the two good horses came right away from the others, Ormonde winning, as I thought, easily by a length and a half.

I believe that Robert Peck, and I know that General Williams and Gurry, thought that Wood rode a bad race in not making enough use of his horse, but I don't think there was anything in it – good as he was, The Bard could not beat Ormonde.

Three weeks after the Derby, The Bard put up a great performance in the Manchester Cup, when he ran second to Riversdale, a very smart horse, giving him no less than 31 lb. After this he was never beaten again.

Minting was sent over to run for the Grand Prix, his old pilot, Archer, to ride. I went over to Paris for the week. At that time the feeling between England and France was not at all friendly, and the authorities were nervous lest there should be a riot if the English horse won. Besides Minting, the Duke of Hamilton's Miss Jummy, winner of the Oaks and the One Thousand, was in the field, ridden by J. Watts.

The race before the Grand Prix was a handicap with a biggish field. Archer got a mount, as he wanted to have a ride round the course before the big race, but said he, 'I am not going to take any risks; they are a rough lot riding, and if they want to put me over the rails they will have to do it on the outside, for that is where I am going this time.' I felt rather sorry for the owner.

In the Grand Prix they went off as usual at a cracking pace; it was a very wet day, and the going was heavy, and half a mile from home Minting was some way behind the leaders, but, coming through quickly, he won in a canter by two lengths.

Archer, having been warned of the danger of a riot, pulled his horse up short, on the post, was into the unsaddling enclosure and off his horse before anyone had time to leave the stands; as smart a performance as I have ever seen.

* * *

To continue the story of the season 1886, Ormonde won the St Leger and every other race he ran for, always without an effort, and The Bard, after his defeat at Manchester, was also unbeaten.

THE HON. GEORGE LAMBTON, *Men and Horses I have Known*

# They're Out to Get the Favourite

*There are times when a horse has more to overcome than his rivals. In 1848 threats were made against Surplice, ante-post favourite for the Derby, after a sensational gallop confirmed he was the horse to beat at Epsom. His trainer, John Kent, describes the precautions he took to prevent any nobbling of the jolly.*

NOTWITHSTANDING the ceaseless vigilance exercised by all to whom the care of watching and guarding Surplice was intrusted after he had been tried, rumours at attempts would be made by fair means or foul to ensure his defeat for the Derby were freely circulated on all sides. Such rumours were naturally to be expected in view of the enormous sums of money laid against him during the winter of 1847–48. Under these circumstances his transportation from Goodwood to Epsom became to me a cause of the deepest anxiety, and endless were the suggestions made as to the best method of effecting it in safety. One of these suggestions was, that I should allow the horse to travel to Epsom under the charge of two of my most trusted men, supervised by a policeman, who was to be specially called in for that purpose. This proposition I met with a decided negative. Having undertaken the responsibility of guarding the horse myself, of feeding and giving him his water with my own hands, of taking care that neither his food nor his drink should be doctored in any way, and, finally, of never allowing him to be out of my sight except when he was locked up and the key was in my pocket, I did not feel inclined to permit a stranger, even though he were a policeman, to take my place. Knowing that many who placed confidence in me had backed Surplice heavily from what I thought of him long before his trial, I felt, as the Derby Day drew nearer and nearer, and the rumours of intended foul practices grew louder and more sustained, that my responsibility was almost more than I could bear.

As the Derby approached, everybody, and especially the 'sharps', had it that my horse was 'a safe un'. Out at exercise on Tuesday morning, every acquaintance that I met kept on asking me, 'What's the matter with Surplice? He's up and down in the market in a very queer way.' To add to my anxiety, Mr Payne refused to give up Flatman, believing that he had a very good chance of winning with Glendower. It was then arranged that James Robinson should ride Surplice, as there seemed no probability that any of his masters would need his services. At the last moment, however, the Duke of Rutland claimed Robinson to ride The Fiddler, and the difficulty of getting a good jockey for Surplice seemed almost insurmountable. At this critical moment, Mr Harry Hill, whose interest in the horse, for Lord George's sake, remained unabated, and who had backed him heavily, recommended, for private reasons, which he stated to Mr Mostyn and Mr Lloyd, that Sim Templeman should be put on Surplice's back.

It was, of course, a great relief to me when this was settled, although I did not think Templeman the best jockey to do justice to a big lazy horse like Surplice, who would make a race with a donkey, and deceived everybody who rode him for the first time. Sim Templeman formed the same unfavourable opinion of his mount, after riding Surplice over the course the day before the Derby, that Jem Robinson had conceived when he rode him in a gallop at Goodwood. What increased Templeman's dislike to Surplice was, that the horse refused to cross the tan road when ridden at a foot's-pace down the course, on his way to the starting-post. All these difficulties and gloomy prognostications tended, of course, to increase my anxiety, and made it difficult for me to fulfil my engagement never to let Surplice out of my sight, unless he was locked up in his loose-box. My favourite old pony, with whom Surplice was well acquainted, enabled me, however, to keep close to him when walking at exercise. The curiosity and excitement of the crowd were so great, that it was extremely difficult for Surplice to make his way through them, so closely was he mobbed. I found Leadbetter and the Goodwood stable lads of great assistance in this emergency; but it was fortunate that Surplice was naturally unexcitable and quiet, as he was followed to his stable-door by a large host of gentlemen on horseback, who would have driven a nervous horse of Bay Middleton's type wild with irritability.

In those days there was on the Sunday, Monday, and Tuesday preceding the Derby, a vast concourse of people assembled at Epsom to see the Derby horses gallop. Never, however, did I witness such a sensational scene, or such intense curiosity as was manifested to catch a glimpse of Surplice. In the midst of the crowds by which he was always surrounded he bore himself with an unruffled calmness and tranquillity which, despite my intimate acquaintance with his disposition and temperament, fairly surprised and delighted me. I endeavoured to form Leadbetter and a small brigade of boys under his charge into a ring around my horse. These human guards quickly lost their tempers, and became violently agitated, but the horse never turned a hair. The same difficulty and disappointment arose when I placed Surplice in the midst of a group of horses, including Loadstone, Sagacity, and other stable companions. Hemmed in by a mob of horsemen, these outposts were always on their hind-legs and dancing about, while Surplice walked sleepily along, as quiet as an old cow. On the night before the Derby a number of roughs surrounded the paddock in the middle of which Lord George's stable stood, and kept watch until midnight – not from any desire to do mischief, I verily believe, but from simple curiosity. In the morning a fresh lot of touts and runners emerged from the Cock Inn and kept watch until Surplice left his stable and walked on to the course, to start for the Derby.

A great favourite is generally unpopular, but never was there one more so than Surplice. All through the winter he had been regarded as a 'dead un', thanks to Mr Francis Villiers's infatuation, and to his reputation for possessing extraordinary talents. Everybody was aware that Mr Villiers had given a never-ceasing commission to lay against Surplice, and, with few exceptions, little backers had staked their money on Loadstone. In an instant Surplice's great trial shattered all their hopes, and he became such a favourite that it was almost impossible to back him. All this tended to make Surplice more disliked than great favourites usually are.

I have entered into all these minute details at the risk of being wearisome, because Surplice's Derby happened at a time when it was more common to poison or lame horses than is now the case, and because the circumstances preceding his attainment of the position of first favourite were of a most peculiar and exceptional kind. Forty or fifty years ago the sums of money betted upon the Derby were so large, and the excitement so great, that it is difficult for a younger generation of racegoers to understand or realise the anxiety and sense of responsibility of a trainer who was in charge of such a favourite as Surplice was in 1848. I was not unaware that tempting overtures had been made surreptitiously to more than one employee in the Goodwood stable to lame Surplice; and if he had run badly in the race, suspicion would doubtless have attached to many innocent persons who were as eager to see him win as my father and I were. It will easily be imagined, therefore, with what feelings I saw the dawn of the Derby Day break.

My father and I rode by the horse's side from Headley to the course. I then dismounted and led Surplice, while his regular lad rode him, and two police officers walked immediately in his rear. On nearing the stand, my father went off to see Templeman weighed, and returned to inform me that even at the eleventh hour Mr Francis Villiers had not given up all hope that Loadstone would prove himself the better horse, and, in order to give Loadstone every chance, had made some considerable pecuniary sacrifice in order to secure Job Marson (one of Mr Villiers's favourite jockeys) to ride him. It was not long before Mr Villiers was undeceived.

* * *

The following description of the race appeared in 'Bell's Life'.

Precisely at the time named on the card the horses were at the starting-post, and we must do the starter, Mr Hibberd, the justice to say that a finer start was never seen on this or any other course. The Fowler jumped off with the lead; but either from not being ambitious, or from inability to keep it, he fell back in half-a-dozen strides, and Great Western went on with the running, followed by Loadstone and Fugleman, Nil Desperandum being fourth on the inside. Behind him came Surplice, Fern, and The Fowler, with The Fiddler and Springy

Jack in their wake. The Fowler kept his place till near the Craven post, where he fell astern of The Fiddler. About the same time Nil Desperandum sprained his off knee, and in the next hundred yards from being fourth became the last horse in the race. Great Western maintained his position until close to the top of the hill, when he was passed by Loadstone, and immediately afterwards gave way altogether, leaving Fugleman second to Loadstone, Surplice following Fugleman, with Fern, Glendower, Springy Jack, and Shylock running in a group close behind. Half-way between the road and the distance-post Loadstone declined, and Fern also had had enough of it. A new formation ensued, Surplice taking a decided lead, followed by Fugleman with Shylock third and Springy Jack by his side. Just inside the distance Fugleman was beaten and dropped behind Shylock and Springy Jack. The race at this moment was very interesting. To all appearances the 'crack' was going very uncomfortably, and Shylock looked so well that 'The favourite's beat!' escaped from a thousand lips. Nor was it until they were half-way up the distance that 'the Jew' was fairly disposed of. Springy Jack now began to look dangerous, as he got to the favourite's quarters, and came with a tremendous rush in the last three or four strides, and almost got up. But it was only 'almost', as Surplice was never quite reached, and won by a neck.

### Wednesday, May 24, 1848

The Derby Stakes of 50 sovs. each, h. ft., for three-year old colts, 8 st. 7 lb.; fillies, 8 st. 2 lb. The new Derby course; a mile and a half.

Lord Clifden's b. c. Surplice, by Touchstone – Crucifix, by Priam (Templeman), 1.

Mr Bowes's b. c. Springy Jack, by Hetman Platoff – Oblivion, by Jerry (F. Butler), 2.

Mr B. Green's bl. c. Shylock, by Simoom – The Queen, by Sir Hercules (S. Mann), 3.

Betting – Even on Surplice, 4 to 1 each v. Glendower and Nil Desperandum, 14 to 1 v. Shylock, 15 to 1 v. Springy Jack,

20 to 1 *v.* Loadstone, 40 to 1 *v.* Great Western, The Fiddler, and Fugleman; 50 to 1 *v.* The Fowler; 1000 to 15 each *v.* Fern and Eagle's Plume; 1000 to 10 *v.* Deerstalker.

Won by a neck; length between second and third.

Sim Templeman assured me after the race that had I not cautioned him so strongly about Surplice's laziness, he might have been beaten, as his horse began to stop directly he steadied him, and would have pulled up altogether had he not kept him going. I had warned him emphatically that directly he ceased to ride him Surplice would cease to run. Had Mr Villiers consented to order Marson to jump off with Loadstone, and to make strong running for half or three-quarters of a mile (which Loadstone was well qualified to do), there would have been no danger of Surplice being beaten, or hard run, as he was as fit as he could be made. So obstinate, however, was Mr Villiers in his own opinion, that he would not hear of Loadstone being sacrificed for Surplice. The result was that, when Loadstone declined, Surplice had to take his own part, and Templeman said that it was all over as soon as Surplice took up the running.

One other extract I am tempted to make from 'Bell's Life' of Saturday, May 27, 1848.

'The Derby nags assembled in the paddock in charge of their respective trainers and grooms, Loadstone and Surplice being foremost in the throng, attended by the elder Kent, Leadbetter, and Thackwell – the former having been in charge of the horse for some nights before the race, with a view of defeating any of those sinister intentions which former experience led to a suspicion might again be put into practice: in fact, every possible care had been taken to protect Surplice from being got at, much to the mortification, it was said, of many who would have been far from displeased to hear that he had had a 'bad night'. Both horses looked remarkably well, especially Surplice, of whom it was said by a competent judge of looks that he was sure to win, as an animal in more splendid condition was never witnessed. In the early part of the day as much as 6 to 5 was laid on Surplice, but a perceptible change took place. Nil Desperandum advanced in favour, and was backed at 5 to 1, and by some parties at 3 to 1, while Surplice went back to 5 and even 6 to 4 – the latter odds being in some instances laid by those who were well on him, and whose confidence was somewhat shaken at the last moment. This change, we have reason to believe, was effected by a *ruse* got up among a party who were opposed to him, and who, by apparently laying odds against him, induced apprehension in the public mind of which they themselves took advantage, thereby getting on at a better price, and saving some £4000 or £5000. The crush to get a position whence a view of the course could be obtained was terrific.

'We have given a description of the race in its usual place, from which it will be seen that it was keenly contested by Surplice, Springy Jack, and Shylock. Surplice was spurred, although the whip was not used; and it was remarked that had the pace been good he would have won more cleverly, being such a sluggish horse and requiring a good deal of riding – evidence of which was afforded in his trial, for when he was nearing the winning-post and experienced the effect of the 'persuaders', he shot out like a dart, and won with consummate ease. These are, however, matters of speculation with which we must leave *cognoscenti* to deal. The winners had their turn of joyous cheering, and the congratulations offered to the Duke of Richmond and to his family, who, we are glad to hear, are large gainers by the result, were loud and vociferous beyond description, – congratulations which were given with equal goodwill to Lord Clifden and to Mr Lloyd, co-proprietors of the winner; both of whom, we also learn have realised a good profit independent of the stakes, which are worth £5500.

Thus terminated this ever-memorable Derby – memorable not only to me, but also to others who are still living, and were vitally interested in it. I perfectly well remember, when I was leading Surplice back to the weighing-place after the race, that a gentleman congratulated me, and added, 'You have now given them the lie direct!' At the time I could not understand what he meant, but from what transpired subsequently, I have no doubt that he congratulated me upon defeating the vile efforts to prevent Surplice from winning the Derby, which were deemed likely to be

successfully accomplished by some of the knaves who were heavy
losers to him.

JOHN KENT, *The Racing Life of Lord George Bentinck*


*Win or lose, a horse's racing career is brief. St Paddy' name does not
crop up in many of today's racing conversations. Nor too, those of
Surplice or Tulyar. A steeplechaser may jump on for ten years, an
honest sprint handicapper can gallop six furlongs for almost as long. A
Classic winner's career can be as short as three or four races. What next?
Philip Larkin saw the horse after his pomp.*

# At Grass

THE eye can hardly pick them out
From the cold shade they shelter in,
Till wind distresses tail and mane;
Then one crops grass, and moves about
– The other seeming to look on –
And stands anonymous again.

Yet fifteen years ago, perhaps
Two dozen distances sufficed
To fable them: faint afternoons
Of Cups and Stakes and Handicaps,
Whereby their names were artificed
To inlay faded, classic Junes –

Silks at the start: against the sky
Numbers and parasols: outside,
Squadrons of empty cars, and heat,
And littered grass: then the long cry
Hanging unhushed till it subside
To stop-press columns on the street.

Do memories plague their ears like flies?
They shake their heads. Dusk brims the shadows.
Summer by summer all stole away,
The starting-gates, the crowds and cries
All but the unmolesting meadows.
Almanacked, their names live; they

Have slipped their names, and stand at ease,
Or gallop for what must be joy,
And not a fieldglass sees them home,
Or curious stop-watch prophesies:
Only the groom, and the groom's boy,
With bridles in the evening come.

PHILIP LARKIN

# OWNERS

'To faithful Earls, Barons and Knights, and
all others to come and tilt at the town.'
*Invitation from Edward II*

*Every racing man, every racing woman has a dream: to own a racehorse,
take up Edward II's invitation and tilt, if not at the town, then at the
betting ring. If this dream has already come true, then the reveries will
be of owning a really good horse. It is this ambition that keeps the round-
about of the thoroughbred world turning, the cycle that takes the
racing man from Newmarket in April through to Cheltenham in March;
the fancy that, maybe this year, it will be his turn to lead Dobbin into
the hallowed turf of the winners' enclosure.*

*Armed with this hope and a cheque book, scores of otherwise sensi-
ble men and women arrive at the sales paddocks each autumn. It is with
this dream that the breeder pours over his charts late into the winter's
evening. Once born or bought, each yearling is vetted and watched as
he grows towards maturity. Nine times out of ten, the owner's dream
ends when the horse is asked to get serious on his racecourse debut and
responds with a turn of foot that is not just pedestrian, but straight from
the plough. For some unfortunates, the dream does not last that long,
dying stillborn on the home gallops. But for those like the prominent
owner, breeder, amateur rider and journalist John Hislop, for whom the
dream comes true, the pleasure is indeed sweet.*

WHEN the Brigadier left for West Ilsley, he was well grown,
but did not strike me as being more than medium sized. I
saw little of him during the winter, but on going to visit him when
he began serious training in February, I was surprised to see how

much he had grown and advanced. Amongst the other two-year-old colts he stood out, not only in looks, but in size, being appreciably bigger than all who were working with him.

The gallops at West Ilsley are excellent, nearly always offering good going at any time of the year; and though standing high up, so that on them it is an overcoat colder than in the valley below and horses trained there tend not to come to hand so early as those working in less exposed surroundings, they enable a trainer to give horses the steady, essential early work which forms the foundation of a horse's preparation and, in particular, the education of two-year-olds.

By the principles on which I was educated at Clarehaven, it is wise to teach two-year-olds their business and get those who are going to race seriously that season about three parts fit in the spring, when the going is usually good. If horses are left uneducated and unfit while the going is suitable, and then a spell of dry weather comes in, a trainer is left in the position of not being able to progress with his horses at all, or risk breaking them down through working them on firm ground. On the other hand, if horses know the business and are reasonably forward in condition, it is easy to get them racing fit in a short time, as soon as the ground comes right.

Dick Hern works to this pattern, so Brigadier Gerard and the other two-year-old colts at West Ilsley knew their job and were forward enough to do sharp work over three or four furlongs by the second half of March.

On 4 April, Jean and I went over to West Ilsley to see the Brigadier do his first important gallop. This was over four furlongs on the trial ground and comprised seven two-year-old colts; these, apart from Brigadier Gerard, were Rugged (Ribot–Rosalba), Grey Sky (Grey Sovereign–Treacle), Colum (Santa Claus–Mitigation), The Bugler (Klarion–La Bastille), Scar (Relic–Cutle) and Don Magnifico (Star Moss–Floria Tosca).

It was a clear, fresh morning and the Brigadier was ridden by Jimmy Lindley. He started the proceedings by whipping round and dropping Jimmy on the way up to the start. As a two-year-old he had a playful habit of doing this, every now and then, but having achieved his objective, just stood still till he was re-mounted. He appeared to single out only licensed jockeys to deposit, his other two victims being Joe Mercer and Bobby Elliott, but having put them on the ground once, he seemed content to leave them in peace thereafter.

Waiting at the four-furlong post, Jean, Dick Hern and I knew nothing of this drama, which was just as well. For Jean and I the next few minutes were going to reveal a dream on the way to realisation, or disillusion and the possible end of our survival as owner–breeders. From the moment that Brigadier Gerard was born, we had always felt that upon him our whole future in this sphere hung: we would never breed a horse like him again, and if he was not a good one the chances were that hope of our producing such a horse had gone for ever.

The professional in racing learns to control his emotions – 'It might have been worse, I only had £5000 on him,' that remarkable owner-trainer, Jack Reardon once observed, without a change of expression, in reply to the condolence of a friend upon a defeated gamble – but he must live with his feelings, however tense or bitter these may be.

As I lifted my glasses to focus them on the horses lining up for the start, I could not help the tension of the moment pervading my senses with a blend of excitement and anxiety. The horses struck off to a level start and before they had gone a furlong it was clear that Jimmy Lindley was going smoothly at the head of the bunch. The nearer they approached the more defined became the Brigadier's advantage, and on reaching us he was a good two lengths clear, with his ears pricked and seeming to be cantering while the others were galloping. Behind, closely bunched, were Grey Sky, Rugged and Colum.

The glow of joy and relief at this impressive performance was tempered by the lessons of past experience: a gallop is only as good as it is proved by form on the racecourse; and until one or more of the horses concerned had run, it was not possible to assess the value of the work in more than terms of conjecture. At the same time, the horses concerned were the most promising of those who, at that time, seemed likely to win as two-year-olds in the stable, so that our immediate reaction was: 'If this isn't a good horse, the others must be very moderate.'

When Jimmy Lindley got back to us after pulling up, he said: 'A very nice colt; he was always going well and will improve a lot; wants a bit of time.' This encouraged us further and we determined to give the Brigadier every chance to develop, by not bringing him out until May or June at the earliest.

The gallop never put him out in any way. He did not fret, never left an oat and pulled out as sound as a bell and fresh as paint the next day.

JOHN HISLOP, *The Brigadier*

*Hislop was to watch his colt reproduce his gallops' form as a two-, three- and four-year-old. The Brigadier went on to win just about every race he ran in – a Guineas, the odd Champion Stakes or two, a King George here, an Eclipse there. The very model of a dream horse.*

# The Debut

*Not all of us will have the good fortune to own a hoof in a Brigadier Gerard or, indeed, John Hislop's eye for greatness in the raw. But there must always be a quiver of anticipation as an owner watches his charge make her racecourse debut. The Duke of Devonshire, describes the evening his Park Top stepped out at Windsor.*

NOT SURPRISINGLY, I did not view the start of the 1967 flat racing season with any great expectations. When the season opened Park Top had got over her troubles of the previous year. The effects of the cough had been shaken off and with patience and care her forelegs had improved.

Her first appearance on a racecourse was delayed until the end of May. The future was to show she never came to her best until the warm weather arrived and she had had some sun on her back. The chosen day was May 22nd, just five days before her third birthday. The race was the Mar Lodge Plate at Windsor over a mile and a quarter and worth £345 to the winner. It was confined to three-year-old maidens, that is horses who have never won a race. It was evening racing, and the last race on the card. I drove down to Windsor, hopeful but far from confident. I had had too many disappointments over the years to be anything other than wary of the chances of any horse of mine winning. In any event, being confident of winning a race beforehand is asking for trouble. Bernard van Cutsem fancied the filly's chance and persuaded me to have my maximum bet. Having backed her, I joined him and Peggy Petre on the stand. Bernard asked me what price I had got and when I told him six to one he could hardly believe I had got such marvellous odds. This encouraged me to return to the rails and double my bet. In the end she started second favourite at five to one. This was to be the longest price she was ever to start at in a race in England.

By choosing a race of a mile and a quarter for Park Top's first appearance Bernard showed he was satisfied that Kalydon had passed on his stamina to the filly. That she would stay was to be expected since what little ability Nellie Park had shown had also been over a distance of ground.

There were fourteen runners of which only two had been placed in a previous race. Three others were, like Park Top, having their first outing. The favourite was Court Gem, trained by K. Cundell, who was to finish third and, like the second, Lord Sing, was to win a small race later in the season. Park Top gave her jockey Russ Maddock no trouble at the start, and the field was soon on its way. Windsor is a figure of eight course, and for races over a mile and a quarter the horses set off going away from the stands. Russ settled Park Top near the rear of the field where she remained for the first three-quarters of a mile of the twisting and turning track. Four furlongs out, she moved closer to the leaders and entering the straight just over two furlongs from home Russ's straw-coloured jacket could be seen close to the leaders.

Now in the early dusk, with the mist beginning to rise from the Thames, my pale yellow silks gleamed as Russ took Park Top to the front rather more than a furlong out and brought her home an easy winner by a length and a half. She won without being seriously pressed and there had been no question of Russ going for his whip.

The instant when victory is assured, and in particular the split second when your colours flash first past the post suddenly, make the whole business of racing worthwhile. All past disappointments are forgotten, the world is transformed into an entirely different place. Walking on air I accompanied Bernard to the unsaddling ring to await the filly's return. This moment in the winner's enclosure is another of the great thrills of racing. The full realisation of success has had time to sink in, and all the tension has gone.

In due course, a smiling Russ Maddock rode Park Top into her place of privilege, to be greeted by Bernard, Maureen and myself, all equally delighted. There was laughter and mutual congratulations all round. Then when she had been led away to the racecourse stables, and Russ had passed the scales, Bernard and I sought the nearest bar to celebrate and discuss future plans.

ANDREW DEVONSHIRE, *Park Top*

*Like Brigadier Gerard, Park Top was to confirm her early promise. Her roll of honour included a King George, a Coronation Cup and two victories at Royal Ascot so the Duke was not disappointed.*

# Two Troublesome Ladies

*Unfortunately there are all too few Brigadier Gerards and Park Tops to share round and most owners find their horses defy their dreams of fleetness. This gulf between expectation and ability can be infuriating, especially if the owner has put the family silver on the beast. But owners have long been renowned for trying the patience of those to whom they have entrusted their horses' care. The trainer Atty Persse once noted: 'At times racehorse owners are a great worry to trainers but they pay the bills and they must be studied.'*

*What would he have made of Dorothy Paget?*

ONE DAY, instead of turning left at the end of the lane from the college, towards the village of Chalfont St Giles, I turned right, down Nightingales Lane, towards Little Chalfont. On either side of the road was woodland, with large, settled houses glimpsed between hedges and sycamores. I turned into one of the drives, and tried to imagine what Hermit's Wood had been like in the 1940s and 1950s, when Dorothy Wyndham Paget lived there.

Miss Paget was the owner of Golden Miller, the only serious rival to Arkle for the title of best steeplechaser ever. Golden Miller won five successive Cheltenham Gold Cups during the 1930s, and remains the only horse to have won the Gold Cup and Grand National in the same year, 1934.

The house hadn't changed much since 1960, when Dorothy Paget died. There was a lodge at the entrance, painted white, where Mr Hall, the gardener and odd job man, used to live. At the side was a shed with a heated floor, installed for the comfort of Miss Paget's Great Danes. At the back of the house was a balcony leading to the room where Dorothy lived, ate and telephoned, and from which her instructions were issued. When the present occupant, Tina Watson, arrived the lawn was in a dreadful state, because Hall was rarely allowed to cut the grass during the day, when Miss Paget was asleep, and it was difficult to cut it at night, when she was awake. 'Tell Hall to grow gladioli,' Paget would say, and the message would reach him through a network of duplicated notes and secretaries. Each secretary was allotted a colour – blue, yellow or pink – to identify both the secretary and her notes.

In the village, Hall was known as 'the eunuch', because the villagers couldn't believe that Miss P would allow an 'entire' on the premises. All her other staff, including drivers and mechanics, were women. Dorothy didn't like men. She told her cousin that the worst experience of her life was being kissed by a drunken Frenchman, and she didn't rate sober Englishmen much more highly. When wartime regulations prevented her from reserving a whole railway carriage for herself, she appealed to the Minister of Transport to exempt her from the restriction, on the ground that sitting next to strange men made her vomit. She did what she could to put them off, with great success. Burdened with a large, round, flat-fronted face, Miss P never wore make-up and her favoured costume was a Girl-Guide-like beret and long, shapeless, tweed coat. When she greeted Golden Miller in the winners' enclosure with a kiss, one wag remarked that it was the first time she had ever kissed a member of the opposite sex. To be fair to her, not many of her suitors had won a Gold Cup.

Dorothy Paget and Golden Miller had little in common, although Golden Miller also ate like a horse. In her younger days, Dorothy had been an accomplished horsewoman, riding side-saddle in point-to-points. Later, though, she discovered food and ate it on a scale which few others have been able to emulate until it was impossible to imagine her – more than twenty stones of her – on horseback. (The RSPCA was founded in 1824.) Few people visited Hermit's Wood, but the house still boasted a day cook, a night cook, and a lot of larders.

When Dorothy ventured out, she took precautions to avoid too much unwelcome human contact. If she wanted to see a film, she booked the whole of Amersham cinema. If she went out to dinner, she was likely to arrive with a thermos flask and a pack of sandwiches. At Wimbledon she booked two seats, one for herself and the other for her handbag. When she went to vote, Miss P took her own pencil. 'In case the horrible socialists should have stolen the public pencils.'

By chance, I met Alice Wilson, who ran a taxi service in Little Chalfont during the war. Alice used to pick Mr Hall up from Hermit's Wood every day and take him to collect 'The Pink 'Un'. The job came to an abrupt end when Mrs Wilson's dog sank its canines into one of the secretary's legs. The crime was not to have bitten her leg but to have bitten the stocking that surrounded it. 'It was the only house in Chalfont with stockings,' Alice explained. 'Dorothy Paget had hers specially made. She had the most enormous legs. No ordinary stockings would fit her.'

Strangers were strongly discouraged from visiting Hermit's Wood, and even members of her family were not encouraged. Dorothy fell out with her father and sister, who lived in Leeds Castle in Kent with a son glorying in the name of Sir Gawaine George Hope Baillie. When I phoned Sir Gawaine, Dorothy's nephew, he told me that he had only met her twice. 'My mother and her sister didn't get on.'

Nor did most people, which seemed to suit the eccentric, frequently unpleasant, but enormously rich Miss Paget. When you know that you are going to be given over £1 million, on the sole condition that you keep breathing until 1926 arrives, along with your twenty-first birthday, pleasing other people becomes an optional extra. Miss P gave it a very low priority. A higher priority, once her inheritance was safely in her handbag, was to set about spending it. Dorothy flirted briefly with motor racing (exciting but no betting), before alighting on horseracing (exciting and with betting). Miss P embraced the blank-cheque approach to bloodstock investment, and chalked up some spectacularly bad buys before spending £12,000 on Insurance, who went on to win the Champion Hurdle in 1932 and 1933, and Golden Miller.

Dorothy declared herself 'terribly pleased' with Golden Miller's Gold Cup–Grand National double, and awarded large chocolate effigies of her champion to the trainer, Basil Briscoe, jockey, Gerry Wilson, and head lad. They deserved their reward, for Miss Paget's daily routine started with dinner at 7.00 a.m., followed by bedtime, followed by breakfast at 8.30 p.m., when her day began. She had an insatiable appetite for discussing her horses with her trainers, and liked to open the debate at about 10.30 p.m. On one occasion she despatched a messenger to Briscoe at 2.30 in the morning, to instruct him to replace the telephone receiver which he had taken off the hook in a vain attempt to claim some sleep.

Briscoe was not temperamentally equipped to deal with Paget's eccentric and despotic ways, and nor were many of the other sixteen English trainers selected for the mixed blessing of her patronage. Fulke Walwyn, who trained more winners for Miss P than anyone else, among them Mont Tremblant, the winner of the 1952 Gold Cup, eventually lost patience and diplomatically suggested a change of trainer.

'She kept such funny hours,' Walwyn told me, 'and was always ringing up. She was a difficult person, so trying, and eventually I got fed up with her constant phone calls and resigned.'

Paget rarely visited her trainers; during the five years Gordon Richards trained for her, she failed to put in a single appearance. This was just as well, because she was habitually unpunctual. An outing to the races was preceded by a frenzy of notes and instructions. Watches were tuned in to Greenwich Mean Time, a precaution which failed to get Dorothy to the racecourse on time, and Hall was told to stand in the middle of Nightingales Lane to keep oncoming traffic at bay, so that Miss P could accelerate uninterrupted out of the drive. On one occasion, her car broke down, forcing Miss P to proceed to the racecourse in a butcher's delivery van, which she had purchased on the spot. After that, a second car always followed her, as a reserve, with a third car joining the convoy on long journeys. She rarely arrived in time to savour the paddock preliminaries, but this didn't trouble her; she was much more interested in the look of the betting market.

Dorothy was a disciplined gambler, betting only from Monday to Saturday. Most of her bets ranged from the equivalent of a modest semi to that of a substantial estate. She would start at £1000 and work her way steadily up to a reputed lifetime best of £160,000. (On an 8–1 on shot. It won.) One of her biggest bets was on Colonel

Payne in the 1939 Cork and Orrery Stakes at Royal Ascot. Fred Darling, the horse's trainer, had made encouraging noises about Colonel Payne's chance, and Dorothy had acted on them, to excess. When Gordon Richards and Colonel Payne returned to the unsaddling enclosure, soundly beaten, Miss P was there to greet them. 'Where's Mr Darling?' she demanded. 'I wouldn't be quite sure, Miss Paget,' Richards replied, 'but I've a shrewd idea he's on the top of the stand, cutting his throat.'

As time went by, the expanding Miss Paget went racing less but bet more. Since she tended to be in bed asleep during racing hours she had a unique arrangement with her bookmaker, who allowed her to bet after the racing was over.

'I'll have £400 on the favourite in the first.'

'Very good, Miss Paget. I'm afraid that one let you down.'

For most of us, it is the only system that would offer a fighting chance of making racing pay, but Miss P still managed to lose houses on a regular basis.

In 1939 Golden Miller joined Insurance in retirement at Paget's Elsenham Stud Farm in Essex. Unlike their owner, they both lived to a ripe old age, dying within three months of each other, both aged thirty, in 1957. Dorothy Paget did not long outlive the horse who made her famous. At her death, aged fifty-four she left no last will and testament, just 'The Heaps': piles of notes and fading copies of the *Sporting Life*.

DAVID ASHFORTH, Hitting the Turf: A Punter's Life

*A second lady who caused her trainers much heartache was Caroline, Duchess of Montrose, whose eccentricities were reported by George Lambton.*

ST MIRIN was the property of 'Mr Manton', the assumed name of Caroline Duchess of Montrose, who, on the death of her second husband, Mr. Crawford, carried on his great racing stud. At the time of which I write she was well over sixty.

She was blessed with a soft and most charming voice, and when things were going right was the best company in the world; but she was hot-tempered and changeable, and was easily put out if she did not get her own way. When at Newmarket she lived at Sefton Lodge, and just on the opposite side of the road was the great Captain Machell, of Bedford Lodge.

Two such strong personalities at such close quarters were bound to clash; at times they were devoted friends, at times most bitter enemies. The Duchess used to tell the most amusing stories about her friends, and had a very lively imagination; once she had told a story she was then firmly persuaded it was true.

One night, coming home from dinner, Captain Machell, in his fly, unfortunately drove over and killed her favourite dog. At the moment they happened to be enemies, and the Duchess, when she told the story, declared that the Captain lifted himself up and came down with a heavy bump on the seat of the fly, so as to make certain of killing her dog.

At that time Reggie Mainwaring was one of the handicappers, and the Duchess, like many owners, always thought her horses were unfairly treated. She took a great dislike to Mainwaring, who was one of the kindest and most amiable of men. He was a tall, dark man, rather like Othello, with an habitual scowl on his face. The Duchess used to refer to him as 'the man who murdered his mother'. So far from this being the case, he had an old mother in Wales to whom he was absolutely devoted, and when I told her of this she said, 'Well, I can't help it, he ought not to look like that.'

The Duchess built and endowed the little church of St Agnes at Newmarket, next door to her house. One very wet summer, when the prospects of the harvest were very bad all over the country, she had a horse in the St Leger particularly suited to the heavy going.

One Sunday, the Rev. Colville Wallis put up a special prayer for fine weather. The Duchess rose from her pew and walked out of church. She sent for Wallis and said, 'How dare you pray for fine weather in my church when you know perfectly well it will ruin my horse's chance, and I shall not allow you to preach in my church again.' Mr Wallis, who knew the old lady well, and had a great affection for her, did not argue the matter, and holds the living to this day.

The Duchess had a big stud-farm at Newmarket, where the Stanley House Stables and Lord Derby's Stud Farm are now situated.

At the dispersal of her stud in 1894, the year of her death, Pilgrimage, carrying Jeddah, winner of the Derby; her daughter Canterbury Pilgrim, winner of the Oaks, and dam of Chaucer and Swynford; and Roquebrune, winner of the New Stakes at Ascot, and dam of Rock Sand, winner of the Derby, were sold. In fact, she owned some of the best blood in England, and she bred and raced many good horses, but their management left much to be desired, and her success was not what it should have been.

She led her trainers an anxious life, with the exception of Alec Taylor, and he was supposed to be the only man she was afraid of. She was very capricious and changeable with regard to her jockeys – a failing not unusual in her sex.

Huxtable used to ride for her when the weights were light at one time. On one occasion, when he was beaten, she was furious, and said to him, 'Why on earth didn't you do as I told you and come along with the horse?' 'I am sorry, Your Grace, but I should have had to come along without the horse,' was the reply.

Huxtable was a quaint little man. Once at Manchester on a very foggy day a certain jockey of rather unsavoury reputation was beaten on a very hot favourite, and, when riding him back to the paddock, kept looking down at his horse's legs, as if he was lame or sore. Huxtable shouted out, 'Don't look at his legs; I think his jaw is broken.'

With all her peculiarities, the Duchess was a great lady, and a good sportswoman. She loved her horses and was a good judge of racing and a great figure on the Turf. She was always wonderfully kind to me and I was very fond of her.

THE HON. GEORGE LAMBTON, *Men and Horses I have Known*

# The Conspiracy

*The two ladies were harmless enough compared with the quartet of owners who established a training centre in the middle of Salisbury Plain, at the Druid's Lodge. The four's dream was not just to win big races, it was to win big races with unexposed horses at long odds and clean up with the bookies. They took Edward II's invitation very seriously.*

PUREFOY liked to say that he made his money in London and spent it in Ireland. And in ensuring that there was always plenty in the coffers, his attention was increasingly focused on racing – and on betting. There were one or two particularly 'hot' establishments to show the way. The long era of the greatest of all gambling owners, Captain James Machell, was drawing to a close. Lord Carnarvon's Whatcombe stable and Captain Bewicke's Grateley syndicate were two contemporaries who had the bookies running for cover. Purefoy decided that racing could be made to pay, and pay handsomely. He had acquired a taste for the turf while racing a few steeplechasers in Germany in the early 1890s. Back at Greenfields, musing with Holmer Peard on the rich pickings available from the London bookmakers, he was on the lookout for a private trainer. His eye fell on a young man from Roscommon called Jack Fallon.

Jack had impeccable credentials. He was the son of a small-time trainer who sent him to England at the age of thirteen to 'do his two' at the Kingsclere stables of John Porter. On returning to Ireland, Fallon spent some time with Michael Dennehy on the Curragh, rode over fences, and then turned to training. Before long he gave every sign of knowing the exact time of day, and just when he might have been looking for bigger challenges and opportunities, along came Purefoy with an offer to set him up in England with a guaranteed supply of horses to train. In September 1894, Fallon was installed with a mixed string of Purefoy's and Peard's flat and jumps horses at Everleigh, north of Salisbury. The stable – now occupied by Richard Hannon – had been owned by 'The Mate', Sir John Astley, a celebrated Victorian owner and gambler who was briefly a Member of Parliament. At one public meeting he was asked what he thought of Sir Wilfred Lawson's Liquor Bill. His reply, which deserved to win any election, was 'I don't know much about Sir Wilfred's liquor bill, but mine's a damned sight too high!'

That winter Pure re-met Percy Cunliffe in South Africa and the two made common cause. Cunliffe too had been nurturing predatory thoughts about bookmakers. Their objective was simple: to part the bookies from their money. The strategies would be to operate private – extremely private – stables, and to spread costs and risks among a few like-minded friends. Pure had the trainer. He and Cunliffe had the friends. Frank Forester, Edward Wigan and Holmer Peard represented an extraordinary resource: all three were horsemen and one was a top vet. And of the five Confederates, four – all but Peard – were millionaires by today's measure. All five were experienced administrators or businessmen. Their roles would be clear-cut. Cunliffe was to be the master strategist, the identifier of targets; Purefoy was the 'racing commissioner', in charge of stable administration and betting; Peard would judge the gallops on his visits from Ireland, besides giving unmatched veterinary advice; Forester and Wigan would add counsel and finance.

One aspect was undecided: location. Cunliffe had the answer. His and Purefoy's scheme necessitated privacy. What could be more private than Salisbury Plain? And as it happened, high up on the Plain in the middle of his estates, Cunliffe owned a property with potential, just two miles south-west of Stonehenge. It was historic terrain for the training and racing of horses. A little to the north of Stonehenge, running for almost two miles east to west is the 300-feet wide *cursus*, or course, dating back 4500 years. Its eighteenth-century discoverer William Stukeley imagined the *cursus* 'Crowded with chariots and horsemen', and hailed it as 'certainly the finest piece of ground that can be imagined for the purpose of a horse race'.

The grass of Salisbury Plain, wrote Stukeley, 'composes the softest and most verdant turf in the world, extremely easy to walk on and [rising] with a spring under one's feet'. The motorist speeding south from Stonehenge to Salisbury today sees little but a modern water tower on the left of the road and a couple of old cottages to the right. When Cunliffe laid his plans, the cottages were a coaching inn, the Druid's Head. It was utterly isolated. The nearest hamlets were a couple of miles away, at Middle Woodford and Berwick St James. A few years before, the Druid's Head had been run by a colourful couple called Guts and Gaiters. They kept a few horses behind the pub, and galloped them on the downs opposite.

On a fine October Wednesday morning in 1895, Jack Fallon walked sixteen of Purefoy's string the few miles from Everleigh to their new home at the Druid's Head stables. Cunliffe had closed the pub. He began the construction of an imposing house a hundred yards back from the road on the open downs. A covered verandah to allow Cunliffe and his guests to enjoy the views across the Plain ran round three sides of the new house, Druid's Lodge. A few yards from the Lodge, Cunliffe built a large U-shaped stable block. The stables were the last word in luxury and attention to detail. They contained individual boxes for forty horses in training, each box lined with metal strips to discourage crib-biting. All the woodwork was oak. The boxes were enclosed, with a covered passage-way running along the front of the doors. This arrangement meant warmth in winter and coolness in summer – not to mention security.

The tack-room, dominated by a beautiful coaching-clock taken from the Druid's Head, had a wood-block floor that wouldn't have disgraced a ballroom. By the tack-room was a kitchen where the lads' meals were prepared. Stairs led up to a dormitory for the lads and apprentices. The dormitory was the entire loft of one leg of the U. In another loft was an elaborate feed-milling machine. A large coal-fired sauna allowed rugged-up horses to be sweated to speed up conditioning. Besides retaining a few of the loose boxes from the Guts and Gaiters days, to house the hacks and horses out of training, Cunliffe built a block of eight hospital boxes a little way away from the main stables to allow the isolation of any coughs or runny noses. They served also as a quarantine area for horses new to the yard. Little or nothing was left to chance.

Between building the Lodge and the stable block and turning some cottages into homes for Fallon and the married lads, Cunliffe sank the best part of *two and a half million pounds* (at today's rates) into Druid's Lodge. Now, the trees and shrubs that he planted have grown to maturity and the Lodge and the stables are hidden from the road. Then, the buildings stood gaunt and exposed on the downs. Any resemblance to a penal institution was intentional. Fallon's former master John Porter used to complain of the unsolicited letters that his lads received. He quoted one:

> Sir, I now venture to ask if you are agreeable to correspond with me for the racing season. You may rest assured it would be quite safe, and it will be kept quite secret between us. If you should favour me by answering, you could name a place where you could get your letters safe.

Very likely, Jack himself received similar missives. He described Druid's Lodge as like 'a fortress in the Sahara':

> Life amid the unending sands couldn't have been more lonely than the existence we led on Salisbury Plain. There was

absolutely nowhere to go. The sight of a horse and trap coming along the road brought all the stable lads to the gates with their eyes popping with curiosity.

Cunliffe and Purefoy were thoroughly alert to the temptations facing low-paid lads. They took every precaution possible. The lads' mail was opened to see who they were writing to, and who was writing to them. A strict curfew was enforced at night. All the staff were locked into their dormitory. The iron concertina gate that barred their exit is now at the National Horseracing Museum in Newmarket.

Occasionally, of course, information leaked. Fallon was down at the hospital boxes when he 'suddenly smelt a most beautiful aroma'. Thinking for a moment that he must be in 'a fashionable restaurant instead of a racing stable', he took another deep sniff – then ordered the lad in charge of the box to turn out his pockets. First appeared a silk handkerchief, drenched in scent. Then a gold fob watch and chain. The lad was rolling in money. He admitted helping himself to the stable's winners. It didn't suit Cunliffe and Purefoy one bit. If each of the fifty or sixty staff employed at Druid's Lodge by the end of the 1890s had his own coterie of punters, what pickings would be left for the Confederates? At the same time, it would have been inconsistent – not to say hypocritical – to expect the lads to be indifferent to betting when the whole *raison d'être* of the stable was plundering the bookies. Purefoy hit on the solution. If any of the lads wanted to back a stable runner, that was fine, but they had to place their bets through him. Winnings and losses would be credited or debited with their wages.

In an establishment run along the lines of Druid's Lodge, it was always possible that things weren't what they seemed. The horse burning up the gallops might not be intended to win; indeed, in races with ante-post betting, it might not even be running. But Purefoy could hardly reveal intimate stable plans when a lad tugged his forelock and asked for 'ten shillings on my horse next week, Sir'. Instead, Pure maintained a charming subterfuge. If a lad had his bet on a horse that wasn't 'intended' or didn't run, Pure never docked the loss from his pay packet. With a perfectly straight face he told his crestfallen employee that – wasn't it just as well?

– he hadn't been able to find a bookmaker. The lads' lot at Druid's Lodge was hard, but not harsh. There wasn't the institutionalised cruelty of some of the stables of the time.

Cunliffe was a remote, unsmiling figure. They said he was terrified of horses, but he wanted to maintain appearances by riding up to the gallops on a hack. So the lads had standing instructions, whenever he was due down from London, to gallop a broad-backed old cob to the point of exhaustion. By the time the enormous Cunliffe was perched on its back, the poor creature scarcely had the energy to put one foot in front of another, still less give him any trouble.

Purefoy was the best sort of paternalist employer. Back at Greenfields, he paid for every medical and dental expense for his staff. He had a kind word for every stable lad, and a genuine interest in their welfare. Many of them came to Druid's Lodge from Tipperary, and they were a raw-boned lot. The sophisticated locals delighted in teaching them to spell: 'd-o-g spells cat', and so on.

Cunliffe used to fret about the Irish lads' visits to confession. On high days and holidays they were taken to mass in Salisbury. Other times, the Catholic priest would visit the stable. Cunliffe asked Fallon if it was possible that the lads might be owning up to more than they should in the confessional box? And if so, could Jack have a quiet word in the reverend's ear? Another reverend, Parson Twining from Middle Woodford, worried about the welfare of the lads in their isolation. He organised football matches and other games. Cunliffe was appreciative and gave Fallon £100 to donate to parish funds.

On another occasion, Cunliffe learned that Salisbury hospital, where any injured lads from the yard were taken, didn't have a lift, so he paid for one to be installed. And more than once he arranged jobs for unhealthy lads in the friendlier climate of South Africa, and paid for their travel. With a reputation to maintain as a hard master, he did all these good works anonymously.

PAUL MATHIEU, *The Druid's Lodge Confederacy*

*The Druid's Lodge confederacy were to land some of the biggest touches ever seen on a racecourse, in particular in the Cambridgeshire, the prestigious nine furlong handicap at Newmarket's October meeting.*

*But the most spectacular win was that of Aboyeur, the 100–1 winner of the infamous 1913 Derby in which suffragette Emily Davidson was killed. Pure had £1000 on with Ladbrokes, a win that netted him over £2 million at today's prices.*

# The Punting Prime Minister

*The list of racehorse owners past and present spans the social world, the dream burning as brightly in the heart of the millhand as it does in the monarch. Once, even politicians were allowed to dream. In the days before political correctness, the colours of an incumbent Prime Minister were led triumphant into the winners' enclosure at Epsom, those of the great Liberal, Lord Rosebery. Like most other owners, Rosebery had tasted the poisoned chalice of defeat before the Gods switched cups. As a youth in 1869, he strongly fancied his Ladas to win at Epsom and encouraged all his former college cronies – forced by the authorities to choose between racehorses and reading for his degree, he quit Oxford University rather than his stable – to steam on to his 66–1 shot, Ladas. His reasoning, though less scientific, is more poetic than the* Sporting Life's *Man On The Spot.*

IT IS the Derby Wednesday, carrier pigeons come in flights, There is terror in St James's street, and agony in White's.
From Hayling Isle to Newmarket they have begun to toast
The foremost horse that stayed the course and foremost passed the
    post.

From Dan and from Beersheba, from Joppa and Gilgal,
The Israelites are flocking, resolved to stand or fall:
From the Baron to the broker each one is like a lion, he
Having staked his bottom shekel on the son of bay *Hermione*.

The Christ Church tutors put a tax on those who came in late,
And they were puzzled how to spend the tribute of the Gate.
So they put it on the Derby, and pitched upon a horse
Who took his rise from *Lambton*'s thighs, and cannot stay the
    course.

There was wailing in the Common Room, the Censors tore
    their hair,

Some scraped themselves with potsherds, and some began to swear,
They d—d the race of *Lambton*, and cursed *Zenobia's* womb,
And wished the race of racehorses a universal tomb.

'They're off!' They stream along the hill at a pace to try the bellows,
Which tomorrow will want mending in the 'Drums and
    *Masaniellos.*
Bright as a scattered rainbow, swift as the dawn of day,
No living horse can stay the course in that breakneck sort of way.

They come along a cracker, now the ruck begins to shirk,
Padwick is flogging *Ethus*, and the Baron is at work;
And from the hill arises a wail of souls in pain,
Where Gad and where Jeshurua bewail their vanished gain.

And now from out the beaten crowd a flogging four there come,
*Pero Gomez* and *Pretender, Ladas* and *Belladrum.*
They have passed the Judge's tribune – Good heavens, what a pot!
And all shout 'What the devil's won?' and Echo answers 'What?'

*The answer was not favourable as Lord Rosebery shamefacedly a admitted in his next verse.*

Now thank your prophet, Gentlemen, ye who plunged upon the
    Drummer,
Who lumped it upon *Rupert* or on *Ladas* went a bummer.
For he told the first two horses who the Judge's tribune passed
Then he wrote a warning comma – and the names of the two last.

*Twenty-five years on and lately installed at Number 10, Rosebery again set out for Epsom with a horse called Ladas. But no 66–1 chance this time. In 1894 Ladas II had swept all before him and was one of the hottest Derby favourites, backed by the elect-orate down to 9–2 on. A freshner to the earlier verses was required.*

So sung your Bard in '69, with cheerful lamentation,
His hopes were past, his horse was last, and all was desolation;
The name of *Ladas* clung to him, a hissing and a scorn,
And he began to sorrow that he ever had been born.

But life is long and youth is young and it is weak to brood,
So his potsherd was discarded and his ashes were shampooed.
And he set himself in earnest a courser to acquire,
That should write the name of *Ladas* in characters of fire.

The search was long and painful, though his horses did abound,
Few, few were swift, and few could stay, and fewer still were sound.
One here and there discredited his colours in a race,
Some vanished into sausages, some vanished into space.

But after patient waiting his drooping hopes were cheered,
For at last the steed of destiny and victory appeared,
As handsome as Apollo and swifter than a bird;
So the flouted name of *Ladas* for him was disinterred.

I trust the hopes of Oxford and the Loders' cash he bor,
And the wounds of '69 were healed in '94:
For *Ladas* won the Derby amid consoling cheers –
After a painful interval of five and twenty years.

A quarter of a century – O vanished years and gold!
Count not the withered thousands, nor the faded years unfold.
Count not the price indeed, for then would victory seem dear;
Let the recording Angel be ready with a tear.

Your Bard was Senior Censor then – or something of the kind –
But there were other censors to his errors far from blind;
Some cursed him as a sportsman, and others still more keen
Damned his followers as faddists – whatever that may mean.

So all he reaped was buffets, applied on either cheek,
Which he bore – all things considered – with resignation meek.
While his winnings were requested for churches and for chapels,
So that Derbies – in fruition – resemble desert apples.

One certain gain alone accrues – experience beyond price –
So let the battered veteran administer advice.
(Of course ye will not take it, ye Loders bold and free),
'Let others own the horses that ye go out to see.'

Another moral yet there is, if moral can be found
In what is so immoral and obviously unsound;
To be may be unlawful, to race may be a sin,
Still in racing, as in everything, it's always best to win.

5<sup>th</sup> EARL OF ROSEBERY

*Rosebery's Liberal Party agreed with the sentiments of the seventh and eighth verses, particularly as the lord was a heavy punter, and after a year in office, Rosebery handed over the keys to Downing Street. He may have done with politics but Rosebery's love affair with the turf continued until his death in 1929. He was another owner to vex his trainers. He once introduced Jack Jarvis with 'This is Mr Jarvis, who trains winners for me', a pause, 'but not recently'. His irascibility was perhaps fired by his love of the betting ring which he visited frequently and heavily. Having dropped almost £1700 in a day at the course, he noted in his diary 'a fair day's racing'.*

# Never Despair

*Few have the resources of a Rosebery to lavish on the best yearlings, the pick of the stallions or the priciest trainers. Most owners have to be content with the pickings. Actor Robert Morley was an enthusiastic owner – he acquired his first horse from the income from his first major part and named the brute The Gloomy Sentry after a character in the play. Together with Wilfred Hyde-White he owned and backed his string with little success but much pleasure.*

ONE OF my happiest extravagances, much recommended to readers of this book is the acquisition from time to time of a young racehorse. This can be in my case a form of advertisement and occasionally partly deductible by the Lord Commissioners of Income Tax, but there is no chance of getting your money back unless you are Arabian or Robert Sangster and able to control the market. Even then it is highly improbable.

But to journey to Newmarket on a warm autumn evening, to forgo dinner and instead bite on a cheese sandwich and then to come home with a yearling you have arbitrarily selected against the advice of the experts, and often of your trainer, is an exhilaration of a special and a unique kind. You don't, of course, exactly come home with the creature. It is wafted away to be broken and schooled on the Downs of Berkshire or the sands of Morecambe. You go home with the cheque-book counterfoil and begin to test your genius in nomenclature. To find a suitable name

– witty but with a hint of the breeding. And then you wait for your trainer's progress reports.

'He is jumping out of his skin . . . he is the best walker in the yard . . . he still needs a bit of time . . . he'll let us know when he's ready to run.'

Then there is all the excitement of Wolverhampton in the late summer when he finishes ninth in a field of eleven – but he really started to race in the last furlong, you tell yourself. One day perhaps! No one ever considers suicide with a two-year-old in training.

ROBERT MORLEY, *The Pleasures of Age*

*The final word can be given to a foreigner, Count von Bismark, Germany's Iron Chancellor who broke away from the Congress of Berlin where the European powers were dividing up the continent of Africa to British Prime Minister Benjamin Disraeli. The substance of the chat was related by Disraeli in a report to Queen Victoria.*

. . . we talked and smoked. If you do not smoke under such circumstances, you look like a spy, taking down his conversation in your mind. Smoking in common puts him at his ease.

He asked me whether racing was still much encouraged in England. I replied never more so; that when I was young, tho' there were numerous race meetings, they were at intervals and sometimes long intervals. . . . Epsom, Ascot, Doncaster, Goodwood . . . and Newmarket frequently; but now there were races throughout the year . . . It might be said, every day of the year . . . and all much attended.

'Then,' cried the Prince eagerly, 'there never will be Socialism in England. You are a happy country. You are safe, as long as the people are devoted to racing. Here a gentleman cannot ride down the street without twenty persons saying to themselves, or each other, "Why has that fellow a horse, and I have not one?" In England the more horses a nobleman has, the more popular he is. So long as the English are devoted to racing, Socialism has no chance with you.'

BENJAMIN DISRAELI

# TRAINERS

'Hard is to teach an old horse amble true.'
SPENSER, *Faerie Queen*

*Once horse and owner have been introduced, they are in need of a train-*
*er to condition the beast, acquaint him with the rudiments of racing and*
*prepare him for the glory that is rightfully his. This can be a thankless*
*task. A trainer has to balance the uselessness of his charge with the*
*aspirations of its owner, a tightrope walk at the best of times. When the*
*horse is very slow and the owner's hopes very high, then there are prob-*
*lems. Tom Oliver, one of the first great trainers of steeplechasers – and*
*before that a mean jockey of the early nineteenth century – came as close*
*to bluntness as any trainer will. 'Honoured Sir,' he wrote in reply to yet*
*another suggestion as to what could be done with a very poor horse, 'your*
*horse can stay four miles but takes a hell of a long time to do it – Yours*
*obediently.' Few trainers are so direct. Most prevaricate and slip into*
*trainerspeak, a language which has one hundred and one ways of*
*saying 'this horse is bloody useless', all of them polite. This trait has won*
*the trainer a poor reputation, at least in certain quarters.*

TRAINERS, by and large, move in mysterious ways. Originally they were known as 'training grooms'. The title was appropriate. They fed and cantered the horses and took their orders from owners who knew as much about the business as they did. It was the Hon. George Lambton who first made racehorse training a posh occupation round about the turn of the century. It was he, by the way, who made my favourite snob remark of all time. As an undergraduate at Cambridge he rode regularly to Newmarket to ride work, and one day on the Heath a gentleman work-watcher asked him what college he went to. 'I don't know,' replied Lambton, 'Trinity I suppose.'

Since then the training of horses has gathered about it an utterly disproportionate glamour – equalled only by the ridiculous reverence heaped on fashion photographers who are known to sleep with their models. I fancy you detect a note of sour grapes in my tone; if there is one, then it is because I'm fairly convinced that with the help of a good Irish head lad I too could train the likes of a Nijinsky, a Sea Bird II or a Shergar. In fact, I'm pretty sure that a horse of the stamp of Nijinsky could be galloped up the side of a slag heap every morning and still win the Derby.

Perhaps it's not quite as simple as that, and yes, of course, there are trainers who are tremendously skilful. Richard Hannon is one. He has won the Two Thousand Guineas twice, both times with comparatively cheap horses – Mon Fils and Don't Forget Me. Cheap horses are a feature of his Marlborough yard. He often takes on the bigger, classier yards and beats them. Such has been his success that he is now capable of training more winners than any but the ten or so biggest stables in the country.

Quite apart from his brilliance as a trainer he is also an unusually inventive gambler. About ten years ago his wife had triplets, two boys and a girl. One night after his wife and children had gone to bed, Richard was downstairs enjoying a drink with a merry band of lunatic, punting mad Irishmen when he had a brilliant idea. He crept upstairs, got hold of the triplets, brought them down to the sitting room and arranged them on the sofa. 'Now,' he announced, 'we're going to play Find the Lady.' So there were the triplets gurgling happily on the sofa while all around them Richard's Irish friends were bunging on ten pound notes, twenties, fifties, until finally a fortune had piled up on each of the babies. Then Richard would remove their nappies with a flourish and pay the punters who had found the lady. Then the game would start again: 'All out of the room,' Richard would bellow, 'while I shuffle them.' This marvellous source of income naturally came to an end when the babies grew old enough for their sexes to become too obvious, but before then fortunes were gambled on this real-life version of the three-card trick.

Richard got very merry when Mon Fils won the Guineas at 50–1. 'Fuck you all,' he told the press. 'I'll never have to work again.'

Of course he was back at the yard on Monday morning as usual.

I used to go to the sales with Dave Hanley, Eddie Reavey, Richard Hannon and my friend from Lambourn Doug Marks. On one occasion one of their number, I won't say who, never actually clapped eyes on a horse. He was in the bar all day every day for three days. But he consulted the catalogue from time to time and, on the strength of the breeding alone, sent someone out to bid for him. He ended up with a couple of decent animals and, as I've already said, it is a system I can recommend, especially to those trainers whose yards are stuffed with hand-picked million-dollar purchases that look good but won't do a tap.

Hanging round the sales is where you meet racing characters more than on the track, and you really do meet some idiots. How they get to be entrusted with millions of pounds worth of horse-flesh is one of racing's enduring mysteries. Typical of this sort is the young, arrogant trainer who treats the stable lads the way he treated fags at school. There's even a PR man in the business who's so shabby that when he was an assistant trainer he actually did beat his stable staff. Anyway, this young idiot trainer appears at the sales in the morning in jodhpurs, roll-neck jersey and Barbour and immediately drops house points for boasting about his hang-over. He then spends most of the morning trying to ingratiate himself with anyone with a title and more than a hundred thousand in his account. A disgusting sight.

In the afternoon he appears on the stands in a curly brimmed soft hat and sounds off at full volume in an accent borrowed from St James's Street until about nine in the evening, at which time the wheels fall off his act and he roars off with his chums to some unspeakable olde worlde pub masquerading as a restaurant. Here they revert to prefect days at school, chuck bread rolls at people and scream at their lady friends, all of whom are called Arabella or Emma.

I know one trainer of this type who managed to book Lester Piggott to ride one of his horses. He had a hefty punt on it, but they were beaten a neck. This twit said to Lester afterwards: 'That's it, Lester. You'll never ride for me again.' Dry as you like Lester replied: 'Oh well, I'd better hang up my boots then, hadn't I?'

A band of trade union officials once bought a horse and sent it to this same idiot. One day they organised a coach trip to the yard to see the animal. There were two coach loads of proud, expectant owners, armed with sandwiches and Thermos flasks, all set for a visit to the stables to see their noble beast followed by an excellent day at the races, all for two quid a head. When they arrived at the training establishment, nothing stirred. Not a cock was crowing, not a stable lad in sight. Baffled, perplexed, they piled out of the coaches and wandered up to the house. They looked through a down-stairs window. All they could see was their chosen trainer, in his dinner jacket, lying on a sofa and snoring, two empty champagne bottles on the table beside him. His career as a trainer was short-lived.

I don't want to give the impression that every trainer is a sozzled prat who looks as if someone's just waved a British Rail Race Day 'Special' pork pie under his nose. Take Bill Marshall, for instance, one of the most likeable characters of the Turf. He flew his own Spitfire from South Africa to England in 1940 and said to the RAF: 'Here's a plane and here's a pilot. Help yourself.' He shot down plenty of German planes and was awarded the DFC. Eventually he was shot down himself and was incarcerated in a prisoner-of-war camp. Needless to say he escaped, walked from Bavaria to the north coast of France, nicked a boat and made it back to England. He couldn't speak a word of German and so anyone who asked awkward questions on the way was making a big mistake. Bill used to train at Edenbridge, from where he sent out Raffingora to break the course record at Epsom over five furlongs (hand timing) and thus become the fastest horse in the world. He's only a tiny skinny fellow, but not one to provoke. After he moved to Newmarket he had a row with a colossus of a lorry driver who was trying to dump some supplies Bill hadn't ordered. When things got really heated, Bill simply laid him out with a punch that wouldn't have disgraced Sugar Ray Robinson.

He was one of the very few trainers who actually rode work rather than watching from the back of a hack. Some days he used to ride out three lots, not bad for a man in his fifties. Some of the old brigade of Newmarket trainers thought he was a bit of a nut, but Bill used to say it kept him fit and cleared the liver of any left-over champagne. When he retired he went to Barbados to sit in the sun and drink rum. But he soon got bored of that and now, [1988 approximately] aged about seventy, he is champion trainer over there. When not working he can be found sitting on a boat with a fishing rod in one hand and a rum punch in the other muttering to himself, 'This is the life.'

I can never understand how some of the biggest trainers who have up to two hundred horses in their yards keep track of them all, but you can't argue with success – look at Henry Cecil, he trains enough horses to fill the card at Newmarket for an entire season. And yet the man has a compulsive habit of collecting white shoes and is tee-total – which, I am reluctant to say, gives the lie to the idea that water is the refuge of half-wits. Barry Hills commands a similarly huge operation at Robert Sangster's complex at Manton. Hills made his money on a horse called Frankincense, which he backed down from 66–1 to 100–8 to win the Lincoln, enabling him to rise overnight from travelling head lad to trainer. That's the sort of story that makes people like me broke.

I suppose you have to love horses to be any good with them, and I don't. The girl who did the late Ryan Price's National winner Kilmore was so deeply attached to the animal that she wanted to take it on holiday with her. 'Where the hell are you going to go?' the Captain asked. 'Well, Guv'nor, I'm going to a hotel in Bournemouth and I thought he could stay on the lawn outside.' He was a great character, Ryan Price. He once employed a stable girl who was rather well-endowed. When he saw her having difficulty mounting a horse he would shout: 'Just throw your tits over and the rest will follow.'

But it doesn't do to get too obsessed with racing at the expense of everything else, though I don't see why you should take that sort of advice from me. One day I was being driven back from the races by an old pisspot of a trainer along with his wife Maisy and one of the gutsiest jockeys ever, whom I'd better call K, a real tough nut. He used to kick dead-beat horses into enormous fences in an absurdly fearless manner, but that day he'd ridden one of this trainer's horses without success. Anyway, this trainer and I were in the front of the car, with Maisy and K in the back. Maisy had her head concealed under an old tartan blanket and it was quite clear to me what was going on. The poor old trainer was rambling away about horses as usual: 'You know, K, I think perhaps we ought to try that horse over a different trip next time . . . Give him two and a half miles in the soft and he could be anything, especially if we let him make his own running . . .' It was lucky he was talking to K not Maisy. Her mouth was full, and it wasn't a lollipop she was sucking.

JEFFREY BERNARD, Talking Horses

# Things Can Only Get Better

*Not everyone is as harsh as Bernard. Times columnist Simon Barnes spent one year following the fortunes of John Dunlop's Arundel stables, a year that started poorly and got worse. It was particularly black for the trainer who tragically lost his son. Barnes picks up the tale after a frustrating Epsom when the stable's Oaks hope, Three Tails had run an enigmatic race to finish third.*

IT WAS 12 June, the day after the general election [1987], and six days after the disaster of the Oaks. The Conservatives had won the election by a huge majority, so naturally there was a bit of talking politics to be done out on the gallops that morning. Most of racing's top people were pretty pleased with that result. The Conservatives had abolished on-course betting tax, and a Conservative government is always more likely, at least in theory, to leave the rich more spending money with which to buy racehorses. Racing survives on spare cash: people bet with it, and pay training fees with it. Racing's survival depends on the rich being rich: the top racing people voted for Maggie in their droves.

This was also the last week before Royal Ascot, which is the biggest meeting of the year. It is not a meeting with one big race: the point about Royal Ascot is that they are all big races. One race of enormous quality is followed by another, and a winner here is a real prize for any trainer in the land. Mind you, for Dunlop's stable a winner in a selling plate at Thirsk or Carlisle would have been a great leap forward.

After Three Tails had disgraced herself in the Oaks, nothing had run very badly. The only problem was that they did not go past the post in front of the others. The cloud of depression still hung over the stable. Every paper you picked up seem to imply in its smallest print that you would have to be an idiot to back a Dunlop horse.

At Castle Stables, the depression expressed itself as bustle. Everyone was charging about, shouting instructions at each other and getting on with things at a great pace: it was all terribly workmanlike and terribly forced. Everyone was putting a Brave Face on things. Because no winners meant that there was something very badly wrong; no winners meant no bonuses; no winners meant that the stable was not doing its job. Where is the job satisfaction in that? And so there was much whistling and bustling and banging of brooms about the yard: well, things must change soon, mustn't they? Well, they couldn't get any worse. Could they?

John Dunlop had still not been to the races since Tim's death. Who can blame him? English people know neither how to give nor how to receive sympathy. He decided to start racing again after Ascot: 'Ascot is such a social meeting, with all those lunches you have to have with people. If I went, I know everyone would be so embarrassed.' Instead, Tony Couch, bustling and sounding more Yorkshire than ever, was flying the flag at the races. His own bustling straightforwardness during these difficult times had set the tone for the rest of the yard. Someone had to look cheerful, after all.

The weather was doing its best. It was a beautiful sunlit morning, and it was a joy to be out on the gallops, to lean against the Japanese Range Rover and wait for the horses to come past. 'What about a nice big Ascot winner to put a spring back into everybody's step?' I said.

'Yes,' Dunlop said. 'That would be the thing. I thought the Oaks would be the race to cheer us all up, in fact. Ah well. It's either feast or famine.' The two-year-olds began to canter past in their tight groups of six. 'The Oaks filly was a total enigma,' Dunlop continued. 'Halfway through the race, I started to tear my hair out. I thought there must be something desperately wrong, the way she was running. I really thought she was going to be tailed off. It was quite remarkable that she managed to finish third in the end. I can't believe that was right. She came back totally sound – and I am totally puzzled.

'She very much slouches at home, she does her work in a very relaxed way. But she has always run her races perfectly normally. But she reverted to that sloppy, disinterested approach to life in the Oaks . . . which was not quite the day to do it. It could have been the course, I suppose, but she was in as much trouble going uphill as she was going down. Yet before the race she looked marvellous, very relaxed, and I thought she really was in tophole condition.'

In one way, Love The Groom's Derby run was less of a disappointment, since less was expected of him. In some ways it was more of one because, for a moment, it looked as if he might have been capable of doing something fairly useful. 'He ran an interesting race,' Dunlop said. You will notice that his habit of pared understatement remained unimpaired. 'I thought for a moment he was going to make it into the first four, which would have been more than pleasing. My feeling at the time was that he didn't get the trip, and Willie felt very much the same. But the thing was, he got baulked, and once that had happened he just couldn't pick up again. In a race run at that sort of pace, once you have been stopped, you can't get going again.'

The two-year-olds were sorted out in their pairs for work, this being a Friday, and of course by now all the younger horses were expected to work for their living. Two by two, they thundered past, each with a lad curled over the withers. Dunlop's work is done on a six-furlong uphill stretch: horsemen love to see a horse do his preparation uphill. You can put a great deal of work into a much smaller amount of space and time, and therefore put the horse under less stress for the same amount of work. And more importantly, you can get the horses to work at the same quality at less speed: and it is speed that causes most training injuries.

The two-year-olds were beginning to come to themselves, and it was a heartwarming sight to see them burning up the gallop with such enthusiasm. They did not look the products of a beaten yard. There were two in particular that caught the eye. The first was a very handsome colt, the white-faced Nureyev, who had acquired enough individuality to be referred to by his name, which was Alwuhush. The second was the delightfully made Lomond filly: 'Can you remember her name this time?' I asked.

'Yes. Ashayer.'

'She does look good.'

'I think she might be quite nice. And I like the way the Nureyev colt covers such a lot of ground. Alwuhush. Even though you can see that he's not properly organized yet.' These young horses tend to crash about on the gallops with great enthusiasm but their galloping action tends to be a little sprawly and babyish, and it fails to convert all their new-found power into speed. But it comes, it comes. And Ashayer had a precocious poise and balance that had Dunlop purring beside me. 'You can tell from the balance and action that she really might be quite nice.'

'Nice? As good as that?'

'Nice. Special.'

'Special means what?'

'Special means proper. Serious.' Dunlop was teasing, but he was also being serious himself. A possible Classic horse, though it would be ridiculously rash and downright improper to say so right now. Simply that here we have a filly that looks tremendous. Here, perhaps, was the great disappointment of the autumn, or of the following season – but perhaps the horse to rescue the season. Or to recall Dunlop's words of a few months back, it was possible that she might be the greatest racehorse ever to set foot on a track. There was still no knowing, but what we did know for certain was that, well, Ashayer was looking gorgeous. That was enough to be going on with.

Earlier that morning, Dunlop had whisked his entire Ascot contingent down to Findon. The idea was to give the horses a change that would put some ginger into them: and it seemed to have worked, at least that morning. They had been on their toes, sharp, excited and ready to show what they were capable of. Richard Baerlein had startled and pleased me that morning by writing a piece in *The Guardian* that flew in the face of the accepted wisdom of the pundits and the obvious non-form of Castle Stables. Strong Dunlop Challenge for Royal Ascot, said the heading.

'John Dunlop, whose horses appear to be on the brink of finding their form, will be saddling nine horses at Ascot next week,' Baerlein wrote. 'Our old friend Patriach will be trying for the double in the Royal Hunt Cup, but the stable's chief moneyspinner, the St Leger winner Moon Madness, will be up against Henry Cecil's Yorkshire Cup winner, Verd-Antique, in the Hardwicke Stakes. . . . It will be the highlight of Friday's card.'

'So how strong is the hand for Ascot?' I asked.

'It could be stronger. But if I get a few to run well, I will be pleased.' So would I, so would everybody in the yard.

The weather remained marvellous until the horses had returned from second lot. What with the sun and the horses beginning to look so good at home, Dunlop was finding himself in a more cheerful mood than of late. Moon Madness had gone particularly well, and Love The Groom had also worked impressively. 'He doesn't seem to have taken too much out of himself in the Derby,' Dunlop said. He had come back from the Derby very sore in front, but he soon recovered, and had worked like a 100 percenter that morning. Unless he had hurt himself in the gallop, he was all set to run on the first day of Royal Ascot, on the following Tuesday. A trainer on a losing streak must nail his colours to the mast again and again before the eyes of the cynical public. The only way of squashing the rumours and restoring public confidence is by producing winners: every blank day added more pressures.

'It has,' I said, choosing my words like a man picking his steps through a minefield, 'been, er, a fairly leanish sort of spell . . .' 'Bloody awful spell.'

'Can you see the light at the end of the tunnel?'

'I hope so. This week, the horses have all been running well, though without winning. A couple of seconds, that sort of thing. I think it is possible, in retrospect, that we've had a little infection rumbling. We've taken tests, we're always taking tests, every kind of test, but nothing has shown up. It is possible that there has been some kind of low key thing that makes all the horses a little off-colour without making them really ill . . . on the other hand, it is possible that they're just not a terribly good lot. We're short of stars, that's for sure.' Moon Madness would doubtless be giving us hurt looks from his box had we been within earshot. 'But it's been a pretty bleak month, really. Things can only get better.'

'I suppose so,' I said. 'But you can't rely on those bloody four-legged things over there.'

'No,' said Dunlop 'That you cannot.' The horses were now helping themselves to a quiet pick of grass, a customary relaxing treat for them after they have done their bit for the day. It was 28 days since Dunlop had last trained a winner.

SIMON BARNES, *Horse Sweat and Tears*

*Dunlop's season turned its corner when Love The Groom won the King Edward VII Stakes, though Moon Madness could not double up in the Hardwicke. And the babies? Ashayer was crowned queen of her sex with a victory in the Prix Marcel Boussac while Alwuhush ran into third place in Ascot's big autumn juvenile prize, the Royal Lodge.*

# Stable Life

*A trainer like John Dunlop may supervise the campaign but the footsoldiers of racing, the stable lads and lasses, do much of the hard work. John Hislop, the owner and breeder of Brigadier Gerard, was, at one time, part of the stable hierarchy and gives the following account of life in the trenches.*

THOUGH I cannot say I enjoyed that winter at Newmarket, it taught me something about this aspect of training and the less glamorous side of a stable-boy's life. For the winter drags heavily in a flat-racing stable and, though it is the season for the lads' holidays, there are a good many 'spares' to do as a result of this and such exigencies as lads being away through illness.

All else equal, the lad who does a horse will ride him out – if he is too heavy, too old, or unsuited to the horse in question, another will take his place, but when this is not the case a lad resents being 'jocked off' his own horse. Thus, when a lad returns from his holiday he usually has some complaint about whoever has been doing the horse and riding him out during his absence. Like a soldier back from leave, he is seldom in the best frame of mind, and any extra excuse to grumble will be welcome.

'Who the hell's been riding my horse out while I've been away? He was going lovely when I left and now he's got a mouth as if he'd been rode by a man with hands like a nigger's feet. I'll bet it was you, Sheenie, you windy old bastard, hanging on to his head like you was rowing a f—— boat. Why don't you pack it in and go back to f—— Petticoat Lane where you came from.'

'Shut yer bleeding mouth, Tommy. I've only rode 'im twice; John's been on 'im three or four times, and Syd and Chester, and one or two of them others.'

'Two rides from you is enough to f—— any horse for life, the way you ride. Look at you now, catching hold of the rings of the f—— bit like you do the door-handle of the Waggon and Horses at opening time.'

'You go and f—— yerself you psalm-singin' f—— pig. I know yer – 'andin' round the hymn-books in the Bible class with one 'and and feelin' the school-marm's fanny with the other. Ride ! – you couldn't sit on a night-stool without fallin' off. I was ridin' winners when you were still wettin' your f—— pants.'

And so the repartee would pass between one lad and another, as tempers frayed in the freezing wind or sleet.

Poor old Sheenie! He always became furious when he had his leg pulled and, in consequence, was the butt of the yard. His especial tormenter was Tommy, who played mercilessly on his tender spots, Sheenie's fondness for beer and his pride in his abililty to ride. 'Watch out, boys, here comes Michael Beary!' Tommy used to call out, using the name of that famous jockey as a pun on Sheenie's chief weakness. Sheenie's replies were framed round Tommy's attendance at some form of religious meeting and his boyish, pink faced appearance. But he usually worked himself up into a state of speechless spluttering, so that he seldom got the best of the argument. Yet, after he retired and became ill before he died, no one could have been more solicitous in going to see him and cheer him up than his former bane, Tommy. I fancy that Sheenie missed their daily verbal battles when he left the stables.

Sheenie was typical of the older generation of stablemen, now almost extinct. He had started in the era when jockeys rode 'long', and though, as a gesture to progress, he pulled his leathers up a hole or two, he never became converted to the modern racing seat. I do not remember where he served his time, but he had been for a while in France and had, in fact, ridden quite successfully as a jockey at some period, but, as not infrequently happens, had lost most of his earnings betting and had gone back to 'doing his two'. He must have been about sixty when I knew him, but his nerve was good and he was quick and alert – if you didn't watch the old villain he would always pinch a length on you at the start of a gallop, on principle, for the spirit of competition had never died in him. A neat little grey-haired man, with a round, merry face, a large mouth, a nose flattened by a fall, and bright steely eyes, he had a faintly simian look about him. He walked with the traditional, bow-legged, rather nautical gait of the stableman, and he frequently hissed through his teeth or blew through his lips.

He always wore the old-fashioned stableman's uniform of boots, leggings, breeches and a coat – as opposed to a wind-breaker, to which the younger lads were then becoming converted; and he never rode out without diving into his tool bag, getting out a boot brush and giving his boots a rub up. Appropriately, in the light of his French associations, he used to do Finglas, of whom he was very fond, in spite of the horse having savaged his arm badly when he was taking him over to run in the Prix de l'Arc de Triomphe: 'It wasn't 'is fault; 'e got frightened when the 'orse-box lurched, and 'e grabbed the first thing 'e could see, so as to keep 'is balance, and it was just bad luck that it 'appened to be my arm.'

I sometimes used to catch a glimpse of Sheenie when I rode out at Newmarket in later years, if the string passed his house in Granby Street and the sound of hooves and a sunny morning brought him to the door to exchange greetings with any lads he knew.

Neat and tidy as ever, he would stand in the sunshine in his shirtsleeves and carpet slippers, with a warm, happy smile on his face, the expression of one enjoying the memories of pleasant times recalled, and a quip ready for old acquaintances.

'Them was good days with the guv'nor at Clarehaven,' he said when I went to visit him in retirement. 'You see, I've still got the old horse's photo,' and he produced a framed photograph of Finglas to show me.

'Yes, 'e was a great 'orse – should 'ave won the Hascot Gold Cup.' Then, as if to himself: 'Never meant to 'urt me when 'e grabbed me; 'e was a kind 'orse really.' It was the last time I saw him.

JOHN HISLOP, *Far from a Gentleman*

# Last of the Great Eccentrics

*The group best placed to appraise the trainer is his staff. They have to bear with the foibles, share the lean and bask in the reflected glory of his success. Appended is their staff's report.*

IF YOU asked a trainer for his opinion of his members of staff, he would either lie and say that he liked and respected us all, or else he would come clean and admit that he thought us a disreputable bunch of uncouth, illiterate undesirables with whom it was his misfortune to have to mix every day. I apologize to those I misjudge, but, alas, I don't think it includes many. I'm sure that the trainers appreciate that they get tremendous value for money, but we are, nevertheless, a necessary evil, and they never seek our company outside the yard, nor know anything about our lives, save what we do for a living. So what do we think of them? The most frequent line heard when the stable lads get to talking about their trainers is, 'The guy's a nutcase!'

I have done a fair bit of travelling around, and I've worked with all sorts of horses – hunters, polo ponies, show jumpers, and in riding schools, and during this time I've come to the conclusion that all rich people who are besotted with horses are eccentric. But not until I began to work in racing and move amongst rich, horsy people, whose lucrative businesses depend upon the whims of luck and fate, did I realize how fine is the line which separates genius from lunacy.

I mean, what other shrewd businessman would invest thousands of pounds over and over again on buying stock which could well prove useless, and gamble money in circumstances where a shower of rain or the mood of an animal may tip the balance? The fact that trainers do all this surely makes them daft; the fact that they can make it pay demonstrates more than a touch of genius.

The bigger and more successful the trainer, the more apparent this becomes. Small trainers dress and behave like farmers. They work alongside their stable lads, and it must keep them down to earth; but as they get more successful, so the eccentricities begin to emerge. It is more than just action and words; there is an aura, a little surrealistic cloud, hovering above the trainer's head, labelled 'loony'. They start to wear strange clothes – silly hats are one of the first signs, followed by ludicrous footwear, and loud-coloured jackets and trousers. While struggling trainers merge into the background on Newmarket Heath, the champion trainer can be seen on a grey horse in a pink sheet, attired in a Donny Osmond hat, red suede knee-length boots, tartan jacket and jeans; and a trainer who had his first Classic successes last season may be in blue corduroy trousers decorated with pink butterflies, little rubber wellies, an electric green quilted coat and a velvet riding hat. These people may then turn around and make a fuss about a stable lad leading up a horse at the races wearing training shoes!

However, I'm not exactly the best dressed person in the world myself (I began to grow my hair because I got sick of shop assistants calling me 'sir'), and I don't believe in judging people by their appearances alone; so I'll tell you what else makes stable lads refer to our employers as nutcases.

There is one who takes his dogs out to dinner. His favourite restaurant, no doubt influenced by large tips, indulges him by providing a table with a heavy tablecloth, which hides the dogs from other diners who may find it anti-social. The trainer sneaks in, and his spoilt, well-trained dogs slip under the table discreetly and await the delivery of medium rare steaks in silence. It seems quite a harmless whim; but you can imagine the surprise of one fellow diner, who watched with interest as the waiter brought four steaks to a table for two, and then saw the trainer cut two of them into pieces, and begin to throw them underneath the tablecloth. 'Excuse me,' said the fellow diner, leaning across with a sour expression, 'but would you mind telling me what on earth you are doing?' The trainer replied calmly, 'I'm feeding my dogs.' The fellow diner contemplated calling the manager, but, as the trainer continued to blithely shove bits of meat under his table, he thought better of it and returned to his own meal, whilst casting occasional anxious glances at the apparent lunatic behind him.

Then there was the incident in a yard when a trainer had a row with his wife, who locked him out of the house and wouldn't let him back in. Far from trying to play it cool, this man rallied the help of his lads, positioned the hay elevator underneath an open bedroom window, and, whilst his staff operated the piece of machinery, rode up to the only available access, and wriggled in.

And what about this tale – a Newmarket trainer, who was

having trouble getting one of his best horses in peak condition, decided that our water contained too much lime and so gave the horse Perrier water to drink by the gallon. It subsequently won a Group race, so he was perhaps right. Is that genius, or lunacy?

I could fill a whole book with this sort of stuff, but it becomes so incredible as to seem downright silly. And anyway, I adore eccentricity; it was one of the things I most missed when I lived abroad. Live and let live is my motto. The only time I find the racehorse trainer's lunacy anything other than amusing is when it endangers my life. One of my old trainers took his string of horses miles from his yard in order to get to a canter which he wanted to use; on arriving, he found that a hurdle had been placed across the bottom of the track, with a large 'Closed' sign. Undeterred, he removed this obstruction, and sent us all up the canter in a tight bunch at a brisk pace. We rounded a bend, and came face to face with a tractor, pulling a chain harrow, raking the ground. By some miracle, we all managed to pull aside in time, and there was a mad stampede of horses, fleeing in all directions across the Heath like frightened mice. It was some time before we reassembled and were able to walk home again in shocked silence. I expect that the trainer duly received a nasty letter from the Jockey Club about the incident, and possibly was fined, too, for using closed ground. But it had little effect. He continued to intrude upon prohibited areas regularly. We staff proceeded with caution forthwith, for it is certain that if the stable lad does not look out for himself, nobody else will.

There is stigma in this business about admitting that you are scared. If a stable lad finds that his name has been placed alongside that of a notoriously dangerous horse on the riding-out board, he should square up his shoulders, stiffen the old upper lip, and say proudly, 'The Guv'nor knows who can ride 'em!'

I'm not sure who is responsible for the stout maintenance of this imbecile tradition, but the trainers certainly exploit it, and those lads who readily leap aboard horses which may well be the death of them ought in theory to be admired and respected. Not so. These lads are silly buggers. I think so, and so do the trainers. Not only do these unrewarded heroes find themselves saddling one crazy horse after another, without relief, but when they do eventually fall off and get hurt, they will get no sympathy.

A young, daring apprentice was once riding a horse which bolted with him. It ran off the Heath and across the main road, but its hooves slipped on the hard road, and, at full gallop, it fell and skidded for several yards, dragging the rider along underneath it. When it finally came to a halt, it scrambled to its feet and sped away, leaving the young lad battered and dazed on the road. Very nasty, but not uncommon. As luck would have it, a police car was waiting at the traffic lights and witnessed the accident. The officers radioed for an ambulance and were removing the recumbent form from the middle of the road when the trainer came along on his hack. The policemen informed him that the horse had galloped home, and hastened to assure him that an ambulance was on its way for the lad. 'Oh, don't bother with that,' said the trainer impatiently, 'I've just got one more lot of horses to work, and then I'll come and collect him.'

That was no isolated incident; that is the normal response to injured lads. The invalid's colleagues, though, will not be any more sympathetic. Once the body has been removed from the scene, the lads will begin to discuss the accident and say things like, 'Well, it was his own fault, the useless bugger. He should/shouldn't have hit it.' And the next day there will be another hero eager to get on board the horse in question and prove that he can manage it, especially if the trainer butters them up with such compliments as, 'I'd better give this to someone who knows what he's doing.' Because the vast majority of lads believe that they are better racehorse trainers than the men they work for.

When lads get to comparing the acts of 'madness' of their respective bosses, they will undoubtedly include such daft things as running what the lad believes to be a five-furlong horse over six, and sending a nervous filly up the gallops before her lad considers that she is ready.

Personally, I think it is daft to *be* a racehorse trainer. If I were a millionaire, I'd be damned if I'd get out of bed at half past five every morning, work seven days a week for months on end, and spend my holidays jetting off to yearling sales and wooing potential clients. The lads do plenty of moaning about all their hard work, but I reckon that the trainers do twice as much. Certainly, they make plenty of money out of it, but what is the point of having a new Mercedes if the only place you are going to go in it is up to the gallops? The small trainers might get some fun out of the job, but the really big ones, with 150 horses in their care? Imagine the paperwork, the phonecalls, the frantic organization when there is one horse running in America, two in Newcastle and three at Sandown, all on the same day, and one of the horses at Sandown is reported to be a bit lame, and one of the runners at Newcastle has arrived without his racing colours, and the phone lines to America are all engaged, and the lads in the yard want to know if they can start a bit later tonight, because there is a football cup final on the telly. No wonder trainers keep getting more and more horses. There's not much about the job to attract new blood, is there? It must be enough to drive anyone crazy!

Trainers are fiercely possessive of their duties. I have often wondered why, in these days of 200-horse yards, they don't go into partnerships; but they are too jealous of their privileged positions, they don't want to share the responsibility, not even with their head lads or assistants. One of my bosses went away to America buying yearlings at the end of the season, leaving his two head lads in charge. A few days later, he phoned up to tell the man in charge to make sure we stable lads washed our grooming kits – nothing else, just that. Why? He never told us to wash our grooming kits when he was at home; he left it to us to keep them clean. But, I suppose, he simply couldn't bear the thought that he no longer had hold of the reins, that we were managing just fine without him, and were not missing him in the least. He just had to keep his oar in. Trainers don't take holidays. They're workaholics.

One of my trainers, on a particularly cold morning in January, must have been in a mood of excessive self-pity, for he began to whine to me about his sorry lot in life. 'I don't have to work this hard,' he grizzled. 'I could make a good living out of just sixty or seventy horses.' I made soothing noises, but wondered to myself: if he felt like that, then why on earth did he persist in slaving away, trying to train twice as many? Musing away the freezing morning, I came to the conclusion that it must be more than an obsession with the racing game. It must be a miserly obsession with money; because he, and most of the other trainers in town, have a strange attitude towards the stuff.

Over and over again, in yards where I have worked, I have seen trainers spend vast amounts of money on gimmicks, while the lads are obliged to share pitchforks and hoof-oil brushes, because there aren't enough to go round. One trainer even made us spend a wet morning darning our mucksacks. It seems to me that to get a trainer to prise open his wallet is no mean achievement, but once he starts to spend, then there is no stopping him – until he realizes what he is doing, and then he snaps his purse shut again in horror and won't get it out again for months. The same trainer who had us repairing worn out mucksacks decided to install, at the cost of some £15,000, a closed-circuit television security system around his yard. He was immensely proud of it – the first in Newmarket – until, to his dismay, he realized that in order for it to be effective he was going to have to leave the stable lights on all night. Horror of horrors! The electricity bill! In an attempt to economize, he removed the 100-watt lightbulbs and replaced them with others of only 40 watts.

Another of my bosses, always reluctant to buy new equipment for the yard, found that as his business prospered and grew he simply did not have enough tack to go around. Some lads were riding out with their horses dressed in rugs which were threadbare, faded and torn, while others were obliged to put two light sheets on their mounts to keep them warm. So he splurged, and bought a great pile of smart new rugs — but then permitted us to use them only when owners were visiting.

SUSAN GALLIER, *One of the Lads*


*Trainers are clubbable animals, congregating in packs at centres like Newmarket, Lambourn or Malton. Despite this pack mentality, there is no collective noun for the breed, though many have suggested disaster and an equal number triumph. A triumph of trainers does have a certain ring. Nestled amid the Berkshire Downs, Lambourn is the most beautiful of the three great training centres and the twin villages have been home to many of the greats from both the flat and jumps. One prominent Lambourn trainer of yesteryear was Aubrey Hastings to whose grave Sir John Betjeman alludes in the following verses.*

# Upper Lambourne

Up the ash-tree climbs the ivy,
  Up the ivy climbs the sun,
With a twenty-thousand pattering
  Has a valley breeze begun,
Feathery ash, neglected elder,
  Shift the shade and make it run –

Shift the shade toward the nettles,
  And the nettles set it free
To streak the stained Carrara headstone
  Where, in nineteen-twenty-three,
He who trained a hundred winners
  Paid the Final Entrance Fee.

Leathery limbs of Upper Lambourne,
  Leathery skin from sun and wind,
Leathery breeches, spreading stables,
  Shining saddles left behind –
To the down the string of horses
  Moving out of sight and mind.

Feathery ash in leathery Lambourne
  Waves above the sarsen stone,
And Edwardian plantations
  So coniferously moan
As to make the swelling downland,
  Far-surrounding, seem their own.

JOHN BETJEMAN

# JOCKEYS

'One who manages or has to do with horses;
a horsedealer. Obs or dial 1638. Hence, a crafty
or fraudulent bargainer, a cheat. 1683.'
*Oxford English Dictionary*

*Jockeys are the front men of racing, the eyecatchers whose names, good
or bad, spring readiest to the public's lips. Cheered and cursed from the
stands, jockeys are like the girl with the curl in the middle of her
forehead. When they are good, they are very, very good but when they
are bad they are horrid. The very, very good are immortalised.*

I ONCE went to Newmarket to interview Lester Piggott for
*The Sunday Times.* He rode two hot-pots for a big trainer on the
gallops that morning and when he got off the second one he said
it was a Derby prospect. On the way back to his house we came
across a loose horse that had obviously thrown its stable lad on
the way home and was now standing stupidly in the middle of
the road. It was the Derby prospect. I pointed it out to Lester and
suggested we stopped and got hold of it – after all, it could easily be smashed up by a car. Lester smiled rather wickedly: 'No,
Jeffrey. You never catch hold of a loose horse. You can spend all
bloody day hanging on to it.' I thought this a charmingly cynical
approach.

At the end of the morning I explained that I had to get back to
Newbury for the races. 'You're an idiot,' he told me succinctly.
'Don't you realise I'm riding there this afternoon? You can have
a lift in my aeroplane.' So we flew to Newbury in his four-seater
with Geoff Wragg and another trainer. I got out at the races, and

said thank you very much and thought nothing more of it. A week later I got a bill for thirty-five quid. A little later, a reminder followed. Incensed by this display of parsimony I told one of the stalls handlers about it. This same man found himself loading Lester into the stalls one day soon after. 'Lester,' he said, 'that thirty-five quid bill you sent to Jeff – he's very annoyed about it . . . ' Apparently when the stalls opened Lester was laughing so much that he almost fell off.

Lester is astute and funny, but his humour is dry and abrasive and when teamed up with a brain that fires on all cylinders it is easily misunderstood. Most of the stories about his meanness are really about Lester winding people up, teasing them – like the day he gave Willie Carson a lift back from York one sweltering August day. Lester told his chauffeur to pull up at a garage selling ice cream. 'Get three,' he told the man, who returned shortly and handed over three cones to Lester. Carson put his hand out for one, but Lester simply turned to him and said: 'They're mine, get your own.' This sort of incident, purely an experiment to see how discomfited Carson could look, has been exaggerated to make Lester seem pathologically mean, which he isn't. He's just tight.

I can remember sitting outside a café in Chantilly feeling bored and depressed and anxious about my fast-dwindling expenses – the afternoons are horribly dead even in that lovely place – and who should walk by but Lester. I never thought that worried, taut, serious face would be a cheering sight off a horse but I nearly burst into a couple of verses of 'We'll Meet Again' *à la* Vera Lynn. But Lester didn't stop to say hello. That might have cost him a glass of red wine.

It's not true either that he never smiles, though it doesn't look as if there'd be room between the crags. I remember a day at Ascot when he landed the King George VI and Queen Elizabeth Diamond Stakes with a brilliant ride on that gutsy horse The Minstrel. He then went on to win the Brown Jack Stakes on the Queen's horse Valuation. In the enclosure afterwards he was talking to the Queen and beaming like the cat that's got the cream. I gather that the Queen had said to him: 'You made it look so easy.' And with an admirable lack of false modesty he had replied: 'Ma'am, it *was* easy.'

Another occasion sticks in the mind. Soon after Vincent

O'Brien sacked him, Lester popped up and beat one of O'Brien's best horses by a short head in a thrilling finish. O'Brien was standing miserably in the unsaddling enclosure. Lester walked past him on his way to the scales and gave him a huge grin. 'Will you be needing me again?' were his only words.

As in all departments, Lester Piggott talks a great deal of sense about gambling. I once told him the story of an Italian waiter in Frith Street who put his life's savings on a horse that Lester was riding and which started at 6–5. You don't back horses like that with your life's savings, not unless you're mad, but this man did, and Lester got stuffed that day – beaten by a very small margin – a neck or half a length. The waiter was reduced to hysteria and suddenly began screaming in the betting shop: 'Alla my life I givva my wife good food . . . My children havva the shoes on their feet . . . They eata well, they're clothed, I paya the rent . . . And now this fucking bastard Piggott, he kill me, he ruin my life . . . ' In a little while he was transferred to the Middlesex Hospital in a straight-jacket. When Lester heard this story, he simply remarked that people like that are idiots. And he was right. After all, no one twists your arm to have a bet. If you lose your wages, well that's your fault.

I don't envy the racing correspondents who, now that he's a trainer (and naturally a successful one), have to try and get statements from Lester after one of his horses has won. He is certainly no orator and tends to reply in short, sharp, grumpy monosyllables. But for my money he's the Guv'nor of all time. There's a long-standing debate about who was the greatest, Lester or Gordon Richards. No contest. After all, Gordon could ride almost anything, but Lester had many fewer mounts because of his weight problems. His genius is unique – he's a Jack Dempsey, a Joe Davis, a Donald Bradman.

JEFFREY BERNARD, *Talking Horses*

# Jockeyship

*It's easy to ride a winner in the stands. Up there you don't have several tons of horseflesh galloping alongside at forty miles an hour, you have a willing partner and everyone else will kindly step aside to allow your winning run through. The novelist Dick Francis, an ex-jockey remembered for his disaster at Aintree rather than his triumphs, describes his former art exhilaratingly.*

THE SIGNAL was given for jockeys to mount, and Dusty, the travelling head-lad who nowadays deputised for Wykeham more often than not, removed North Face's rug with a flick and gave me a deft leg-up into the saddle.

The princess said, 'Good luck', and I said cheerfully, 'Thank you.'

No one in jump racing said 'Break a leg' instead of 'Good luck', as they did in the theatre. Break a leg was all too depressingly possible.

North Face was feeling murderous: I sensed it the moment I sat on his back and put my feet in the irons. The telepathy between that horse and myself was particularly strong always, and I simply cursed him in my mind and silently told him to shut up and concentrate on winning, and we went out on to the windy track with the mental dialogue continuing unabated.

One had to trust that the urge to race would overcome his grouchiness once the actual contest started. It almost always did, but there had been days in the past when he'd refused to turn on the enthusiasm until too late. Days, like this one, when his unfocussed hatred flowed most strongly.

There was no way of cajoling him with sweet words, encouraging pats, pulling his ears. None of that pleased him. A battle of wills was what he sought, and that, from me, was what he habitually got.

We circled at the starting point, seven runners in all, while the roll was called and girths were tightened. Waited, with jockeys' faces turning pale blue in the chilly November wind, for the seconds to tick away to start-time, lining up in no particular order as there were no draws or stalls in jump races, watching for the starter to raise the tapes and let us go.

North Face's comment on the proceedings took the form of a lowered head and arched back, and a kick like a bronco. The other riders cursed and kept out of his way, and the starter told me to stay well to the rear.

It was the big race of the day, though heavier in prestige than prize money, an event in which the sponsors, a newspaper, were getting maximum television coverage for minimum outlay. The Sunday Towncrier Trophy occurred annually on a Saturday afternoon (naturally) for full coverage in the *Sunday Towncrier* itself the next morning, with self-congratulatory prose and dramatic pictures jostling scandals on the front page. Dramatic pictures of Fielding being bucked off before the start were definitely not going to be taken. I called the horse a bastard, a sod and a bloody pig, and in that gentlemanly fashion the race began.

He was mulish and reluctant and we got away slowly, trailing by ten lengths after the first few strides. It didn't help that the start was in plain view of the stands instead of decently hidden in some far corner. He gave another two bronco kicks to entertain the multitude, and there weren't actually many horses who could manage that while approaching the first fence at Cheltenham.

He scrambled over that fence, came almost to a halt on landing and bucked again before setting off, shying against coercion from the saddle both bodily and clearly in mind.

Two full circuits ahead. Nineteen more jumps. A gap between me and the other runners of embarrassing and lengthening proportions. I sent him furious messages: Race, you bastard, race, or you'll end up as dogmeat, I'll personally kill you, you bastard, and if you think you'll get me off, think again, you're taking me all the way, you sod, so get on with it, start racing, you sod, you bastard, you know you like it, so get going . . .

We'd been through it before, over and over, but he'd never been worse. He ignored all take-off signals at the second fence and made a mess of it and absolutely refused to gallop properly round the next bend.

Once in the past when he'd been in this mood, I'd tried simply not fighting him but letting him sort out his own feelings, and he'd brought himself to a total halt within a few strides. Persevering was the only way: waiting until the demonic fit burned itself out.

He stuck his toes in as we approached the next fence as if the downhill slope there alarmed him, which I knew it didn't; and over the next, the water jump, he landed with his head down by his feet and his back arched, a configuration almost guaranteed to send a jockey flying. I knew his tricks so well that I was ready for him and stayed in the saddle, and after that jolly little manoeuvre we were more than three hundred yards behind the other horses and seriously running out of time.

My feelings about him rose to somewhere near absolute fury. His sheer pigheadedness was again going to lose us a race we could easily have won, and as on other similar occasions I swore to myself that I'd never ride the brute again, never. Not ever. Never. I almost believed I meant it.

As if he'd been a naughty child who knew its tantrums had gone too far, he suddenly began to race. The bumpy uneven stride went smooth, the rage faded away, the marvellous surge of fighting spirit returned, as it always did in the end. But we were a furlong and a half to the rear, and to come from more than three hundred yards behind and still win meant theoretically that one could have won by the same margin if one had tried from the start. A whole mile had been wasted; two left for retrieval. Hopeless.

Never give up, they say.

Yard by flying yard over the second circuit we clawed back the gap, but we were still ten lengths behind the last tired and trailing horse in front as we turned towards the final two fences. Passed him over the first of them. No longer last, but that was hardly what mattered. Five horses in front, all still on their feet after the long contest, all intent on the final uphill battle.

All five went over the last fence in front of North Face. He must have gained twenty feet in the air. He landed and strode away with smooth athletic power as if sticky bronco jumps were the peccadillo of another horse altogether.

I could dimly hear the crowd roaring, which one usually couldn't. North Face put his ears back and galloped with a flat, intense, bloody-minded stride, accelerating towards the place he knew was his, that he'd so wilfully rejected, that he wanted in his heart.

I flattened myself forward to the line of his neck to cut the wind resistance; kept the reins tight, my body still, my weight steady over his shoulders, all the urging a matter of mind and hands, a matter of giving that fantastic racing creature his maximum chance.

The others were tiring, the incline slowing them drastically, as it did always to so many. North Face swept past a bunch of them as they wavered and there was suddenly only one in front, one whose jockey thought he was surely winning and had half dropped his hands.

One could feel sorry for him, but he was a gift from heaven. North Face caught him at a rush a bare few strides from the winning post, and I heard his agonised cry as I passed.

Too close for comfort, I thought, pulling up. Reprieved on the scaffold.

There was nothing coming from the horse's mind: just a general sort of haze that in a human one would have interpreted as smugness. Most good horses knew when they'd won: filled their lungs and raised their heads with pride. Some were definitely depressed when they lost. Guilt they never felt, nor shame nor regret nor compassion: North Face would dump me next time if he could.

The princess greeted us in the unsaddling enclosure with starry eyes and a flush on her cheeks. Stars for success, I diagnosed, and the flush from earlier embarrassment. I unbuckled the girths, slid the saddle over my arm and paused briefly before going to weigh in, my head near to hers.

'Well done,' she said.

I smiled slightly. 'I expected curses.'

'He was especially difficult.'

'And brilliant.'

'There's a trophy.'

'I'll come right out,' I said, and left her to the flocking newsmen, who liked her and treated her reverently, on the whole.

I passed the scales. The jockey I'd beaten at the last second was looking ashamed, but it was his own fault, as well he knew. The Stewards might fine him. His owners might sack him. No one else paid much attention either to his loss or to my win. The past was the past: the next race was what mattered.

DICK FRANCIS, *Break In*

*A professional earning his money at the top end of the scale. At the other end, there are the amateurs who bump round three or four times a season on their own horses in a point-to-point.*

# What the Captain Said at the Point-to-Point

I've had a good bump round; my little horse
Refused the brook first time,
Then jumped it prime;
And ran out at the double,
But of course
There's always trouble at a double:
And then – I don't know how
It was – he turned it up
At that big, hair fence before the plough;
And some young silly pup
(I don't know which),
Near as a toucher knocked me into the ditch;
But we finished full of running, and quite sound:
And anyhow I've had a good bump round.

SIEGFRIED SASSOON

*Amateur or pro, good or indifferent, it comes down to bottle. How many times can one go out there and play dodgems, pick one's teeth out of the turf and get back on board. Rudyard Kipling, in this short story, tells of one jockey who had had enough.*

# Broken-Link Handicap

T HERE are more ways of running a horse to suit your book than pulling his head off in the straight. Some men forget this. Understand clearly that all racing is rotten – as everything connected with losing money must be. In India, in addition to its inherent rottenness, it has the merit of being two-thirds sham; looking pretty on paper only. Everyone knows everyone else far too well for business purposes. How on earth can you rack and harry and post a man for his losings when you are fond of his wife, and live in the same Station with him? He says, 'On the Monday following. I can't settle just yet.' You say, 'All right, old man,' and think yourself lucky if you pull off nine hundred out of a two thousand-rupee debt. Any way you look at it, Indian racing is immoral, and expensively immoral; which is much worse. If a man wants your money he ought to ask for it, or send round a subscription-list, instead of juggling about the country with an Australian larrikin; a 'brumby', with as much breed as the boy; a brace of *chumars* in goldlaced caps; three or four *ekka*-ponies with hogged manes, and a switch-tailed demirep of a mare called Arab because she has a kink in her flag. Racing leads to the *shroff* quicker than anything else. But if you have no conscience and no sentiments, and good hands, and some knowledge of pace, and ten years' experience of horses, and several thousand rupees a month, I believe that you can occasionally contrive to pay your shoeing-bills.

Did you ever know Shackles – b. w. g., 15.1 $^3/_8$ – coarse, loose, mule-like ears – barrel as long as a gate-post – tough as a telegraph-wire – and the queerest brute that ever looked through a bridle? He was of no brand, being one of an ear-nicked mob taken into the *Bucephalus* at £4:10s. a head to make up freight, and sold raw and out of condition at Calcutta for Rs.275. People who lost money on him called him a 'brumby'; but if ever any horse had Harpoon's shoulders and The Gin's temper, Shackles was that horse. Two miles was his own particular distance. He trained himself, ran himself, and rode himself; and, if his jockey insulted him by giving him hints, he shut up at once and bucked the boy off. He objected to dictation. Two or three of his owners did not understand this, and lost money in consequence. At last he was bought by a man who discovered that, if a race was to be won, Shackles, and Shackles only, would win it in his own way, so long as his jockey sat still. This man had a riding-boy called Brunt – a lad from Perth, West Australia – and he taught Brunt, with a trainer's whip, the hardest thing a jock can learn – to sit still, to sit still, and to keep on sitting still. When Brunt fairly grasped this truth, Shackles devastated the country. No weight could stop him at his own distance; and the fame of Shackles spread from Ajmir in the South, to Chedputter in the North. There was no horse like Shackles, so long as he was allowed to do his work in his own way. But he was beaten in the end; and the story of his fall is enough to make angels weep.

At the lower end of the Chedputter race course, just before the turn into the straight, the track passes close to a couple of old brick-mounds enclosing a funnel-shaped hollow. The big end of the funnel is not six feet from the railings on the off-side. The astounding peculiarity of the course is that, if you stand at one particular place, about half a mile away, inside the course, and speak at ordinary pitch, your voice just hits the funnel of the brick-mounds and makes a curious whining echo there. A man discovered this one morning by accident while out training with a friend. He marked the place to stand and speak from with a couple of bricks, and he kept his knowledge to himself. Every peculiarity of a course is worth remembering in a country where rats play the mischief with the elephant-litter, and Stewards build jumps to suit their own stables. This man ran a very fairish country-bred, a long, racking high mare with the temper of a fiend, and the paces of an airy wandering seraph – a drifty, glidy stretch. The mare was, as a delicate tribute to Mrs Reiver, called 'The Lady Regula Baddun'– or for short, Regula Baddun.

Shackles' jockey, Brunt, was a quite well-behaved boy, but his nerve had been shaken. He began his career by riding jump-races in Melbourne, where a few Stewards want lynching, and was one of the jockeys who came through the awful butchery – perhaps you will recollect it – of the Maribyrnong Plate. The walls were colonial ramparts – logs of *jarrah* spiked into masonry – with wings as strong as Church buttresses. Once in his stride, a horse had to jump or fall. He couldn't run out. In the Maribyrnong Plate twelve horses were jammed at the second wall. Red Hat, leading, fell this side, and threw out The Gled, and the ruck came up behind and the space between wing and wing was one struggling, screaming, kicking shambles. Four jockeys were taken out dead; three were very badly hurt, and Brunt was among the three. He told the story of the Maribyrnong Plate sometimes; and when he described how Whalley on Red Hat, said, as the mare fell under him – 'God ha' marcy, I'm done for!' and how, next instant, Sithee

104

There and White Otter had crushed the life out of poor Whalley, and the dust hid a small hell of men and horses, no one marvelled that Brunt had dropped jump-races and Australia together. Regula Baddun's owner knew that story by heart. Brunt never varied it in the telling. He had no education.

Shackles came to the Chedputter Autumn races one year, and his owner walked about insulting the sportsmen of Chedputter generally, till they went to the Honorary Secretary in a body and said, 'Appoint handicappers, and arrange a race which shall break Shackles and humble the pride of his owner.' The Districts rose against Shackles and sent up of their best; Ousel, who was supposed to be able to do his mile in 1–53; Petard, the stud-bred, trained by a cavalry regiment who knew how to train; Gringalet, the ewe-lamb of the 75th; Bobolink, the pride of Peshawar; and many others.

They called that race The Broken-Link Handicap, because it was to smash Shackles; and the Handicappers piled on the weights, and the Fund gave eight hundred rupees, and the distance was 'round the course for all horses'. Shackles' owner said, 'You can arrange the race with regard to Shackles only. So long as you don't bury him under weight-cloths, I don't mind.' Regula Baddun's owner said, 'I throw in my mare to fret Ousel. Six furlongs is Regula's distance, and she will then lie down and die. So also will Ousel, for his jockey doesn't understand a waiting race.' Now, this was a lie, for Regula had been in work for two months at Dehra, and her chances were good, always supposing that Shackles broke a blood-vessel – or Brunt moved on him.

The plunging in the lotteries was fine. They filled eight thousand-rupee lotteries on the Broken-Link Handicap, and the account in the *Pioneer* said that 'favouritism was divided'. In plain English, the various contingents were wild on their respective horses; for the Handicappers had done their work well. The Honorary Secretary shouted himself hoarse through the din; and the smoke of the cheroots was like the smoke, and the rattling of the dice-boxes like the rattle of small-arm fire.

Ten horses started – very level – and Regula Baddun's owner cantered out on his hack to a place inside the circle of the course, where two bricks had been thrown. He faced towards the brick-mounds at the lower end of the course and waited.

The story of the running is in the *Pioneer*. At the end of the first mile, Shackles crept out of the ruck, well on the outside, ready to get round the turn, lay hold of the bit and spin up the straight before the others knew he had got away. Brunt was sitting still, perfectly happy, listening to the 'drum-drum-drum' of the hoofs behind, and knowing that, in about twenty strides, Shackles would draw one deep breath and go up the last half-mile like the 'Flying Dutchman'. As Shackles went short to take the turn and came abreast of the brick-mound, Brunt heard, above the noise of the wind in his ears, a whining, wailing voice on the offside, saying – 'God ha' mercy, I'm done for!' In one stride, Brunt saw the whole seething smash of the Maribyrnong Plate before him, started in his saddle, and gave a yell of terror. The start brought the heels into Shackles' side, and the scream hurt Shackles' feelings. He couldn't stop dead; but he put out his feet and slid along for fifty yards, and then, very gravely and judicially, bucked off Brunt – a shaking, terror-stricken lump, while Regula Baddun made a neck-and-neck race with Bobolink up the straight, and won by a short head – Petard a bad third. Shackles' owner, in the Stand, tried to think that his fieldglasses had gone wrong. Regula Baddun's owner, waiting by the two bricks, gave one deep sigh of relief, and cantered back to the Stand. He had won, on lotteries and bets, about fifteen thousand.

It was a Broken-Link Handicap with a vengeance. It broke nearly all the men concerned, and nearly broke the heart of Shackles' owner. He went down to interview Brunt. The boy lay, livid and gasping with fright, where he had tumbled off. The sin of losing the race never seemed to strike him. All he knew was that Whalley had 'called' him, that the 'call' was a warning; and, were he cut in two for it, he would never get up again. His nerve had gone altogether, and he only asked his master to give him a good thrashing, and let him go. He was fit for nothing, he said. He got his dismissal, and crept up to the paddock, white as chalk, with blue lips, his knees giving way under him. People said nasty things in the paddock; but Brunt never heeded. He changed into tweeds, took his stick and went down the road, still shaking with fright, and muttering over and over again – 'God ha' mercy, I'm done for!' To the best of my knowledge and belief he spoke the truth.

So now you know how the Broken-Link Handicap was run and

won. Of course you don't believe it. You would credit anything about Russia's designs on India, or the recommendations of the Currency Commission; but a little bit of sober fact is more than you can stand.

RUDYARD KIPLING

# The Losing Streak

*Like Torriano's racehorse and whore, a jockey is only as good as his reputation. For the top twenty riders this is not often a problem, their retaining stables provide them with a constant stream of winners whose success attracts outside rides like flies to a midden. But beyond the elite, life becomes harder and the infamous Catch 22 comes into play. If a jockey hits a drought of winners, the rides dry up, especially the good ones. Without a decent horse beneath him, the jockey struggles to return his name to the winners' enclosure. The former jockey and trainer Jack Leach examines this problem.*

TO RETURN to the subject of luck, I have known many top-flight jockeys nearly go out when a run of bad luck has lasted a long time. Bill Rickaby, who is riding so well nowadays, had an atrocious run of luck and was practically out when it suddenly changed. Freddie Fox was another who had a long spell in the wilderness before he came back with a bang to win classics and head the list. Henry Spencer (the Ice Man), a great jockey before my time, was sent back to America because the heads kept going against him, although some of the best judges said he was a great rider and he certainly proved it in America.

And, of course, there must have been a lot of good ones that did go clean out. I have only known two jockeys that never had a bad run, or anyway not a long one. They were Richards and Charlie Elliott. I once had a very bad trot and went to Yarmouth one day for a single ride on a poor horse. I remember standing near the weighing room before the first race, feeling depressed and thinking, as somebody once said, 'the prospect presents but few attractions', when along came Harvey (Jack) Leader and asked me to ride Duteons in the second and Rock Dove in the fifth as Michael Beary had not arrived back from Ireland. Both horses won, and that started a combination of Leader and Leach that was very successful for quite a few years – in fact until I got too heavy to ride and had to retire.

Billy Rickaby's case was extraordinary. At one period he couldn't get a ride at all. Nobody would wear him and, in fact, he seriously thought of packing up altogether and going abroad to try his luck. I like to think that I had a lot to do with him staying on here until the luck turned, and I am sure Bill will not mind me telling the story.

One evening I went into the Craven Club at Newmarket and saw Bill looking down in the mouth and talking very seriously to a couple of other boys. Suddenly he turned to me and said, 'What do you think?' As I had not been listening to the conversation I said, 'About what?' Bill then told me that he hadn't ridden a winner for months and hadn't been offered a ride on anything that could keep itself warm for the last three weeks. He could see no prospects whatsoever, and did I think he ought to try to get a job somewhere abroad. I thought it over and said, 'No. You are a good jockey, the weight is not too bad, everybody knows you are straight, and the luck will turn one day, especially when you least expect it.'

It was not long afterwards that the luck did turn for Bill. He came up on a couple of long shots, got some more riding, won a few races, and two years afterwards was riding for one of the most powerful stables in the country and has never looked back.

The case of Henry Spencer was long before my time. This American boy had a great record in the States and had won all the big races including the Kentucky Derby, the Preakness, the Belmont, the Futurity, in fact the lot. He was known as the 'Ice Man' because he had great patience and would sit still until the last few strides and then snap them up on the post. This was when he was riding against Tod Sloan and other great jockeys.

He was first jockey for James R. Keene, who had then about the most powerful stable in America. Somewhere around 1902 Keene decided to race in England, brought his horses over to be trained by my father, Felix Leach, and Spencer came over to ride them. I remember years later my father telling me that he thought Spencer was the best jockey he had ever seen, even better than Tod Sloan and Danny Maher.

However, things went badly at first. Good things had a habit of getting narrowly beaten, and Spencer got the blame. The old man told me that he rode a beautiful race in the Chester Cup but was beaten a short head and was booed by the crowd as he returned to weigh in. The Hon. George Lambton asked him to ride a horse in a big race. This was also beaten a head and although Mr. Lambton said that Spencer rode perfectly the owners would not put him up again. His quiet style of riding did not suit the English racegoers, who in those days liked to see a lot of action, and plenty of whip and spur in a tight finish.

The lack of success or luck or whatever it was did not suit James R. Keene, a self-made millionaire who wanted results – winning ones. And so there was a conference at Graham Place in Newmarket where my father trained. Mr. Keene led off: 'Spencer is not riding half as well as he was in America. He must go back.' My father said: 'It's not Spencer's fault; he's riding better than any jockey in the country. The horses are all carrying top weight and are just getting beaten.' Spencer jumped up and said, 'I don't need anybody to stick up for me, Mr. Leach. To hell with Keene. I'm going home.' It was a lively conference while it lasted, but Spencer went back to America; my old man said it was a tragedy as we lost a great jockey. Back in the States Spencer again went to the top and stayed there for many years.

These are a few isolated cases that I happen to know of personally. There must have been many more. Any competent jockey can win if he gets on the 'goods'. But you must have a bit of luck.

Here is another illustration. A bad jockey might have won the Derby on Colombo. This is what I said when perhaps the greatest controversy there has ever been about this race, and believe me there have been plenty, was raging. Freddy Fox agreed with me but we were in a minority of two, except perhaps for the unfortunate jockey himself, Rae Johnstone, who said less than anybody in the racing world. In fact he only made two remarks that I know of. One was: 'Well, anyway, no lives were lost,' and later, when he got fed up with all the questions: 'A jockey would have won by ten minutes.'

Why I say that a bad jockey might have won on that horse (although, as the form worked out afterwards, it is doubtful) is that at the most critical part of the race, half way down the hill to Tattenham Corner, Johnstone had Colombo perfectly balanced and going beautifully in a position that jockeys dream of. He was on the leaders' heels on the inside, not losing an inch of ground and ready to move whenever he liked after turning for home.

A bad jockey would almost certainly not have been in the position. But here the luck of the race stepped in. Steve Donoghue was on Medieval Knight which had won a mile-and-a-half race and, although the class had not been great, certainly could not have been expected by anybody to stop. Suddenly, going downhill after only 7½ furlongs, that is just what he did, and Colombo was stuck right in his heels with no chance to move. In that split second three other horses moved quickly up on the outside, and so Colombo was in a perfect pocket – although Rae Johnstone had another word for it. Johnstone had two alternatives: to jump Steve and Medieval Knight or to stay where he was. He stayed where he was until the horses on his outside passed him, and then he pulled out. Colombo was then unbalanced and three good horses had got first run on him. He made a gallant effort and for a few strides about a furlong from home looked as if he might still win, but the effort was too much and he died out on his run.

The post-mortems were terrific. Some people said that Steve had ridden to beat Colombo; but this was ridiculous. Medieval Knight stopped as if he was shot when Steve was determined to get round Tattenham Corner, in front if possible. But the majority of the critics slammed Rae Johnstone. 'Steve would have won a hundred yards on that horse,' was the remark of most of the thousands of great riders on the stand.

Rae rode a few more races for Lord Glanely, the owner, before he got the sack and went back to ride with great success in France. But he came back to England later to win three Derbies and many other classics, and so it goes to prove that there is only one thing certain about luck, it always changes – especially in racing and generally when you least expect it. And anyway no lives were lost.

JACK LEACH, *Sods I Have Cut on the Turf*

*Ernest Hemingway's Old Man was pinned to the wings of this dilemma in this classic story.*

# My Old Man

I GUESS looking at it, now, my old man was cut out for a fat guy, one of those regular little roly fat guys you see around, but he sure never got that way, except a little towards the last, and then it wasn't his fault, he was riding over the jumps only and he could afford to carry plenty of weight then. I remember the way he'd pull on a rubber shirt over a couple of jerseys and a big sweat shirt over that, and get me to run with him in the forenoon in at the hot sun. He'd have, maybe, taken a trial trip with one of Razzo's skins early in the morning after just getting in from Torino at four o'clock in the morning and beating it out to the stables in a cab and then with the dew all over everything and the sun just starting to get going, I'd help him pull off his boots and he'd get into a pair of sneakers and all these sweaters and we'd start out.

'Come on, kid,' he'd say, stepping up and down on his toes in front of the jocks' dressing-room, 'let's get moving.'

Then we'd start off jogging around the infield once, maybe, with him ahead, running nice, and then turn out the gate and along one of those roads with all the trees along both sides of them that run out from San Siro. I'd go ahead of him when we hit the road and I could run pretty stout and I'd look around and he'd be jogging easy just behind me and after a little while I'd look around again and he'd begun to sweat. Sweating heavy and he'd just be dogging it along with his eyes on my back, but when he'd catch me looking at him he'd grin and say, 'Sweating plenty?' When my old man grinned, nobody could help but grin too. We'd keep right on running out towards the mountains and then my old man would yell, 'Hey, Joe!' and I'd look back and he'd be sitting under a tree with a towel he'd had around his waist wrapped around his neck.

I'd come back and sit down beside him and he'd pull a rope out of his pocket and start skipping rope out in the sun with the sweat pouring off his face and him skipping rope out in the white dust with the rope going cloppetty, cloppetty, clop, clop, clop, and the sun hotter, and him working harder up and down a patch of

**111**

the road. Say, it was a treat to see my old man skip rope, too. He could whirr it fast or lop it slow and fancy. Say, you ought to have seen wops look at us sometimes, when they'd come by, going into town walking along with big white steers hauling the cart. They sure looked as though they thought the old man was nuts. He'd start the rope whirring till they'd stop dead still and watch him, then give the steers a cluck and a poke with the goad and get going again.

When I'd sit watching him working out in the hot sun I sure felt fond of him. He sure was fun and he done his work so hard and he'd finish up with a regular whirring that'd drive the sweat out on his face like water and then sling the rope at the tree and come over and sit down with me and lean back against the tree with the towel and a sweater wrapped around his neck.

'Sure is hell keeping it down, Joe,' he'd say and lean back and shut his eyes and breathe long and deep, 'it ain't like when you're a kid.' Then he'd get up before he started to cool and we'd jog along back to the stables. That's the way it was keeping down to weight. He was worried all the time. Most jocks can just about ride off all they want to. A jock loses about a kilo every time he rides, but my old man was sort of dried out and he couldn't keep down his kilos without all that running.

I remember once at San Siro, Regoli, a little wop, that was riding for Buzoni, came out across the paddock going to the bar for something cool; and flicking his boots with his whip, after he'd just weighed in and my old man had just weighed in too, and came out with the saddle under his arm looking red-faced and tired and too big for his silks and he stood there looking at young Regoli standing up to the outdoors bar, cool and kid-looking, and I says, 'What's the matter, Dad?' 'cause I thought maybe Regoli had bumped him or something and he just looked at Regoli and said, 'Oh, to hell with it,' and went on to the dressing-room.

Well, it would have been all right, maybe, if we'd stayed in Milan and ridden at Milan and Torino, 'cause if there ever were any easy courses, it's those two, 'Pianola, Joe,' my old man said when he dismounted in the winning stall after what the wops thought was a hell of a steeplechase. I asked him once. 'This course rides itself. It's the pace you're going at, that makes riding the jumps dangerous, Joe. We ain't going any pace here, and they ain't any really bad jumps either. But it's the pace always – not the jumps that makes the trouble.'

San Siro was the swellest course I'd ever seen but the old man said it was a dog's life. Going back and forth between Mirafiore and San Siro and riding just about every day in the week with a train ride every other night.

I was nuts about the horses, too. There's something about it, when they come out and go up the track to the post. Sort of dancy and tight looking with the jock keeping a tight hold on them and maybe easing off a little and letting them run a little going up. Then once they were at the barrier it got me worse than anything. Especially at San Siro with that big green infield and the mountains way off and the fat wop starter with his big whip and the jocks fiddling them around and then the barrier snapping up and that bell going off and them all getting off in a bunch and then commencing to string out. You know the way a bunch of skins gets off. If you're up in the stand with a pair of glasses all you see is them plunging off and then the bell goes off and it seems like it rings for a thousand years and then they come sweeping round the turn. There wasn't ever anything like it for me.

But my old man said one day, in the dressing-room, when he was getting into his street clothes, 'None of these things are horses, Joe. They'd kill that bunch of skates for their hides and hoofs up at Paris.' That was the day he'd won the Premio Commercio with Lantorna shooting her out of the field the last hundred metres like pulling a cork out of a bottle.

It was right after the Premio Commercio that we pulled out and left Italy. My old man and Holbrook and a fat wop in a straw hat that kept wiping his face with a handkerchief were having an argument at a table in the Galleria. They were all talking French and the two of them were after my old man about something. Finally he didn't say anything any more but just sat there and looked at Holbrook, and the two of them kept after him, first one talking and then the other, and the fat wop always butting in on Holbrook.

'You go out and buy me a *Sportsman*, will you, Joe?' my old man said, and handed me a couple of soldi without looking away from Holbrook.

So I went out of the Galleria and walked over to in front of the

Scala and bought a paper, and came back and stood a little way away because I didn't want to butt in and my old man was sitting back in his chair looking down at his coffee and fooling with a spoon and Holbrook and the big wop were standing and the big wop was wiping his face and shaking his head. And I came up and my old man acted just as though the two of them weren't standing there and said, 'Want an ice, Joe?' Holbrook looked down at my old man and said slow and careful, 'You son of a bitch,' and he and the fat wop went out through the tables.

My old man sat there and sort of smiled at me, but his face was white and he looked sick as hell and I was scared and felt sick inside because I knew something had happened and I didn't see how anybody could call my old man a son of a bitch, and get away with it. My old man opened up the *Sportsman* and studied the handicaps for a while and then he said, 'You got to take a lot of things in this world, Joe.' And three days later we left Milan for good on the Turin train for Paris, after an auction sale out in front of Turner's stables of everything we couldn't get into a trunk and a suitcase.

We got into Paris early in the morning in a long, dirty station the old man told me was the Gare de Lyon. Paris was an awful big town after Milan. Seems like in Milan everybody is going somewhere and all the trams run somewhere and there ain't any sort of a mix-up, but Paris is all balled up and they never do straighten it out. I got to like it, though, part of it, anyway, and say, it's got the best racecourses in the world. Seems as though that were the thing that keeps it all going and about the only thing you can figure on is that every day the buses will be going out to whatever track they're running at, going right out through everything to the track. I never really got to know Paris well, because I just came in about once or twice a week with the old man from Maisons and he always sat at the Café de la Paix on the Opéra side with the rest of the gang from Maisons and I guess that's one of the busiest parts of the town. But, say, it is funny that a big town like Paris wouldn't have a Galleria, isn't it?

Well, we went out to live at Maisons-Laffitte, where just about everybody lives except the gang at Chantilly, with a Mrs Meyers that runs a boarding house. Maisons is about the swellest place to live I've ever seen in all my life. The town ain't so much, but there's a lake and a swell forest that we used to go off bumming in all day, a couple of us kids, and my old man made me a sling shot and we got a lot of things with it but the best one was a magpie. Young Dick Atkinson shot a rabbit with it one day and we put it under a tree and were all sitting around and Dick had some cigarettes and all of a sudden the rabbit jumped up and beat it into the brush and we chased it but we couldn't find it. Gee, we had fun at Maisons. Mrs Meyers used to give me lunch in the morning and I'd be gone all day. I learned to talk French quick. It's an easy language.

As soon as we got to Maisons, my old man wrote to Milan for his licence and he was pretty worried till it came. He used to sit around the Café de Paris in Maisons with the gang; there were lots of guys he'd known when he rode up at Paris, before the war, lived at Maisons, and there's a lot of time to sit around because the work around a racing stable, for the jocks, that is, is all cleaned up by nine o'clock in the morning. They take the first batch of skins out to gallop them at 5.30 in the morning and they work the second lot at 8 o'clock. That means getting up early all right and going to bed early, too. If a jock's riding for somebody too, he can't go boozing around because the trainer always has an eye on him if he's a kid and if he ain't a kid he's always got an eye on himself. So mostly if a jock ain't working he sits around the Café de Paris with the gang and they can all sit around about two or three hours in front of some drink like a vermouth and seltz and they talk and tell stories and shoot pool and it's sort of like a club or the Galleria in Milan. Only it ain't really like the Galleria because there everybody is going by all the time and there's everybody around at the tables.

Well, my old man got his licence all right. They sent it through to him without a word and he rode a couple of time. Amiens, up country and that sort of thing, but he didn't seem to get any engagements. Everybody liked him and whenever I'd come in to the cafe in the forenoon I'd find somebody drinking with him because my old man wasn't tight like most of these jockeys that have got the first dollar they made riding at the World's Fair in St Louis in nineteen ought four. That's what my old man would say when he'd kid George Burns. But it seemed like everybody steered clear of giving my old man any mounts.

We went out to wherever they were running every day with the car from Maisons and that was the most fun of all. I was glad when the horses came back from Deauville and the summer. Even though it meant no more bumming in the woods, 'cause then we'd ride to Enghien or Tremblay or St Cloud and watch them from the trainers' and jockeys' stand. I sure learned about racing from going out with that gang and the fun of it was going every day.

I remember once out at St Cloud. It was a big two-hundred-thousand-franc race with seven entries and War Cloud a big favourite. I went around to the paddock to see the horses with my old man and you never saw such horses. This War Cloud is a great big yellow horse that looks like just nothing but run. I never saw such a horse. He was being led around the paddock with head down and when he went by me I felt all hollow inside he was so beautiful. There never was such a wonderful, lean, running-built horse. And he went around the paddock putting feet just so and quiet and careful and moving easy like he knew just what he had to do and not jerking and standing up on his legs and getting wild-eyed like you see these selling platers with a shot of dope in them. The crowd was so thick I couldn't see him again except just his legs going by and some yellow and my old man started out through the crowd and I followed him over to the jocks' dressing-room back in the trees and there was a big crowd around there, too, but the man at the door in a derby nodded to my old man and we got in and everybody was sitting around and getting dressed and pulling shirts over their heads and pulling boots on and it all smelled hot and sweaty and linimenty and outside was the crowd looking in.

The old man went over and sat down beside George Gardner that was getting into his pants and said, 'What's the dope, George?' just in an ordinary tone of voice 'cause there ain't any use him feeling around because George either can tell him or he can't tell him.

'He won't win,' George says very low, leaning over and buttoning the bottoms of his pants.

'Who will?' my old man says, leaning over close so nobody can hear.

'Foxless,' George says, 'and if he does, save me a couple of tickets.'

My old man says something in a regular voice to George and George says, 'Don't ever bet on anything, I tell you,' kidding like, and we beat it out and through all the crowd that was looking in over to the 100 franc mutuel machine. But I knew something big was up because George is War Cloud's jockey. On the way he gets one of the yellow odds-sheets with the starting prices on and War Cloud is only paying 5 for 10, Cefisidote is next at 3 to 1 and fifth down the list this Foxless at 8 to 1. My old man bets five thousand on Foxless to win and puts on a thousand to place and we went around back of the grandstand to go up the stairs and get a place to watch the race.

We were jammed in tight and first a man in a long coat with a grey tall hat and a whip folded up in his hand came out and then one after another the horses, with the jocks up and a stable-boy holding the bridle on each side and walking along, followed the old guy. That big yellow horse War Cloud came first. He didn't look so big when you first looked at him until you saw the length of his legs and the whole way he's built and the way he moves. Gosh, I never saw such a horse. George Gardner was riding him and they moved along slow, back of the old guy in the grey tall hat that walked along like he was the ringmaster in a circus. Back of War Cloud, moving along smooth and yellow in the sun, was a good-looking black with a nice head with Tommy Archibald riding him; and after the black was a string of five more horses all moving along slow in a procession past the grandstand and the *pesage*. My old man said the black was Foxless and I took a good look at him and he was a nice-looking horse, all right, but nothing like War Cloud.

Everybody cheered War Cloud when he went by and he sure was one swell-looking horse. The procession of them went around on the other side past the *pelouse* and then back up to the near end of the course and the circus master had the stable-boys turn them loose one after another so they could gallop by the stands on their way up to the post and let everybody have a good look at them. They weren't at the post hardly any time at all when the gong started and you could see them way off across the infield all in a bunch starting on the first swing like a lot of little toy horses. I was watching them through the glasses and War Cloud was running well back, with one of the bays making the pace. They swept down and around and come pounding past and War Cloud was way back when they passed us and this Foxless horse in front and going smooth. Gee, it's awful when they go by you and then you have to watch them go farther away and get smaller and smaller and then all bunched up on the turns and then come around towards you into the stretch and you feel like swearing and goddamning worse and worse. Finally they made the last turn and came into the straightway with this Foxless horse way out in front. Everybody was looking funny and saying 'War Cloud' in a sort of sick way and them pounding nearer down the stretch, and then something come out of the pack right into my glasses like a horse-headed yellow streak and everybody began to yell 'War Cloud' as though they were crazy. War Cloud came on faster than I'd ever seen anything in my life and pulled up on Foxless that was going fast as any black horse could go with the jock flogging hell out of him with the gad and they were right dead neck and neck for a second but War Cloud seemed about twice as fast with those great jumps and that head out – but it was while they were neck and neck that they passed the winning post and when the numbers went up in the slots the first one was 2 and that meant Foxless had won.

I felt all trembly and funny inside, and then we were all jammed in with the people going downstairs to stand in front of the board where they'd post what Foxless paid. Honest, watching the race I'd forgot how much my old man had bet on Foxless. I'd wanted War Cloud to win so damned bad. But now it was all over it was swell to know we had the winner.

'Wasn't it a swell race, Dad?' I said to him.

He looked at me sort of funny with his derby on the back of his head. 'George Gardner's a swell jockey, all right,' he said. 'It sure took a great jockey to keep that War Cloud horse from winning.'

Of course I knew it was funny all the time. But my old man saying that right out like that sure took the kick all out of it for me and I didn't get the real kick back again ever, even when they posted the numbers up on the board and the bell rang to pay off and we saw that Foxless paid 67.50 for 10. All round people were saying, 'Poor War Cloud! Poor War Cloud!' And I thought, I wish I were a jockey and could have rode him instead of that son of a bitch. And that was funny, thinking of George Gardner as a son of a bitch because I'd always liked him and besides he'd given us the winner, but I guess that's what he is, all right.

My old man had a big lot of money after that race and he took to coming into Paris oftener. If they raced at Tremblay he'd have them drop him in town on their way back to Maisons, and he and I'd sit out in front of the Café de la Paix and watch the people go by. It's funny sitting there. There's streams of people going by and all sorts of guys come up and want to sell you things, and I loved to sit there with my old man. That was when we'd have the most fun. Guys would come by selling funny rabbits that jumped if you squeezed a bulb and they'd come up to us and my old man would kid with them. He could talk French just like English and all those kind of guys knew him 'cause you can always tell a jockey – and then we always sat at the same table and they got used to seeing us there. There were guys selling matrimonial papers and girls selling rubber eggs that when you squeezed them a rooster came out of them and one old wormy-looking guy that went by with postcards of Paris, showing them to everybody, and, of course, nobody ever bought any, and then he would come back and show the under side of the pack and they would all be smutty postcards and lots of people would dig down and buy them.

Gee, I remember the funny people that used to go by. Girls around supper time looking for somebody to take them out to eat and they'd speak to my old man and he'd make some joke at them in French and they'd pat me on the head and go on. Once there was an American woman sitting with her kid daughter at the next table to us and they were both eating ices and I kept looking at the girl and she was awfully good-looking and I smiled at her and she smiled at me but that was all that ever came of it because I looked for her mother and her every day and I made up ways that I was going to speak to her and I wondered if I got to know her if her mother would let me take her out to Auteuil or Tremblay but I never saw either of them again. Anyway, I guess it wouldn't have been any good, anyway, because looking back on it I remember the way I thought out would be best to speak to her was to say, 'Pardon me, but perhaps I can give you a winner at Enghien today?' and, after all, maybe she would have thought I was a tout instead of really trying to give her a winner.

We'd sit at the Café de la Paix, my old man and me, and we had a big drag with the waiter because my old man drank whisky and it cost five francs, and that meant a good tip when the saucers were counted up. My old man was drinking more than I'd ever seen him, but he wasn't riding at all now and besides he said that whisky kept his weight down. But I noticed he was putting it on, all right, just the same. He'd busted away from his old gang out at Maisons and seemed to like just sitting around on the boulevard with me. But he was dropping money every day at the track. He'd feel sort of doleful after the last race, if he'd lost on the day, until we'd get to our table and he'd have his first whisky and then he'd be fine.

He'd be reading the *Paris-Sport* and he'd look over at me and say, 'Where's your girl, Joe?' to kid me on account I had told him about the girl that day at the next table. And I'd get red, but I liked being kidded about her. It gave me a good feeling. 'Keep your eye peeled for her, Joe,' he'd say, 'she'll be back.'

He'd ask me questions about things and some of the things I'd say he'd laugh. And then he'd get started talking about things. About riding down in Egypt, or at St Moritz on the ice before my mother died, and about during the war when they had regular races down in the south of France without any purses, or betting or crowd or anything just to keep the breed up. Regular races with the jocks riding hell out of the horses. Gee, I could listen to my old man talk by the hour, especially when he'd had a couple or so of drinks. He'd tell me about when he was a boy in Kentucky and going coon hunting, and the old days in the States before everything went on the bum there. And he'd say, 'Joe, when we've got a decent stake, you're going back there to the States and go to school.'

'What've I got to go back there to go to school for when everything's on the bum there?' I'd ask him.

'That's different,' he'd say and get the waiter over and pay the pile of saucers and we'd get a taxi to the Gare St Lazare and get on the train out to Maisons.

One day at Auteuil, after a selling steeplechase, my old man bought in the winner for 30,000 francs. He had to bid a little to get him but the stable let the horse go finally and my old man had his permit and his colours in a week. Gee, I felt proud when my old man was an owner. He fixed it up for stable space with

Charles Drake and cut out coming in to Paris, and started his running and sweating out again, and him and I were the whole stable gang. Our horse's name was Gilford; he was Irish bred and a nice, sweet jumper. My old man figured that training him and riding him, himself, he was a good investment. I was proud of everything and I thought Gilford was as good a horse as War Cloud. He was a good, solid jumper, a bay, with plenty of speed on the flat, if you asked him for it, he was a nice-looking horse, too.

Gee, I was fond of him. The first time he started with my old man up, he finished third in a 2,500 metre hurdle race and when my old man got off him, all sweating and happy in the place stall, and went in to weigh, I felt as proud of him as though it was the first race he'd ever placed in. You see, when a guy ain't been riding for a long time, you can't make yourself really believe that he has ever rode. The whole thing was different now, 'cause down in Milan, even big races never seemed to make any difference to my old man, if he won he wasn't ever excited or anything, and now it was so I couldn't hardly sleep the night before a race and I knew my old man was excited, too, even if he didn't show it. Riding for yourself makes an awful difference.

Second time Gilford and my old man started, was a rain Sunday at Auteuil, in the Prix du Marat, a 4,500 metre steeplechase. As soon as he'd gone out I beat it up in the stand with the new glasses my old man had bought for me to watch them. They started way over at the far end of the course and there was some trouble at the barrier. Something with goggle blinders on was making a great fuss and rearing around and busted the barrier once, but I could see my old man in our black jacket, with a white cross and a black cap, sitting up on Gilford, and patting him with his hand. Then they were off in a jump and out of sight behind the trees and the gong going for dear life and the pari-mutuel wickets rattling down. Gosh, I was so excited, I was afraid to look at them, but I fixed the glasses on the place where they would come out back of the trees and then out they came with the old black jacket going third and they all sailing over the jump like birds. Then they went out of sight again and then they came pounding out and down the hill and all going nice and sweet and easy and taking the fence smooth in a bunch, and moving away from us all solid. Looked as though you could walk across on their backs they were all so bunched and going so smooth. Then they bellied over the big double Bullfinch and something came down. I couldn't see who it was, but in a minute the horse was up and galloping free and the field, all bunched still sweeping around the long left turn into the straightway. They jumped the stone wall and came jammed down the stretch towards the big water-jump right in front of the stands. I saw them coming and hollered at my old man as he went by, and he was leading by about a length and riding way out, and light as a monkey, and they were racing for the water-jump. They took off over the big hedge of the water-jump in a pack and then there was a crash, and two horses pulled sideways out off it, and kept on going, and three others were piled up. I couldn't see my old man anywhere. One horse kneed himself up and the jock had hold of the bridle and mounted and went slamming on after the place money. The other horse was up and away by himself, jerking his head and galloping with the bridle rein hanging and the jock staggered over to one side of the track against the fence. Then Gilford rolled over to one side off my old man and got up and started to run on three legs with his off hoof dangling and there was my old man laying there on the grass flat out with his face up and blood over the side of his head. I ran down the stand and bumped into a jam of people and got to the rail and a cop grabbed me and held me and two big stretcher bearers were going out after my old man and around on the other side of the course I saw three horses, strung way out, coming out of the trees and taking the jump.

My old man was dead when they brought him in and while a doctor was listening to his heart with a thing plugged in his ears, I heard a shot up the track that meant they'd killed Gilford. I lay down beside my old man, when they carried the stretcher into the hospital room, and hung on to the stretcher and cried and cried, and he looked so white and gone and so awfully dead, and I couldn't help feeling that if my old man was dead maybe they didn't need to have shot Gilford. His hoof might have got well. I don't know. I loved my old man so much.

Then a couple of guys came in and one of them patted me on the back and then went over and looked at my old man and then pulled a sheet off the cot and spread it over him; and the other was telephoning in French for them to send the ambulance to take

him out to Maisons. And I couldn't stop crying, crying and chok-
ing, sort of, and George Gardner came in and sat down beside
me on the floor and put his arm around me and says, 'Come on,
Joe, old boy. Get up and we'll go out and wait for the ambulance.'

George and I went out to the gate and I was trying to stop bawl-
ing and George wiped off my face with his handkerchief and we
were standing back a little ways while the crowd was going out
of the gate and a couple of guys stopped near us while we were
waiting for the crowd to get through the gate and one of them
was counting a bunch of mutuel tickets and said, 'Well, Butler got
his, all right.'

The other guy said, 'I don't give a good goddamn if he did,
the crook. He had it coming to him on the stuff he's pulled.'

'I'll say he had,' said the other guy, and tore the bunch of
tickets in two.

And George Gardner looked at me to see if I'd heard and I had
all right and he said, 'Don't you listen to what those bums said,
Joe. Your old man was one swell guy.'

But I don't know. Seems like when they get started they don't
leave a guy nothing.

ERNEST HEMINGWAY

# A Royal Rumpus

*Jockeys must be like Caesar's wife if they want to be jocked up on a
regular basis. A reputation which would fit the OED's obsolete defini-
tion of jockeyship will scare off the trainers. A proven cheat is banned.
Sam Chifney, the most famous jockey of his day and the progenitor of a
line of great riders, was asked to take a hike from Newmarket Heath in
a notorious scandal of the eighteenth century. The Prince of Wales, whose
horse, Escape, Chifney was riding, was himself advised to end his asso-
ciation with the turf, lest other owners refused to match their horses against
his. Chifney protested his innocence of any wrongdoing and published
his defence.*

ABUSES THAT ARE GONE ABROAD

I AM repeatedly told, by respectable people, and from all quarters, that it is talked in their counties that Chifney lost

123

intentionally upon His Royal Highness the Prince of Wales's horse Escape, on the 20th of October 1791; and after Escape had pulled up on this said race to walk back to scale, that Chifney was laughing to the Prince of Wales because he had got Escape beat; and then, to suit their wicked construction, they said, and I find that it is sent out to the world, that the Prince won such an immense sum of money upon Escape the following day; and that the Prince gives Chifney two hundred guineas a year for his life after losing this said race with Escape.

* * *

On the 20th October 1791, as I was going on the race-ground in company with others, His Royal Highness from on horse back called to me, saying, 'Sam Chifney, Escape is sure of winning to-day, is not he?' I immediately rode up and informed His Royal Highness that I did not know that Escape was sure of winning to-day.

His Royal Highness said, 'yes, Escape is sure of winning to-day'. I then wished His Royal Highness not to bet him; for the odds are likely to be high upon him; that His Royal Highness might lose a deal of money to winning very little.

His Royal Highness then turned short from me, saying, 'no, I shall not bet upon him, but he is sure of winning'; and immediately joined the company that was riding down the lower side of the running ground to the turn of the lands.

I now found myself under a peculiar embarrassment, for I very much wanted to tell His Royal Highness that I was doubtful about Escape being quite fit to run, and that this was my only reason for wishing His Royal Highness not to bet upon him; and yet I thought Escape might win without being quite well to run; therefore, if I made any complaint about Escape's condition, and he should afterwards win, I thought I should be represented by some as mischievous. Those thoughts were what made me so slow in trying to break my opinion to His Royal Highness, that I was doubtful about Escape not being fit to run; under these impressions, I wished to be well timed in acquainting His Royal Highness with my doubts about Escape's fitness to run.

After there had been a race or two over, His Royal Highness was in the carriage with Lord Barrymore, standing near the lower end of the rails, by the turn of the lands; and I was on horse-back, standing at a small distance from the carriage, when His Royal Highness called to me, and asked me if Escape's race was coming next, I answered, 'yes, your Royal Highness'.

His Royal Highness said, 'come this way, Sam Chifney, I will give you your orders how to ride Escape'. I immediately got up to the side of the carriage, and His Royal Highness said, 'Sam Chifney, I wish you to make very strong play with Escape'; then made a pause, as I thought, for me to make answer: I did not make answer. His Royal Highness then said, 'Sam Chifney, I am never afraid when that I am giving South and you orders, for I know you are both too good jockeys to over-mark your horses; but now I will not compel you to make play with Escape; providing there should be good play made by any other horse, you may wait with Escape; but should there be no other horse make such as you think good play, you must take care to make good play with Escape. I hope, Sam Chifney, you perfectly understand.' I said, 'yes, your Royal Highness, I perfectly understand.' His Royal Highness then ordered the carriage to drive to the betting-post.

Mr W. Lake had been standing with his horse in his hand, near the carriage, but on the other side of the rails, whilst His Royal Highness was giving me my orders how to ride Escape.

Directly the carriage was gone, I was then passing near to Mr W. Lake: he said, 'well Chifney, has the Prince given you orders how to ride Escape?'. I said, 'yes, Sir'. Mr W. Lake said, 'what are your orders?'. I told Mr Lake that His Royal Highness wished me to make very strong play with Escape; but after, His Royal Highness gave me leave to wait, with Escape, provided there should be any other horse make good play; but should there be no other horse make such as I thought good play, that I must take care to make good play with Escape.

Mr W. Lake then asked me if I thought that the best way for Escape to run? I replied, 'no Sir, if I had my life depending upon Escape's winning to-day, I should wish Escape to wait by all means; but as his Royal Highness told me he should not bet upon him, and as I am so often contradicting my orders, and as I was not asked my opinion, I thought it would be impertinent of me to offer to give His Royal Highness any more trouble.'

Mr Lake said, 'well, Chifney, I think as you do, that Escape had better wait, so you will wait at all events; and I see the Prince's carriage, I will go immediately and make everything perfectly pleasant.'

I immediately went over to saddle; when I was saddling Escape, I asked if he had had a sweat since he ran last; and I was answered that he had not had a sweat since his running against Grey Diamond. The horses started, I waited with Escape, and was beaten.

Immediately that the race was over, Escape pulled up to walk back to scale. His Royal Highness came up to me, saying, 'Sam Chifney, you have lost this race by not making play with Escape as I desired you.' I answered, 'I don't know that I have, your Royal Highness.' His Royal Highness then said, 'Yes, you certainly have lost the race by not making strong play with Escape.' I then hoped His Royal Highness had not lost much money upon the race. His Royal Highness said, 'No, I have not lost a stiver; but that don't argue, for Escape certainly would have won, if you had made strong play with him, as I desired you; and I do tell you, Sam Chifney, that I am a better jockey than Mr. Lake and you both, for you have lost the race by not running as I desired you.' His Royal Highness turned from me, for I was got to the scale-house to light and weigh.

Whilst I was in the weighing-house, I received a message to attend His Royal Highness. Immediately I got my clothes on I went immediately to His Royal Highness, who was on horse-back with Mr W. Lake, standing close to the farther winning-post of the Beacon Course. His Royal Highness said, 'Sam Chifney, what is the meaning of Escape's being beaten to-day, for you tell me that Escape is the best horse in the world?'.

I replied, 'I did tell your Royal Highness that Escape was much the best horse in England, and I think the same of him now, your Royal Highness.' His Royal Highness continued, 'Sam Chifney, tell me your motive immediately why Escape is beaten to-day.'

'I will tell your Royal Highness my motive immediately why I think Escape is beat today. It is a fortnight, or a fortnight and a day, I think, since Escape ran last, which was with Grey Diamond. During that time, Escape has not had a sweat, neither has he been tried since, but he has been tenderly treated; and notwithstanding he looks straight and handsome to the eye, he is unfit to run;

and this I believe is the reason of his being beat to-day, your Royal Highness'.

His Royal Highness said, 'Very well'. I then bowed and drew back to a small distance, facing His Royal Highness and Mr Lake, not knowing whether His Royal Highness had quite done with me; and while I was thus waiting, I heard His Royal Highness or Mr Lake say something about Escape's running tomorrow. I immediately took the liberty of asking His Royal Highness if Escape were to run to-morrow. His Royal Highness said, 'Yes, I certainly shall run Escape to-morrow.'

I said, 'I am very glad your Royal Highness does run Escape to-morrow, for I think Escape will win to-morrow; and I wish your Royal Highness to back him to-morrow to losing six or seven hundred; and I wish you to back him, Mr Lake, and I will back him, your Royal Highness; and had not Escape run to-day, I should not have wished your Royal Highness to back him to-morrow, for this sharp rally to-day will not fatigue him; it has caused a good perspiration, so as to lighten him of his flesh, and opened his pores, that he will run both faster and longer to-morrow; and his running to-day is my only reason for wishing your Royal Highness to back him to-morrow; for had he not run to-day, I should not have wished your Royal Highness to back him to-morrow.'

\* \* \*

On the 21st of October 1791, when I was on the race-ground, His Royal Highness came to me near or in the Round Course, over against the Well Gap, as there had been a race over some part of the Round Course before Escape's coming on.

His Royal Highness then said, 'Sam Chifney, I will give you your orders again to-day; and let me beg of you to take care that you make no mistake to-day. I wish, Sam Chifney, for you to make play with Escape to-day; but I will not compel you to make play to-day. Should there be tolerable good play made by any other horse, you may then wait with Escape; but should no other horse make tolerable good play, you must make tolerably good play with Escape. God bless you!' As His Royal Highness was leaving me, I said, 'I wish your Royal Highness to back Escape'; and he called to me, saying, 'Yes, I will'.

SAM CHIFNEY, *Genius Genuine*

*Win he did and with plenty in hand. Too comfortably for the Jockey Club who immediately banned Chifney, and his patron, from the Heath. The Prince of Wales took his horses to Brighton while Chifney, who was awarded a pension of £200 a year, proceeded to invent the Chifney bit and sired a champion jockey of greater probity than himself.*

# The Death of a Legend

*Chifney was the original star turn in the saddle. For each new pretender jockeying for glory, there is an old timer with whom he will be compared. Jeffrey Bernard had his top two in Lester Piggott and Sir Gordon Richards. Before them there was Steve Donoghue. But the greatest of all may have been Fred Archer who defied a height of 5' 10" and a natural bodyweight of close to 11 stone – ferociously held in check at 8 st 10 lb by Turkish baths and the infamous purgative, Archer's mixture – to win thirteen consecutive jockey's championships. The last was posthumous, for in 1886 he took his own life. Sir George Chetwynne describes the end of a legend.*

IN THE Jockey Club St Gatien gave 3 lb to Melton, and with Eurasian to make the running, galloped him to a standstill, and this was the last race but one these two Derby winners ever ran. They were very different types of a racehorse, Melton being small, symmetrical, all quality, and gifted with speed rather than stamina; whilst St Gatien was a great strong, big-boned horse, a trifle coarse, but with a wonderful swinging stride, and he could stay for a month. There was a doubt about Melton's courage, I should add, and so much whisky was given to him before this race that Tom Cannon, who rode him, declared that the horse was quite drunk. The one other race I allude to is the Liverpool Autumn Cup, which Melton won easily, giving any amount of weight away. He was ridden by his old jockey Archer no more, Watts having the mount, for on the Monday of this meeting a terrible event had happened. Poor Archer, under the influence of delirium, had shot himself. The week before he said he felt very ill, and although he rode in the first two races at Lewes on Thursday (Tommy Tittlemouse being the last mount he ever had), he was persuaded to leave the course at once and to go home. When he reached Newmarket he was violently ill, was put to bed, and, having a pistol in his room

128

by his bedside, ended his life. Whatever faults he had, poor fellow, he was the finest 'backers' jockey' that has ever lived. He only thought of winning the race on the horse he rode somehow, and although he often got into trouble about foul riding, it was probably excessive anxiety to win that led him astray in the excitement of the moment. I do not mean to advance this in the least as an excuse, but it may, perhaps, be in some degree accepted as an extenuating circumstance. He finished very powerfully, almost tying his long legs under the horse he was riding, though sometimes he let their heads go at a finish. His hands were perfect, and he rode more by balance than grip. Some of his best races were ridden over the Epsom course, notably Master Kildare's City and Suburban, and the Derbies he won on Bend Or and Melton. He had the most gentlemanly manners when talking to anyone, and that was to a great extent the reason of his popularity. At his funeral his grave was heaped up many feet high with flowers sent from admirers and friends from all parts of the world. It is sad as one drives to the Cambridgeshire Stand to look at that quiet little cemetery with his grave standing a few yards from the road, and to think how often he has galloped up in hot haste to the course, little imagining how shortly his career would be checked, and that soon he would be lying in that little churchyard which he had so often heedlessly passed, laughing and chatting with his companions. No doubt excessive wasting and the exhaustion occasioned by Turkish baths hurried him to his end.

SIR GEORGE CHETWYNNE,
*Racing Reminiscences and Experiences of the Turf*

# *A Tragic Death*

*George Lambton, whose first encounter with the great jockey was blessed with a tip for the 16–1 winner of the Manchester Cup in 1880, has also told of Fred Archer's last days.*

THE HOUGHTON Meeting at Newmarket of 1886, when St Mirin was beaten in the Cambridgeshire, had been a very bad one for backers, especially for the numerous followers of Fred Archer. On the Friday morning, at exercise on the Heath, Archer rode up to me, saying, 'I suppose you have had a very bad week.' I answered that I had. 'Well,' he said, 'you get out on Queen Bee' (a mare of Robert Peck's); 'she can't be beat, but I have only told you and the Captain, and I know you will give Peck time to get his money on; he also has had a very bad week, so don't say any thing to a soul.'

When the race came off, Queen Bee was beaten the shortest of heads by Wood on Draycot, no one knowing which had won till the number went up. Machell was standing next to a friend of his, Mrs Chaine, always an ardent supporter of Archer, and who, as the numbers appeared in the frame, exclaimed, 'Thank God!' Machell turned to her saying that he thought she always backed Archer. 'So I do,' she replied, 'but he told me not to this time.' The Captain threw up his hands saying, 'God save me from my friends.'

When he passed Archer in the paddock he cut him dead. Archer came to me after the races, looking worn to a shadow, saying that he had ridden the mare into the ground, so anxious was he to win. He was cut to the heart by Machell's behaviour to him. 'I had to put all those touting people off,' he said, 'and the Captain thinks I put him wrong.'

Ten days after Archer was dead. For a long time Machell was a miserable man; this episode preyed on his mind, and he could never forgive himself for his treatment of one who had been such a good friend and servant. 'Could you believe it possible,' he said to me, 'that, after seeing a horse beaten a short head in a desperate finish, I should think Archer was not trying, and yet I allowed myself to think so, and I am haunted by the look on his face when I refused to speak to him after the race.'

There is no doubt that Archer, when he rode this race, was already sickening for the illness which was the cause of his death.

The following week was Brighton and Lewes. Archer went to Brighton, which was one of his favourite courses, where he rode several well-fancied horses without success. On the Thursday, at Lewes, I saw him just before he was getting up on Tommy Tittlemouse (the last horse he ever rode), an eleven-to-eight-on chance. He looked very ill, and said, 'My horse ought to win, but I am dead out of luck and can't win a race.' He was unplaced, and after the race said he would not ride any more that week, but was going home to Newmarket. Just before he left he said 'good-bye' to me. He was walking away when he turned back and said, 'If you see a two-year-old called Eunuch in a mile selling race to-morrow you ought to back him; I got beat on him in a five furlong race, but he is a certain stayer.'

Sure enough Eunuch, the property of the American sportsman, Mr Ten Broeck, was entered, and won easily at five to one; so, curiously enough, on my first acquaintance with Archer, he put me on a good winner in Isonomy, and the last words he ever spoke to me were to back this Eunuch.

On his arrival at Newmarket he was found to be seriously ill with what turned out to be typhoid fever. Unfortunately, he always kept a loaded revolver in his bedroom, and this had not been taken away. He had overcome the crisis of his illness, and was a little better, when his sister, who was nursing him, left his room for a moment, and he jumped out of bed and shot himself.

I was at Liverpool when the news of his tragic death came. It was a terrible blow to me and many others. As Lord Marcus Beresford said, when he heard the news, 'Backers have lost the best friend they have ever had.' He certainly was the most attractive figure that I have ever come across on a racecourse, and, apart from my admiration for him as a jockey, I was very fond of him as a man.

THE HON. GEORGE LAMBTON, *Men and Horses I have Known*

*Though not strictly about racing, Adam Lindsay-Gordon's poem, A Hunting Song, namechecks the great Tom Oliver, rendered Olliver, and Bendigo. Lindsay-Gordon was taught to ride by Oliver, his fellow Cheltonian, but became so enthusiastic for the world of racing and gambling he was banished to Australia by his father. Despite cleaning up on the local racing scene he, like Archer, took his life at an early age. 'The Most Fun You Can Have With Your Trousers On,' might be a suitable sub-title for this poem which was penned while in an exuberant mood.*

# A Hunting Song

HERE'S a health to every sportsman, be he stableman or lord,
If his heart be true, I care not what his pocket may afford;
And may he ever pleasantly each gallant sport pursue,
If he takes his liquor fairly, and his fences fairly, too.

He cares not for the bubbles of Fortune's fickle tide,
Who like Bendigo can battle, and like Olliver can ride.
He laughs at those who caution, at those who chide he'll frown,
As he clears a five-foot paling, or he knocks a peeler down.

The dull, cold world may blame us, boys! but what care we the
    while,
If coral lips will cheer us, and bright eyes on us smile?
For beauty's fond caresses can most tenderly repay
The weariness and trouble of many an anxious day.

Then fill your glass, and drain it, too, with all your heart and soul,
To the best of sports – The Fox-hunt, The Fair Ones, and The
    Bowl,
To a stout heart in adversity through every ill to steer,
And when Fortune smiles, a score of friends like those around us
    here.

                                                    ADAM LINDSAY-GORDON

# THE PLAYERS

'Horse-races are desports of great men, and
good in themselves, though many gentlemen by
such means gallop quite out of their fortunes.'
*Burton, Anatomy of Melancholy*

I'LL TAKE the odds against Caravan.'
'In ponies?'
'Done.'
And Lord Milford, a young noble, entered in his book the bet which
he had just made with Mr. Latour, a grey-headed member of the
Jockey Club.

It was the eve of the Derby of 1837. In a vast and golden
saloon, that in its decorations would have become, and in its splen-
dour would not have disgraced, Versailles in the days of the grand
monarch, were assembled many whose hearts beat at the thought
of the morrow, and whose brains still laboured to control its
fortunes to their advantage.

'They say that Caravan looks puffy,' lisped, in a low voice, a
young man, lounging on the edge of a buhl table that had once
belonged to a Mortemart, and dangling a rich cane with affected
indifference, in order to conceal his anxiety from all, except the
person whom he addressed.

'They are taking seven to two against him freely over the way,'
was the reply. 'I believe it's all right.'

'Do you know I dreamed last night something about Mango?'
continued the gentleman with the cane, and with a look of un-
easy superstition.

His companion shook his head.

'Well,' continued the gentleman with the cane, 'I have no opinion of him. I betted Charles Egremont the odds against Mango this morning; he goes with us, you know. By-the-bye, who is our Fourth?'

'I thought of Milford,' was the reply in an under tone. 'What say you?'

'Milford is going with St. James and Punch Hughes.'

'Well, let us come in to supper, and we shall see some fellow we like.'

So saying, the companions, taking their course through more than one chamber, entered an apartment of less dimensions than the principal saloon, but not less sumptuous in its general appearance. The gleaming lustres poured a flood of soft yet brilliant light over a plateau glittering with gold plate, and fragrant with exotics embedded in vases of rare porcelain. The seats on each side of the table were occupied by persons consuming, with a heedless air, delicacies for which they had no appetite; while the conversation in general consisted of flying phrases referring to the impending event of the great day that had already dawned.

'Come from Lady St. Julians', Fitz?' said a youth of tender years, and whose fair visage was as downy and as blooming as the peach from which, with a languid air, he withdrew his lips to make this inquiry of the gentleman with the cane.

'Yes; why were not you there?'

'I never go anywhere,' replied the melancholy Cupid, 'everything bores me so.'

'Well, will you go to Epsom with us to-morrow, Alfred?' said Lord Fitzheron. 'I take Berners and Charles Egremont, and with you our party will be perfect.'

'I feel so cursed blasé!' exclaimed the boy in a tone of elegant anguish.

'I will give you a fillip, Alfred,' said Mr Berners; 'do you all the good in the world.'

'Nothing can do me good,' said Alfred, throwing away his almost untasted peach; 'I should be quite content if anything could do me harm. Waiter, bring me a tumbler of Badminton.'

'And bring me one too,' sighed our Lord Eugene de Vere, who was a year older than Alfred Mountchesney, his companion and brother in listlessness. Both had exhausted life in their teens, and all that remained for them was to mourn, amid the ruins of their reminiscences, over the extinction of excitement.

'Well, Eugene, suppose you come with us,' said Lord Fitzheron. 'I think I shall go down to Hampton Court and play tennis,' said Lord Eugene. 'As it is the Derby, nobody will be there.'

'And I will go with you, Eugene,' said Alfred Mountchesney, 'and we will dine together afterwards at the Toy. Anything is better than dining in this infernal London.'

'Well, for my part,' said Mr Berners, 'I do not like your suburban dinners. You always get something you can't eat, and cursed bad wine.'

'I rather like bad wine,' said Mrs Mountchesney; 'one gets so bored with good wine.'

'Do you want the odds against Hybiscus, Berners?' said a guardsman, looking up from his book, which he had been intently studying.

'All I want is some supper, and as you are not using your place – '

'You shall have it. Oh! here's Milford, he will bet me them.'

And at this moment entered the room the young nobleman whom we have before mentioned, accompanied by an individual who was approaching perhaps the termination of his fifth lustre, but whose general air rather betokened even a less experienced time of life. Tall, with a well-proportioned figure and a graceful carriage, his countenance touched with a sensibility that at once engages the affections, Charles Egremont was not only admired by that sex whose approval generally secures men enemies among their fellows, but was at the same time the favourite of his own.

'Ah, Egremont! come and sit here,' exclaimed more than one banqueter.

'I saw you waltzing with the little Bertie, old fellow,' said Lord Fitzheron, 'and therefore did not stay to speak to you, as I thought we should meet here. I am to call for you, mind.'

'How shall we all feel this time to-morrow?' said Egremont, smiling.

'The happiest fellow at this moment must be Cockie Graves,' said Lord Milford. 'He can have no suspense. I have been looking over his book, and I defy him, whatever happens, not to lose.'

'Poor Cockie,' said Mr Berners; 'he has asked me to dine with him at the Clarendon on Saturday.'

'Cockie is a very good Cockie,' said Lord Milford, 'and Caravan is a very good horse; and if any gentleman sportsman present wishes to give seven to two, I will take him to any amount.'

'My book is made up,' said Egremont: 'and I stand or fall by Caravan.'

'And I.'

'And I.'

'And I.'

'Well, mark my words,' said a fourth, rather solemnly, 'Rat-trap wins.'

'There is not a horse except Caravan,' said Lord Milford, 'fit for a borough stake.'

'You used to be all for Phosphorus, Egremont,' said Lord Eugene de Vere.

'Yes; but fortunately I have got out of that scrape. I owe Phip Dormer a good turn for that. I was the third man who knew he had gone lame.'

'And what are the odds against him now?'

'Oh! nominal; forty to one; what you please.'

'He won't run,' said Mr Berners, 'John Day told me he had refused to ride him.'

'I believe Cockie Graves might win something if Phosphorus came in first,' said Lord Milford, laughing.

BENJAMIN DISRAELI, Sybil

# The System

*It is a truth universally acknowledged, that a single man in possession of a good fortunes must be in want of a bet. To retain that fortune, he will be in want of a system. The system is a nebulous web of do's and don'ts to be disregarded in the heat of battle. Sir George Chetwynne had a system for the nineteenth century.*

I RECOMMEND the beginner to pay the greatest attention to public form. It is not always trustworthy – very far from it – but it is twenty times more so than private trials. Over and over again

I have been told of the marvellous prowess exhibited by young-
sters at home. It is said that they can 'climb trees' and do everything but talk; but as a rule, when they make their first appearance
in public their number is taken down by a tried public performer.
What puzzles the student of private and public form, and leads
to innumerable contradictory results, is the fact that some animals
do their best at home in trials, but do not run up to their form
out, owing to nervousness, ill-temper, or cowardice; whilst
others do not exert themselves in private trials, but are excited,
and have their nerves strung to concert pitch on the racecourse,
where they run many pounds better than on their own home
grounds. Needless to say, the latter sort are the ones that cost their
backers the least money.

It is a good plan for a man who bets always to carry a 'Racing
Guide' in his pocket, also the latest issues of the weekly guide published at the offices of some of the sporting papers, and of course
containing all the latest returns of racing up to date. Make up your
mind what animal you are going to back before you go near the
Ring, and if you are a fair judge of the looks and condition of a
horse, try and get a chance of inspecting him in the saddling
paddock before the race. Avoid touting as much as possible, though
it is desirable, if it can be done, to ascertain from those who should
know most about him if an animal is well. If you fancy a horse
very much, and find that he is a great favourite at what you
consider to be a false price, do not on that account put on more
money than you originally proposed to risk. It is foolish, though
at the same time it is a by no means uncommon practice in such
cases, to back another animal in the race instead of your original
fancy. If you can really make out on form that your second choice
actually has a choice of beating the favourite, it may be that the
price you would get about him in the face of a hot favourite would
be worth your taking. Above all, abstain from plunging when you
are losing. 'Cut your losses and play up your winnings,' is the
best advice I can give to beginners, or indeed, to every backer of
horses, though it is advice which requires no little resolution to
act upon, as we almost daily see.

Do not be led away by fairy tales of what horses can do or have
done at home. During my racing career I have had hundreds
of trials, often employing the best jockeys to ride in them, and

taking every possible care and pains to arrive at a really accurate and trustworthy result; but my experience is that four out of six of them – I state the proportion deliberately – turn out to be wrong, as shown afterwards by the public form of the horses. If a good two-year-old comes out, stick to him till he is beaten, unless he has to carry such a penalty that his victory would seem impossible. Remember that to a speedy and early two-year-old, running six furlongs is nearly equivalent to a five-furlong horse of maturer age running a mile. You cannot make some two-year-olds get six furlongs. They stop after going five as if they were shot. If two animals of apparently the same class have to run a longer course than they have travelled before, back the gamer of the two, the one that you believe will run the longer. You have much greater pleasure during the race if you do so, and although the other one may be pulling over your selection in the early part of the struggle, the moment his jockey begins to ride him you know you have won your money.

If you find an animal is at a longer price in the betting than you anticipated, and you know of no good reason for his being so, put a little more money on him than you intended to wager. It will pay you in the long run for having to take short prices about 'good things'. It is a good plan in the morning to go over the performances of horses that you intend to back, but if you keep a handicap book – that is, if you handicap the first three or four horses in races, by putting on to or taking off weight from what they carried, so as to reduce them as nearly as possible to 'a dead heat on paper', as all good handicappers ought to do – do not rely implicitly on your calculation, or you are sure to lose. Your book cannot take into consideration the improvement of horses with age, or with work, or with *less work* (which latter is, I generally find, a very frequent cause of improved form). Backers, again, are far too apt to forget what very great differences exist in various courses that races are run over, although the distances may be the same. A horse may distinguish himself greatly on the five furlongs at Epsom, all down hill; and be wholly unable to show to advantage over the severe five furlongs at Sandown, all up hill. No doubt there might well be a difference of a stone in a horse's running at these two places, and where would your book be then?

For several years I kept a handicap book, and took the greatest pains with it, but when I had thoroughly tested it I gave it up in disgust. One particular reason for doing so was the following: One day two horses were in a race. It lay between them, as the others were outclassed. I made up my mind to have five hundred pounds on one of them, but before doing so I consulted my book, and found to my horror that the other had five pounds in hand. I was greatly puzzled what to do, but in the end I chanced my book (having had misgivings about it on several occasions before) and backed my own fancy, which won cleverly a length and a half. During the race my feelings were extremely mixed. I was apprehensive and bothered at the idea that my carefully compiled book would very likely prove to be wrong, but still more apprehensive and bothered at the idea that it might prove right and I should lose my money. Now, I only handicap certain horses from one week to another, relying always on the latest form, provided I can ascertain that there is no particular reason why that form should not be right. I say, also, to the beginner, Provide yourself with a good pair of glasses, watch each race with the greatest attention – not only the horse you have backed in it but all the others, or as many of the others as you can and note what you think was second and third best if an animal wins easily and the rest are not persevered with right past the post. Do not bet on every race – that is fatal – but pay the same attention to those you do not bet on, and you will find the pleasure of watching them is the same, if not greater. Never bet on selling handicaps, which are the most odious kind of races run on the contemporary turf, and detrimental to the good of the sport and the breed of racehorses, inasmuch as a certain number of worthless animals are kept in training every year, especially for this class of race. If a gentleman says to his trainer, 'I must get rid of this brute,' his answer is sure to be, 'Oh, keep him a little longer, sir; I think I can get him through a selling handicap!' Besides, my great objection to this class of race is that it is not fair for horses to be entered all to be sold for one price, £100, and for one horse to be called on to give another of the same age two stone or more. I hope to see selling handicaps done away with, but some years ago when, as already remarked, I proposed at a Jockey Club meeting that they should cease to exist, many members rose and protested against my motion, as if they were Clerks of Courses themselves. Their defence of these wretched affairs was based on the fact that Catterick Bridge and other small northern meetings would cease to exist if selling handicaps were abolished, so they still continue in great force, and anyone who likes to go down to Alexander Park (of late years, I must say, an admirably conducted meeting, in spite of the occasional presence of 'the rough element') may, after one of these races, become possessed of half-a-dozen or a dozen 'racehorses', sold at auction for prices varying from five to twenty-five guineas each.

It is bad, again, to bet on big nurseries at what is called 'the back end'. Even if your money is on the horse that really has the best chance, it does not at all follow that he will be returned the winner, as the starter has immense trouble with the lads and apprentices that ride the lighter-weighted horses, and after a long delay at the post, caused by repeated false starts, the fractiousness of the horses, and, I regret to say, sometimes of the jockeys, he is so sick and disgusted with them that he is often glad to drop his flag to even the semblance of a good start; hence the result of the race is often a lottery, and you might as well toss up or draw numbers out of a bag for your money.

Far and away the best races to bet on are the weight-for-age races, and to my taste they are also the most interesting. I go so far as to say, from long experience, that if a shrewd and careful backer keeps his head, does not plunge or risk more than he can con-veniently pay on the Monday, and confines himself to betting on weight-for-age races, he can make a certainty of winning money every year; but he must work hard at the public form of horses, be unprejudiced, and have a certain knowledge, which may come to him instinctively or be acquired by years of well-paid-for experience.

Try and lose and win your money with equal imperturbability. A boasting, boisterous winner is almost more odious than a whining loser, though there are occasions when some fine performance of a favourite horse may draw from his owner or some enthusiastic supporter expressions of satisfaction and approval. When you are in a winning vein for several weeks be thankful for your good luck and do not forget that the reverse of the medal is quite certain to be presented shortly, perhaps when you are least prepared for it. Still, I am all for making hay whilst the sun shines, and confidence often makes one's wits clearer. The late Mr E. Brayley once exclaimed that 'he was tired of winning'. His luck quickly changed after this speech – for years he won very few races, and died in very moderate circumstances.

It is related that when Black Tommy, the property of Mr Drinkald, passed the post for the Derby, locked together with another horse, believing he had won, his owner shouted out excitedly, 'Thank Heaven I have won the Derby, and nobody is on!' meaning that none of his friends had backed the horse. A second later, when the number went up, to his intense mortification, and to the frantic delight of his friends who had heard his remark, he found his horse had been beaten a short head.

I recollect seeing poor Charles Brewer – when Robert the Devil was sailing away in front at the Bell in the Derby, and Archer was seen to be riding Bend Or two lengths behind – surrounded by an admiring crowd of friends who were patting him on the back whilst he was complacently pointing to his horse as much as to say, 'There's a horse for you!' and even after they had passed the post, believing he had won; but five minutes afterwards, great as the disappointment must have been to him after his acceptance of victory, he was talking it over as coolly and collectedly as if it had been a small selling plate.

The owner of Paradox, too, took defeat well in Melton's year, measuring with his hands what the distance of a head would be, and exclaiming, 'By Jove! to be only that much off winning the Derby: I shall never get as close again!'

You never could tell by Lord Rosebery's face whether he had won or lost. Still, sometimes it is refreshing to see the beaming face of some young man pulled off a good bet, particularly if you happen to know that it is a 'retriever' to get him home on a bad week. I have pleasurable recollection of a grin from ear to ear of a friend of mine only last year at Brighton August Meeting when he had taken 1600 to 200 about Kaikoura in the Light Weight Plate. Things had been going very badly before with him, and this win meant much.

However, it is these very retrievers that I want to warn inexperienced and reckless backers against, as they generally turn out disastrously, and, whereas before you found yourself within *measurable* distance from home, the matter has now assumed such proportions that you only thirst for the numbers of the next race to go up to plunge madly on the favourite again, and so on till the last race is out and you turn hopelessly away, knowing that it is impossible you can settle your account in full on Monday. It is then that thoughts get into your head that ought to be banished at once if you wish to remain strictly honourable. 'If they make any row about my not settling I'll see them somewhere before they ever get a shilling', is a remark that has been made after a disastrous Ascot or Houghton week.

All the same, if men will be, I strongly advocate betting at Ascot. Many weight-for-age races are run, and the best horses in training are always seen out there and at Goodwood – both favourite places of mine for winning money. Beware of Newmarket! awful are the upsets that take place on the famous heath. I believe the reason of it is that horses can see such a long way in front of them *beyond* the winning post, especially on the T.Y.C., Ditch, and Abingdon Mile courses. They do not know where the post is (nor do most of the jockeys, by the way), and this discourages them. The Rous course contains many traps for a favourite if he happens to be back at the knees, or if his shoulders are wrong. No sooner are they at the top of the hill than down they go into the Dip, and it takes a lot of getting out of, and up the hill home. That Dip has been fatal to many a horse's chance when he is beginning to tire, and is all abroad, floundering, in fact, before his jockey has time to pull him together. If you walk over the Rowley Mile you will be surprised at the many changes that take place in the course, and if you walk briskly up to and past the winning post, and, not stopping to do so, thrust your stick in the ground exactly in what you think is a straight line between the two posts, when you have contemplated your attempt you will be charitable in future about any jockey not much accustomed to ride at Newmarket whom you see beaten a head on the post. Here, by the way, let me add, that if you bet about the result of a race before the number goes up you should never do so 'absolutely', which is the way the Ring will want you to bet. If you say, 'so-and-so has won for ten *absolutely*', and it is a dead heat, you lose your money. From the stand at Newmarket, it is very difficult at times to tell what has won after a close finish, and I can recommend the backer to follow Steel, who always bets on such a result and is nearly always right.

SIR GEORGE CHETWYNNE,
*Racing Reminiscences and Experiences of the Turf*

*Easy isn't it? But not all punters follow such sage advice. The spur of the moment is a terrible thing, as is the hot tip. With this kind of ammunition, John Self's dad cared little for systems.*

THREE years ago, when I started to make some real money as opposed to all that other stuff I'd been making, my father hit bad trouble on the tables and the track and he ... Do you know what he *did*, that funker? He submitted a bill for all the money he had spent on my upbringing. That's right – he fucking invoiced me. It wasn't that expensive, either, my childhood, because I spent seven years of it with my mum's sister in the States. I still have the document somewhere. It was six sheets of foolscap, thumb typed. *To* 30 pairs of shoes (approx.) ... *To* 4 caravan holidays in Nailsea ... *To* share of petrol to same ... He tabbed me for everything, pocket-money, ice-creams, rug-rethinks, everything. He enclosed a cover note, explaining in his clerkly style that it was of course only a rough estimate, and that I wasn't beholden to reimburse him penny for penny. Inflation had been taken into account. I'd cost him nineteen thousand pounds.

Anyway, we both behaved in character – the same character. On receipt of my father's letter, I got drunk and sent him a cheque for twenty grand. On receipt of my cheque, my father got drunk and put the money on a horse running in the Cheltenham Golden Shield called, I don't know, Handjob or Bumboy or whatever. The horse was young for a chaser and didn't have much in the way of form – but Barry had a hot tip. 100–8 looked good to him. He placed the bet by messenger. One of his villain mates, Morrie Dubedat, set up the deal and vouched for dad's punt ... Ten minutes later Barry panicked and tried to cancel. But the bookie was already out hiring frighteners and the bet had to stand. Jackknifed over the whisky bottle, Barry listened to the radio commentary in closing-time light. Sure enough, Bumboy came lolloping out of its stall, each leg going somewhere different, neighing and dumping in its blinkers and Dobbin hat. Eventually flogged into submission by the jockey, Bumboy set off after its vanishing playmates. The horse received the odd joke mention from the commentator, until my father smashed the radio, finished the whisky, and suffered a near-fatal nosebleed.

Barry has since acquired a video recording of the race and still gloats over it even now. Bumboy not only won: it was more or less the sole survivor. There was one of those churning, drowning pile-ups at the penultimate jump. Bumboy tripped snorting through the chaos – and was clear with one fence to beat. The lone horse pranced flimsily on. It didn't leap that last hedge: it just munched its way through. Then, with only flat green ahead, ten yards from the post, Bumboy fell over. The jockey, who was all whipped out by now, tried to remount. Some of his grounded colleagues got the same idea. After about ten minutes – several riderless horses had skipped over the line by now, and another contender had cleared the last jump, and was gaining – Bumboy was finally scourged out of a series of circles and flopped over the line, home by half a length.

Now this bookie was a middleman, not legal, and my dad took Morrie Dubedat, Fat Paul and two shooters when he went to collect his winnings. Also, I had sobered up by then and caused some complications by trying to stop the cheque – until my father came squealing on to the line. He got his money, after a month of gang warfare – not the full whack by any means, but enough to pay his debts, buy out the brewery, gut the Shakespeare, install the pool table, the stripper and the strobes . . . He says he's going to repay me, one of these days. Who cares? It doesn't matter.

MARTIN AMIS, Money

*But Damon Runyon's Unser Fritz did have a system. Unser Fritz's system had got him into trouble thirty years previously and his fiancée ran off as his readies ran out. Since then he's been living hand-to-mouth and hoping his figures will come right and he'll get together enough scratch to entice his Emma back.*

NO,' Unser Fritz says, 'You see, I never make a scratch since then. I am never since in the money, so there is no reason for Emma to return to me. But,' he says, 'wait until I get going good again and you will see.'

Well, I always figure Unser Fritz must be more or less of an old screwball for going on thinking there is still a chance for him around the tracks, and now I am sure of it, and I am about to bid him good evening, when he mentions that he can use about two dollars if I happen to have a deuce on me that is not working, and I will say one thing for Unser Fritz, he seldom comes right out and asks anybody for anything unless things are very desperate with him, indeed.

'I need it to pay something on account of my landlady,' he says. 'I room with old Mrs Crob around the corner for over twenty years, and,' he says, 'she only charges me a finnif a week, so I try to keep from getting too far to the rear with her. I will return it to you the first score I make.'

Well, of course I know this means practically never, but I am feeling so good about my success at the track that I slip him a deucer, and it is half an hour later before I fully realize what I do, and go looking for Fritz to get anyway half of it back. But by this time he disappears, and I think no more of the matter until the next day out at the course when I hear Unser Fritz bets two dollars on a thing by the name of Speed Cart, and it bows down at 50 to 1, so I know Mrs. Crob is still waiting for hers.

Now there is Unser Fritz with one hundred slugs, and this is undoubtedly more money than he enjoys since Hickory Slim is a two-year-old. And from here on the story becomes very interesting, and in fact remarkable, because up to the moment Speed Cart hits the wire, Unser Fritz is still nothing but a crumbo, and you can say it again, while from now on he is somebody to point out and say can you imagine such a thing happening?

He bets a hundred on a centipede called Marchesa, and down pops Marchesa like a trained pig at 20 to 1. Then old Unser Fritz bets two hundred on a caterpillar by the name of Merry Soul, at 4 to 1, and Merry Soul just laughs his way home. Unser Fritz winds up the day betting two thousand more on something called Sharp Practice, and when Sharp Practice wins by so far it looks as if he is a shoo-in, Fritz finds himself with over twelve thousand slugs, and the way the bookmakers in the betting ring are sobbing is really most distressing to hear.

Well, in a week Unser Fritz is a hundred thousand dollars in front, because the way he sends it in is quite astonishing to behold, although the old-timers tell me it is just the way he sends it when he is younger. He is betting only on horses that he personally figures out, and what happens is that Unser Fritz's figures suddenly come to life again, and he cannot do anything wrong.

He wins so much dough that he even pays off a few old touches, including my two, and he goes so far as to lend Joe Palladino three dollars on the Betsy that Solly and I hock with Joe for the pound note, as it seems that by this time Joe himself is practically on his way to the poorhouse, and while Unser Fritz has no use whatsoever for a Betsy he cannot bear to see a character such as Joe go to the poorhouse.

But with all the dough Unser Fritz carries in his pockets, and plants in a safe-deposit box in the jug downtown, he looks just the same as ever, because he claims he cannot find time from working on his figures to buy new clothes and dust himself off, and if you tell anybody who does not know who he is that this old crutch is stone rich, the chances are they will call you a liar.

In fact, on a Monday around noon, the clerk in the branch office that a big Fifth Avenue jewellery firm keeps in the lobby of the States Hotel is all ready to yell for the constables when Unser Fritz leans up against the counter and asks to see some jewellery on display in a showcase, as Unser Fritz is by no means the clerk's idea of a customer for jewellery.

I am standing in the lobby of the hotel on the off chance that some fresh money may arrive in the city on the late trains that I may be able to connect up with before the races, when I notice Unser Fritz and observe the agitation of the clerk, and presently I see Unser Fritz waving a fistful of bank notes under the clerk's beak, and the clerk starts setting out the jewellery with surprising speed.

I go over to see what is coming off, and I can see that the jewellery Unser Fritz is looking at consists of a necklace of emeralds and diamonds, with a centrepiece the size of the home plate, and some eardrops, and bracelets, and clips of same, and as I approach the scene I hear Unser Fritz ask how much for the lot as if he is dickering for a basket of fish.

'One hundred and one thousand dollars, sir,' the clerk says. 'You see, sir, it is a set, and one of the finest things of the kind in the country. We just got it in from our New York store to show a party here, and,' he says, 'she is absolutely crazy about it, but she states she cannot give us a final decision until five o'clock this afternoon. Confidentially, sir,' the clerk says, 'I think the real trouble is financial, and doubt that we will hear from her again.' In fact, he says, 'I am so strongly of this opinion that I am prepared to sell the goods without waiting on her. It is really a bargain at the price,' he says.

'Dear me,' Unser Fritz says to me, 'this is most unfortunate as the sum mentioned is just one thousand dollars more than I possess in all this world. I have twenty thousand on my person, and eighty thousand over in the box in the jug, and not another dime. But,' he says, 'I will be back before five o'clock and take the lot. In fact,' he says, 'I will run in right after the third race and pick it up.'

Well, at this the clerk starts putting the jewellery back in the case, and anybody can see that he figures he is on a lob and that he is sorry he wastes so much time, but Unser Fritz says to me like this:

'Emma is returning to me,' he says.

'Emma who?' I say.

'Why,' Unser Fritz says, 'my Emma. The one I tell you about not long ago. She must hear I am in the money again, and she is returning just as I always say she will.'

'How do you know?' I say. 'Do you hear from her, or what?'

'No,' Unser Fritz says, 'I do not hear from her direct, but Mrs Crob knows some female relatives of Emma's that lives a Ballston Spa a few miles from here, and this relative is in Saratoga this morning to do some shopping, and she tells Mrs. Crob and Mrs Crob tells me. Emma will be here to-night. I will have these emeralds waiting for her.'

Well, what I always say is that every guy knows his own business best, and if Unser Fritz wishes to toss his dough off on jewellery, it is none of my put-in, so all I remark is that I have no doubt Emma will be very much surprised indeed.

'No,' Unser Fritz says, 'She will be expecting them. She always expects emeralds when she returns to me. I love her,' he says. 'You have no idea how I love her. But let us hasten to the course,' he says, 'Cara Mia is a right good thing in the third, and I will make just one bet to-day to win the thousand I need to buy these emeralds.'

'But, Fritz,' I say, 'you will have nothing left for operating expenses after you invest in the emeralds.'

'I am not worrying about operating expenses now,' Unser Fritz says. 'The way my figures are standing up, I can run a spool of thread into a pair of pants in no time. But I can scarcely wait to see the expression on Emma's face when she sees her emeralds.

I will have to make a fast trip into town after the third to get my dough out of the box in the jug and pick them up,' he says. 'Who knows but what this other party that is interested in the emeralds may make her mind up before five o'clock and pop in there and nail them?'

Well, after we get to the race track, all Unser Fritz does is stand around waiting for the third race. He has his figures on the first two races, and ordinarily he will be betting himself a gob on them, but he says he does not wish to take the slightest chance of cutting down his capital at this time, and winding up short of enough dough to buy the emeralds.

It turns out that both of the horses Unser Fritz's figures make on top in the first and second races bow down, and Unser Fritz will have his thousand if he only bets a couple of hundred on either of them, but Unser Fritz says he is not sorry he does not bet. He says the finishes in both races are very close, and prove that there is an element of risk in these races. And Unser Fritz says he cannot afford to tamper with the element of risk at this time.

He states that there is no element of risk whatever in the third race, and what he states is very true, as everybody realizes that this mare Cara Mia is a stick-out. In fact, she is such a stick-out that it scarcely figures to be a contest. There are three other horses in the race, but it is the opinion of one and all that if the owners of these horses have any sense they will leave them in the barn and save them a lot of unnecessary lather.

The opening price offered by the bookmakers on Cara Mia is 2 to 5, which means that if you wish to wager on Cara Mia to win you will have to put up five dollars to a bookmaker's two dollars, and everybody agrees that this is a reasonable thing to do in this case unless you wish to rob the poor bookmaker.

In fact, this is considered so reasonable that everybody starts running at the bookmakers all at once, and the bookmakers can see if this keeps up they may get knocked off their stools in the betting ring and maybe seriously injured, so they make Cara Mia 1 to 6, and out, as quickly as possible to halt the rush and give them a chance to breathe.

This 1 to 6 means that if you wish to wager on Cara Mia to win, you must wager six of your own dollars to one of the bookmaker's dollars, and means that the bookies are not offering any prices whatsoever on Cara Mia running second or third. You can get almost any price you can think of right quick against any of the other horses winning the race, and place and show prices, too, but asking the bookmakers to lay against Cara Mia running second or third will be something like asking them to bet that Mr Roosevelt is not President of the United States.

Well, I am expecting Unser Fritz to step in and partake of the 2 to 5 on Cara Mia for all the dough he has on his person the moment it is offered, because he is very high indeed on this mare, and in fact I never see anybody any higher on any horse, and it is a price Unser Fritz will not back off from when he is high on anything.

Moreover, I am pleased to think he will make such a wager, because it will give him plenty over and above the price of the emeralds, and as long as he is bound to purchase the emeralds, I wish to see him have a little surplus, because when anybody has a surplus there is always a chance for me. It is when everybody runs out of surpluses that I am handicapped no little. But instead of stepping in and partaking, Unser Fritz keeps hesitating until the opening price gets away from him, and finally he says to me like this:

'Of course,' he says, 'my figures show Cara Mia cannot possibly lose this race, but,' he says, 'to guard against any possibility whatever of her losing, I will make an absolute cinch of it. I will bet her third.'

'Why, Fritz,' I say, 'I do not think there is anybody in this world outside of an insane asylum who will give you a price on the peek. Furthermore,' I say, 'I am greatly surprised at this sign of weakening on your part on your figures.'

'Well,' Unser Fritz says, 'I cannot afford to take a chance on not having the emeralds for Emma when she arrives. Let us go through the betting ring and see what we can see,' he says.

So we walk through the betting ring, and by this time it seems that many of the books are so loaded with wagers on Cara Mia to win that they will not accept any more under the circumstances, and I figure that Unser Fritz blows the biggest opportunity of his life in not grabbing the opening. The bookmakers who are loaded are now looking even sadder than somewhat, and this makes them a pitiful spectacle indeed.

Well, one of the saddest-looking is a character by the name of Slow McCool, but he is a character who will usually give you a gamble and he is still taking Cara Mia at 1 to 6, and Unser Fritz walks up to him and whispers in his ear, and what he whispers is he wishes to know if Slow McCool cares to lay him a price on Cara Mia third. But all that happens is that Slow McCool stops looking sad a minute and looks slightly perplexed, and then he shakes his head and goes on looking sad again.

Now Unser Fritz steps up to another sad-looking bookmaker by the name of Pete Phozzler and whispers in his ear, and Pete also shakes his head, and after we leave him I look back and see that Pete is standing up on his stool watching Unser Fritz and still shaking his head.

Well, Unser Fritz approaches maybe a dozen other sad-looking bookmakers, and whispers to them, and all he gets is the old head-shake, but none of them seem to become angry with Unser Fritz, and I always say that this proves that bookmakers are better than some people think, because, personally, I claim they have a right to get angry with Unser Fritz for insulting their intelligence, and trying to defraud them, too, by asking a price on Cara Mia third.

Finally we come to a character by the name of Willie the Worrier, who is called by this name because he is always worrying about something, and what he is generally worrying about is a short bank roll, or his ever-loving wife, and sometimes both, though mostly it is his wife. Personally, I always figure she is something to worry about, at that, though I do not consider details necessary.

She is a red-headed Judy about half as old as Willie the Worrier, and this alone is enough to start any guy worrying, and what is more she is easily vexed, especially by Willie. In fact, I remember Solly telling me that she is vexed with Willie no longer ago than about 11am this very day, and gives him a public reprimanding about something or other in the telegraph office downtown when Solly happens to be in there hoping maybe he will receive an answer from a mark in Pittsfield, Mass., that he sends a tip on a horse.

Solly says the last he hears Willie the Worrier's wife say is that she will leave him for good this time, but I just see her over on the clubhouse lawn wearing some right classy-looking garments, so I judge she does not leave him as yet, as the clubhouse lawn is not a place to be waiting for a train.

Well, when Unser Fritz sees that he is in front of Willie's stand, he starts to move on, and I nudge him and motion at Willie, and ask him if he does not notice that Willie is another bookmaker, and Unser Fritz says he notices him all right, but that he does not care to offer him any business because Willie insults him ten years ago. He says Willie calls him a dirty old Dutch bum, and while I am thinking what a wonderful memory Unser Fritz has to remember insults from bookmakers for ten years, Willie the Worrier, sitting on his stool looking out over the crowd spots Unser Fritz and yells at him as follows:

'Hello, Dirty Dutch,' he says. 'How is the soap market? What are you looking for around here, Dirty Dutch? Santa Claus?'

Well, at this Unser Fritz pushes his way through the crowd around Willie the Worrier's stand, and gets close to Willie, and says:

'Yes,' he says, 'I am looking for Santa Claus. I am looking for a show price on number two horse, but,' he says, 'I do not expect to get it from the shoemakers who are booking nowadays.'

Now the chances are Willie the Worrier figures Unser Fritz is just trying to get sarcastic with him for the benefit of the crowd around his stand in asking for such a thing as a price on Cara Mia third, and in fact the idea of anybody asking a price third on a horse that some bookmakers will not accept any more wagers on first, or even second, is so humorous that many characters laugh right out loud.

'All right,' Willie the Worrier says. 'No one can ever say he comes to my store looking for a marker on anything and is turned down. I will quote you a show price, Dirty Dutch,' he says. 'You can have 1 to 100.'

This means that Willie the Worrier is asking Unser Fritz for one hundred dollars to the book's one dollar if Unser Fritz wishes to bet on Cara Mia dropping in there no worse than third, and of course Willie has no idea Unser Fritz or anybody else will ever take such a price, and the chances are if Willie is not sizzling a little at Unser Fritz, he will not offer such a price, because it sounds foolish. Furthermore, the chances are if Unser Fritz offers Willie a comparatively small bet at this price, such as may enable him to chisel just a couple of hundred out of Willie's book, Willie will find some excuse to wiggle off, but Unser Fritz leans over and says in a low voice to Willie the Worrier:

'A hundred thousand.'

Willie nods his head and turns to a clerk alongside him, and his voice is as low as Unser Fritz's as he says to the clerk:

'A thousand to a hundred thousand, Cara Mia third.'

The clerk's eyes pop open and so does his mouth, but he does not say a word. He just writes something on a pad of paper in his hand, and Unser Fritz offers Willie the Worrier a package of thousand-dollar bills, and says:

'Here is twenty,' he says. 'The rest is in the jug.'

'All right, Dutch,' Willie says, 'I know you have it, although,' he says, 'this is the first crack you give me at it. You are on, Dutch,' he says. 'P.S.,' Willie says, 'The Dirty does not go any more.'

Well, you understand Unser Fritz is betting one hundred thousand dollars against a thousand dollars that Cara Mia will run in the money, and personally I consider this wager a very sound business proposition indeed, and so does everybody else, for all it amounts to is finding a thousand dollars in the street.

There is really nothing that can make Cara Mia run out of the money, the way I look at it, except what happens to her, and what happens is she steps in a hole fifty yards from the finish when she is on top by ten, and breezing, and down she goes all spread out, and of course the other three horses run on past her to the wire, and all this is quite a disaster to many members of the public including Unser Fritz.

I am standing with him on the rise of the grandstand lawn watching the race, and it is plain to be seen that he is slightly surprised at what happens, and personally, I am practically dumbfounded because, to tell the truth, I take a nibble at the opening price of 2 to 5 on Cara Mia with a total of thirty slugs, which represents all my capital, and I am thinking what a great injustice it is for them to leave holes in the track for horses to step in, when Unser Fritz says like this:

'Well,' he says, 'it is horse racing.'

DAMON RUNYON, *All Horse Players Die Broke*

# The Fix

*As Unser Fritz discovered, even a successful system needs a level playing field. Accidents at Saratoga – or even at Doncaster where in 1989 the earth opened up and swallowed some of the field – are one thing. Deliberate foul play is quite another.*

THE LEGER this year was to be run on the 14th September, and while Lord Silverbridge was amusing himself with the deer at Crummie Toddie and at Killancodlem with the more easily pursued young ladies, the indefatigable Major was hard at work in the stables. This came a little hard on him. There was the cub-hunting to be looked after, which made his presence at Runnymede necessary, and then that 'pig-headed fellow, Silverbridge', would not have the horses trained anywhere but at Newmarket. How was he to be in two places at once? Yet he was in two places almost at once, cub-hunting in the morning at Egham and Bagshot, and sitting on the same evening at the stable-door at Newmarket, with his eyes fixed upon Prime Minister.

Gradually had he and Captain Green come to understand each other, and though they did at last understand each other, Tifto would talk as though there were no such correct intelligence – when for instance he would abuse Lord Silverbridge for being pig-headed. On such occasions the Captain's remark would generally be short. 'That be blowed!' he would say, implying that that state of things between the two partners, in which such complaints might be natural, had now been brought to an end. But on one occasion, about a week before the race, he spoke out a little plainer. 'What's the use of your going on with all that before me? It's settled what you've got to do.'

'I don't know that anything is settled,' said the Major.

'Ain't it? I thought it was. If it aren't you'll find yourself in the wrong box. You've as straight a tip as a man need wish for, but if you back out you'll come to grief. Your money's all on the other way already.'

On the Friday before the race Silverbridge dined with Tifto at the Beargarden. On the next morning they went down to Newmarket to see the horse get a gallop, and came back the same evening. During all this time, Tifto was more than ordinarily pleasant to his patron. The horse and the certainty of the horse's success were the only subjects mooted. 'It isn't what I say,' repeated Tifto, 'but look at the betting. You can't get five to four against him. They tell me that if you want to do anything on the Sunday the pull will be the other way.'

'I stand to lose over £20,000 already,' said Silverbridge, almost frightened by the amount.

'But how much are you on to win?' said Tifto. 'I suppose you could sell your bets for £5000 down.'

'I wish I knew how to do it,' said Silverbridge. But this was an arrangement, which, if made just now, would not suit the Major's views.

They went to Newmarket, and there they met Captain Green. 'Tifto,' said the young Lord, 'I won't have that yellow with us when the horse is galloping.'

'There isn't an honester man, or a man who understands a horse's paces better in all England,' said Tifto.

'I won't have him standing alongside of me on the Heath,' said his Lordship.

'I don't know how I'm to help it.'

'If he's there I'll send the horse in; – that's all.' Then Tifto found it best to say a few words to Captain Green. But the Captain also said a few words to himself. 'D—— young fool; he don't know what he's dropping into.' Which assertion, if you lay aside the unnecessary expletive, was true to the letter. Lord Silverbridge was a young fool, and did not at all know into what a mess he was being dropped by the united experience, perspicuity, and energy of the man whose company on the Heath he had declined.

The horse was quite a 'picture to look at'. Mr Pook the trainer assured his Lordship that for health and condition he had never seen anything better. 'Stout all over,' said Mr Pook, 'and not an ounce of what you may call flesh. And bright! Just feel his coat, my Lord! That's 'ealth, that is; not dressing, nor yet macassar!'

And then there were various evidences produced of his pace – how he had beaten that horse, giving him two pounds; how he had been beaten by that, but only on a mile course, the Leger distance was just the thing for Prime Minister, how by a lucky chance that marvellous quick rat of a thing that had won the Derby had not been entered for the autumn race, how Coalheaver was known to have had bad feet. 'He's a stout 'orse, no doubt, is the 'Eaver,' said Mr Pook, 'and that's why the betting-men have stuck to him. But he'll be nowhere on Wednesday. They're beginning to see it now, my Lord. I wish they wasn't so sharp-sighted.'

In the course of the day, however, they met a gentleman who was of a different opinion. He said loudly that he looked on the Heaver as the best three-year-old in England. Of course as matters stood he wasn't going to back the Heaver at even money – but he'd take twenty-five to thirty in hundreds between the two. All this ended in the bet being accepted and duly booked by Lord Silverbridge. And in this way Silverbridge added two thousand four hundred pounds to his responsibilities.

But there was worse than this coming. On the Sunday afternoon he went down to Doncaster, of course in company with the Major. He was alive to the necessity of ridding himself of the Major, but it had been acknowledged that that duty could not be performed till after this race had been run. As he sat opposite to his friend on their journey to Doncaster, he thought of this in the train. It should be done immediately on their return to London after the race. But the horse, his Prime Minister, was by this time so dear to him that he intended if possible to keep possession of the animal.

When they reached Doncaster the racing-men were all occupied with Prime Minister. The horse and Mr Pook had arrived that day from Newmarket, via Cambridge and Peterborough. Tifto, Silverbridge, and Mr Pook visited him together three times that afternoon and evening, and the Captain also visited the horse, though not in company with Lord Silverbridge. To do Mr Pook justice, no one could be more careful. When the Captain came round with the Major Mr Pook was there. But Captain Green did not enter the box, had no wish to do so, was of opinion that on such occasions no one whose business did not carry him there should go near a horse. His only object seemed to be to compliment Mr Pook as to his care, skill, and good fortune.

It was on the Tuesday evening that the chief mischief was done. There was a club at which many of the racing-men dined, and there Lord Silverbridge spent his evening. He was the hero of the hour, and everybody flattered him. It must be acknowledged that his head was turned. They dined at eight and much wine was drunk.

No one was tipsy, but many were elated; and much confidence in their favourite animals was imparted to men who had been sufficiently cautious before dinner. Then cigars and soda-and-brandy became common, and our young friend was not more abstemious than others. Large sums were named, and at last in three successive bets Lord Silverbridge backed his horse for more than forty thousand pounds. As he was making the second bet Mr Lupton came across to him and begged him to hold his hand. 'It will be a nasty sum for you to lose, and winning it will be nothing to you,' he said. Silverbridge took it good-humouredly, but said that he knew what he was about. 'These men will pay,' whispered Lupton; 'but you can't be quite sure what they're at.' The young man's brow was covered with perspiration. He was smoking quick and had already smoked more than was good for him. 'All right,' he said. 'I'll mind what I'm about.' Mr Lupton could do no more, and retired. Before the night was over bets had been booked to the amount stated, and the Duke's son, who had promised that he would never plunge, stood to lose about seventy thousand pounds upon the race.

While this was going on Tifto sat not far from his patron, but completely silent. During the day and early in the evening a few sparks of the glory which scintillated from the favourite horse flew in his direction. But he was on this occasion unlike himself, and though the horse was to be run in his name had very little to say in the matter. Not a boast came out of his mouth during dinner or after dinner. He was so moody that his partner, who was generally anxious to keep him quiet, more than once endeavoured to encourage him. But he was unable to rouse himself. It was still within his power to run straight, to be on the square, if not with Captain Green, at any rate with Lord Silverbridge. But to do so he must make a clean breast with his Lordship and confess the intended sin. As he heard all that was being done, his conscience troubled him sorely. With pitch of this sort he had never soiled himself before. He was to have three thousand pounds from Green, and then there would be the bets he himself had laid against the horse – by Green's assistance! It would be the making of him. Of what use had been all his 'square' work to him? And then Silverbridge had behaved so badly to him! But still, as he sat there during the evening, he would have given a hand to have been free from the attempt. He had had no conception before that he could become subject to such misery from such a cause. He would make it straight with Silverbridge this very night – but that Silverbridge was ever lighting fresh cigars and ever having his glass refilled. It was clear to him that on this night Silverbridge could not be made to understand anything about it And the deed in which he himself was to be the chief actor was to be done very early in the following morning. At last he slunk away to bed.

On the following morning, the morning of the day on which the race was to be run, the Major tapped at his patron's door about seven o'clock. Of course there was no answer though the knock was repeated. When young men overnight drink as much brandy-and-water as Silverbridge had done, and smoke as many cigars, they are apt not to hear knocks at their door made at seven o'clock. Nor was his Lordship's servant up – so that Tifto had no means of getting at him except by personal invasion of the sanctity of his bedroom. But there was no time, not a minute, to be lost. Now, within this minute that was pressing on him, Tifto must choose his course. He opened the door and was standing at the young man's head.

'What the d—— does this mean?' said his Lordship angrily, as soon as his visitor had succeeded in waking him. Tifto muttered something about the horse which Silverbridge failed to understand. The young man's condition was by no means pleasant. His mouth was furred by the fumes of tobacco. His head was aching. He was heavy with sleep, and this intrusion seemed to him to be a final indignity offered to him by the man whom he now hated. 'What business have you to come in here?' he said, leaning on his elbow. 'I don't care a straw for the horse. If you have anything to say send my servant. Get out.'

'Oh; very well,' said Tifto; and Tifto got out.

It was about an hour afterwards that Tifto returned, and on this occasion a groom from the stables, and the young Lord's own servant, and two or three other men were with him. Tifto had been made to understand that the news now to be communicated, must be communicated by himself, whether his Lordship were angry or not. Indeed, after what had been done his Lordship's anger was not of much moment. In his present visit he was only carrying out the pleasant little plan which had been arranged for him by

Captain Green. 'What the mischief is up?' said Silverbridge, rising in his bed.

Then Tifto told his story, sullenly, doggedly, but still in a perspicuous manner, and with words which admitted of no doubt. But before he told the story he had excluded all but himself and the groom. He and the groom had taken the horse out of the stable, it being the animal's nature to eat his corn better after slight exercise, and while doing so a nail had been picked up.

'Is it much?' asked Silverbridge, jumping still higher in his bed. Then he was told that it was very much – that the iron had driven itself into the horse's frog, and that there was actually no possibility that the horse should run on that day.

'He can't walk, my Lord,' said the groom in that authoritative voice which grooms use when they desire to have their own way, and to make their masters understand that they at any rate are not to have theirs.

'Where is Pook?' asked Silverbridge. But Mr Pook was also still in bed.

It was soon known to Lord Silverbridge as a fact that in very truth the horse could not run. Then sick with headache, with a stomach suffering unutterable things, he had, as he dressed himself, to think of his seventy thousand pounds. Of course the money would be forthcoming. But how would his father look at him? How would it be between him and his father now? After such a misfortune how would he be able to break that other matter to the Duke, and say that he had changed his mind about his marriage – that he was going to abandon Lady Mabel Grex and give his hand and a future Duchess's coronet to an American girl whose grandfather had been a porter?

A nail in his foot! Well! He had heard of such things before. He knew that such accidents had happened. What an ass must he have been to risk such a sum on the well-being and safety of an animal who might any day pick up a nail in his foot. Then he thought of the caution which Lupton had given him. What good would the money have done him had he won it? What more could he have than he now enjoyed? But to lose such a sum of money! With all his advantages of wealth he felt himself to be as forlorn and wretched as though he had nothing left in the world before him.

ANTHONY TROLLOPE, *The Duke's Children*

*But then there has always been a less-than-honest element in racing. Some even boast of it.*

I LIKE yourself,' said I, 'know, to a certain extent, what may be done with animals.'

'Then how would you, Mr. Romany Rye, pass off the veriest screw in the world for a flying drummedary?'

'By putting a small live eel down his throat; as long as the eel remained in his stomach, the horse would appear brisk and lively in a surprising degree.'

'And how would you contrive to make a regular kicker and biter appear so tame and gentle, that any respectable fat old gentleman of sixty, who wanted an easy goer, would be glad to purchase him for fifty pounds?'

'By pouring down his throat four pints of generous old ale, which would make him so happy and comfortable, that he would not have the heart to kick or bite anybody, for a season at least.'

'And where did you learn all this?' said the jockey.

'I have read about the eel in an old English book, and about the making drunk in a Spanish novel, and, singularly enough, I was told the same things by a wild blacksmith in Ireland.'

GEORGE BORROW, *Romany Rye*

*Some counsel against it.*

# Sound Advice

I HAD a mind to visit the horse-races in company with Mr Beau-clerk. However, I did not dare to endure the possible strictures of my illustrious friend in the enterprise and thought it wiser to introduce the more general topick. Finding him at the Mitre with a small company, I mentioned that I had observed many of the nobility and gentry setting forth for Goodwood, and questioned whether morality was served by such devotion to horseflesh.

*Johnson:* Sir, you are not to suppose that they are animated solely by care for the horses. They hope to get money by biting into their patrimony. They are baiting a trap with a piece of cheese in hopes of capturing an entire Stilton.

*Boswell:* But, Sir, you have often said that circulation of money is advantageous, by whatsoever means it be achieved.

*Johnson:* No, Sir. I can regard without disfavour the spending of money in vicariously equestrian pursuits by persons of noble birth whose equinal interests compel them to maintain their positions by an affectation of zeal; but when I find their example emulated by the offscourings of the Fleet Ditch I am not in the least edified. And those persons who abet them, where they should admonish, I would treat as rascals and set to cool their heels in the stocks.

*Goldsmith:* I should like to see a horse which I have chosen arrive first at the post, and I should be glad of the money he secured me.

*Boswell:* It would be a great satisfaction for a man of quality to hob and nob with other genteel persons in the enclosure.

*Johnson:* Sir, you may be in civil company in church as well as in playing at chuck-farthing on the Piazza. Thrale was disposed, a sennight since, to visit Newmarket and stake some wealth on the doubtful issue of competing quadrupeds, but I dissuaded him. Sir, said I, consider how, when you brew a vat of ale, you have at your service the knowledge and experience of a lifetime. But when you seek to brew the gainer in an horse-race you are setting your prentice wits against those of the master-brewers.

*Boswell:* Thrale, Sir, would be in the position of a Member of the House of Commons who attempted to bandy arguments with Dr. Johnson.

*Johnson:* Sir, that is justly observed.

Here Mr. Langton, who was also present, suggested that horse-racing was an healthy and even improving pastime, since it induced numerous persons to pass a day amid rural scenes in place of idling in fœtid and ill-aired taverns.

*Johnson:* Come, Sir, let us have none of this foppish talk. Should you desire rural scenes you may go to St James's Park and have your bellyful of nature; and as to the air of a tavern, if it be sweetened with elegant and informed conversation, there is no purer to be found this side Paradise. I beseech you, Sir, to think before you utter sentiments which can have no effect save to lower your reputation in the eyes of the company.

*Goldsmith:* But may not a man enjoy himself well on a day at Goodwood? Consider, Sir; there would be wine and wenches on the coach and we should find good taverns by the way.

*Johnson:* Sir, what has this to do with Goodwood? A man may find these on any journey; and you, Sir, I warrant, will find them when you travel to Tyburn.

Such was the great lexicographer's instant rebuke to one whose levity of mind often led him to talk profanely of the great issues of morals and conduct.

*A Gentleman:* But, Sir, if a man found himself at Goodwood, would he not be innocently employed in hazarding some guineas with the intention of distributing in alms whatever he might gain.

*Johnson:* No, Sir. If a man found himself at Bedlam he need not imitate the anticks of the inmates. The receivers of alms would reap a more certain gain from the free gift of the original guineas than from this conjectural benefaction. Depend upon it, Sir, the motive is not sound and (looking sternly at the gentleman) can only serve a rogue for an excuse to undermine his own morality and to favour his own gust for low pleasures. A man who throws his guineas into the Thames from London Bridge may be supposed to rob the publick of that amount of wealth, but he may perhaps defend himself by the undeniable assertion that he is not enriching the makers of books. Both they and their customers are rogues, and there's an end on't.

I soon experienced the soundness of my illustrious friend's judgment in regard to this worldly pastime, for, having gone, according to intention, in Mr. Beauclerk's company to the Downs, I failed to predict the gainer in any single event of the day.

E. P. WHITE, *Boswell The Optimist*

*Others believe that a sound analysis will win through.*

# A Process of Elimination

THE FORM of the year's two-year-olds contains perhaps the ideal problem for the long winter evenings, and besides being a problem it is a pleasure. When icicles hang by the wall, the pages of the Form Book can take a man back to longer and warmer days spent at Sandown or Ascot or on Newmarket Heath in the previous summer, and the labour of pure thinking can be lightened by the memory of the flowers in the paddock at Gatwick. Of course it is not all sunshine and flowers (that is not the way in which Derby winners are picked). These hours of retrospect are also hours of constructive thought, of breeding, of weights, of distances, and their result will be, or should be, that sooner or later (the speed of the process will vary with the habit and aptitude of the individual) there will crystallize in one's mind an Idea, and this Idea, when it comes, is to be watched and treated carefully, it is to be tended and cherished lest the frosts nip it or the rough winds sweep it away, because the fact of the matter is that this Idea is one's Winter Selection for the Derby next summer.

Let us suppose that we are safely through the winter, and find ourselves blowing the dust off our glasses on a cold Monday morning in March, but feeling ten years younger because 'the Flat' has started again. Stamped on our brain in letters of fire (but also written in our pocket-book in case of accidents) is the name of our Winter Selection, and our daily task and pleasure, from now to the first Wednesday in June, will be to keep an eye on him, literally when we can (when he runs in public), but failing this at second-hand, in the pages of the sporting press, which kindly keeps us informed of the training and work of nearly every horse in the country. This will be one part of our task, to follow the progress of our hope; but the other part, and much the more important, is to compare his progress with that of other horses considered by us in the winter but rejected, and to compare it, too, with the progress of yet others whom we never considered at all because they never ran, or never ran seriously, as two-year-olds. The truth is that our Winter Selection *may* be of some real use to us still when we come to make our final selection at the end of May, but its first, and sometimes its only, use is that it will have saved us from going mad during the winter, as no doubt we should if we had nothing but Christmas and the House of Commons to occupy our minds. By all means, then, let us remember our Winter Selection, but let us be prepared to change our minds as the season advances, prepared if necessary to change them more than once, and above all, let us be prepared to take trouble.

Early in the season probably the correct attitude of mind towards the winner of the coming Derby is one of quiet vigilance and a suspended judgment: one knows that the vision will come, and the wise man will wait for it to come. There are those to whom it comes almost daily (and different every time) throughout the merry months of April and May, but they seldom thrive, and usually end by doing themselves some serious mischief. We said just now that the Derby is not won by horses that have never won a race or have won only races of poor class, but that does not mean that we can expect the Derby winner always to stare us in the face, and more particularly if we are to detect him at the earliest possible moment we need to keep awake and examine the form every day of any three-year-olds that can have any possible pretensions. It is safest to glance at every three-year-old race that is run; but there are certain races in particular which are useful guides, whether the horse that wins them attracts our notice, or whether, as more often happens, these races expose the limitations of a Derby 'possible' and so help us in our process of elimination.

GUY GRIFFITH AND MICHAEL OAKESHOTT,
*A Guide to the Classics*

# *Pay, Pay*

*And when the race is run and the selection booted home, there is the problem of collecting. Evelyn Waugh has Adam, one drunken night, gambling his everything, £1000, on an outsider for the November Handicap, Indian Runner, only to learn the horse is completely unfancied by its connections. He cannot track down the drunk Major with whom he has placed the bet in order to lay it off. He cannot even find the Major at Manchester, where the race was run. Indian Runner bolts home at 35–1 but he has no idea what has happened to his worldly assets. Later at a motor race meeting, he sees the Major.*

THE FIRST person they saw when they reached the refreshment tent was the drunk Major.

'Your boy friend again,' said Miles.

'Well, there you are,' said the Major. 'D'you know I've been chasing you all over London. What have you been doing with yourself all this time?'

'I've been staying at Lottie's.'

'Well, she said she'd never heard of you. You see, I don't mind admitting I'd had a few too many that night, and to tell you the truth I woke up with things all rather a blur. Well then I found a thousand pounds in my pocket, and it all came back to me. There'd been a cove at Lottie's who gave me a thousand pounds to put on Indian Runner. Well, as far as I knew, Indian Runner was no good. I didn't want to lose your money for you, but the devil of it was I didn't know you from Adam.' ('I think that's a perfect joke,' said Miss Runcible.) 'And apparently Lottie didn't either. You'd have thought it was easy enough to trace the sort of chap who deals out thousands of pounds to total strangers, but I couldn't find one fingerprint.'

'Do you mean,' said Adam, a sudden delirious hope rising in his heart, 'that you've still got my thousand?'

'Not so fast,' said the Major. 'I'm spinning this yarn. Well, on the day of the race I didn't know what to do. One half of me said, keep the thousand. The chap's bound to turn up some time, and it's his business to do his own punting – the other half said, put it on the favourite for him and give him a run for his money.'

'So you put it on the favourite?' Adam's heart felt like lead again.

'No, I didn't. In the end I said, well, the young chap must be frightfully rich. If he likes to throw away his money, it's none of my business, so I planked it all on Indian Runner for you.'

'You mean . . .'

'I mean I've got the nice little packet of thirty-five thou. waiting until you condescend to call for it.'

'Good heavens . . . look here, have a drink, won't you?'

'That's a thing I never refuse.'

'Archie, lend me some money until I get this fortune.'

'How much?'

'Enough to buy five bottles of champagne.'

'Yes, if you can get them.'

The barmaid had a case of champagne at the back of the tent. ('People often feel queer through watching the cars go by so fast – ladies especially,' she explained.) So they took a bottle each and sat on the side of the hill and drank to Adam's prosperity.

'Hullo, everybody,' said the loudspeaker. 'Car No. 28, the Italian Omega, driven by Captain Marino, has just completed the course in twelve minutes one second, lapping at an average speed of 78.3 miles per hour. This is the fastest time yet recorded.'

A burst of applause greeted this announcement, but Adam said, 'I've rather lost interest in this race.'

'Look here, old boy,' the Major said when they were well settled down, 'I'm rather in a hole. Makes me feel an awful ass, saying so, but the truth is I got my notecase pinched in the crowd. Of course, I've got plenty of small change to see me back to the hotel and they'll take a cheque of mine there, naturally, but the fact is I was keen to make a few bets with some chaps I hardly know. I wonder, old boy, could you possibly lend me a fiver? I can give it to you at the same time as I hand over the thirty-five thousand.'

'Why, of course,' said Adam. 'Archie, lend me a fiver, can you?'

'Awfully good of you,' said the Major, tucking the notes into his hip pocket. 'Would it be all the same if you made it a tenner while we're about it?'

'I'm sorry,' said Archie, with a touch of coldness. 'I've only just got enough to get home with.'

'That's all right, old boy, *I* understand. Not another word . . . Well, here's to us all.'

'I was on the course at the November Handicap,' said Adam. 'I thought I saw you.'

'It would have saved a lot of fuss if we'd met, wouldn't it? Still, all's well that ends well.'

'What an *angelic* man your Major is,' said Miss Runcible.

When they had finished their champagne, the Major – now indisputably drunk – rose to go.

'Look here, old boy,' he said. 'I must be toddling along now. Got to see some chaps. Thanks no end for the binge. So jolly having met you all again. Bye-bye, little lady.'

'When shall we meet again?' said Adam.

'Any time, old boy. Tickled to death to see you any time you care to drop in. Always a pew and a drink for old friends. So long everybody.'

'But couldn't I come and see you soon? About the money, you know.'

'Sooner the better, old boy. Though I don't know what you mean about money.'

'My thirty-five thousand.'

'Why, yes, to be sure. Fancy my forgetting that. I tell you what. You roll along tonight to the Imperial and I'll give it to you then. Jolly glad to get it off my chest. Seven o'clock at the American bar – or a little before.'

EVELYN WAUGH, *Vile Bodies*

*Finally there are those who are born losers. Like Whistling Bob Smith.*

# *A Good Exit*

Throughout his long career Whistling Bob sent out many great winners but, despite his success, he was never far from the bread line because of his inability to allow his horses to race without his financial support. In 1942 he had a heart attack and was whisked, seemingly unconscious, to a hospital. Anxious friends gathered round. One asked the doctor what were Whistling Bob's chances. The doctor shook his head, ummed and ahhed, and concluded things were not looking good. 'One chance in ten,' he avowed. At which point, Whistling Bob opened his eyes, took 100–10 and then died.

*The serious racing man must applaud such an exit and vow he too will go out with his betting boots on.*

# Festivals

## The Races

Crowds assembled
Colourful scene
Jockeys mounted
Gaunt and lean
Hopeful owners
Trainers too
Tipsters punters
Ballyhoo.

Sprinters stayers
Chestnuts greys
Starters orders
White flag raised
Photo finish
Objection too
Winners losers
Ballyhoo.

ROBERT HUGHES

## Newmarket

*Racing begins at Newmarket. Though there are older racecourses and arenas staging more prestigious races, Newmarket has been known as Headquarters since Charles I and II took their courts to East Anglia for the sport. Even before the latter, Old Rowley, graced the windswept heath, the course was popular: a 15th century verse describes a day at Newmarket.*

IN SOMMER at Whitsontyde
When knights most on horsebacke ride;
A cours, let them make on a daye
Steedes and palfreyes, for to assaye;
Which horse, that best may ren
Three myles the cours was then
Who that might ryde him shoulde
Have forty pounds of redy golde.

SIR BEVIS OF SOUTHAMPTON

*Charles II made Newmarket more of a social event, building himself a palace in the town and encouraging his court to throw themselves into the sport and other diversions. It is his nickname, Old Rowley, after which the spring and autumn course is named, and he is certainly the only English monarch whose life was saved by his love of horses, albeit inadvertently. The Rye House murder conspiracy of 1683 was foiled when the king made an unexpectedly early return to London after his palace at Newmarket burnt to the ground. His frequent presence at the races meant the niceties of court often had to be conducted between the 2.30 and the 3.00. One foreign visitor in Newmarket on business in 1669 was the diplomat, Cosmo, Duke of Tuscany, who recorded his impressions in his memoirs.*

THE racecourse is a tract of ground in the neighbourhood of Newmarket, which extending to the distance of four miles over a spacious and level meadow, covered with very short grass, is marked out by tall wooden posts, painted white. These point out the road that leads directly to the goal, to which they are continued the whole way; they are placed at regular distances from one another, and the last is distinguished by a flag mounted upon it, to designate the termination of the course. The horses intended for this exercise, in order to render them more swift, are kept always girt; that their bellies may not drop, and thereby interfere with the agility of their movements; and when the time of the races draws near, they feed them with the greatest care, and very sparingly, giving them for the most part, in order to keep them in full vigour, beverages composed of soaked bread and fresh eggs. Two horses only started on this occasion, one belonging to Bernard

Howard, of Norfolk, and the other to Sir — Elliot (*sic*). They left Newmarket saddled in a very simple and light manner after the English fashion, led by the hand, and at a slow pace by the men who were to ride them, dressed in taffeta of different colours, that of Howard being white; and that of Elliot green. When they reached the place where they were to start, they mounted, and loosening the reins, let the horses go; keeping them in at the beginning that they might not be too eager at first setting off, and their strength fail them in consequence at the more important part of the race; and the farther they advanced in the course, the more they urged them, forcing them to continue it at full speed. When they came to the station where the King and the Duke of York, with some lords and gentlemen of His Majesty's court were waiting on horseback till they should pass, the latter set off after them at the utmost speed, which was scarcely inferior to that of the racehorses; for the English horses, being accustomed to run, can keep up with the racers without difficulty; and they are frequently trained for this purpose in another race ground, out of London, situated on a hill which swells from the plain with so gradual and gentle a rise that at a distance it cannot be distinguished from a plain; and there is always a numerous concourse of carriages there to see the races, upon which considerable bets are made. Meanwhile His Highness, with his attendants and others of his court, stopping on horseback at a little distance from the goal, rode along the meadows waiting the arrival of the horses, and of His Majesty, who came up close after them with a numerous train of gentlemen and ladies, who stood so thick on horseback, and galloped so freely, that they were no way inferior to those who had been for years accustomed to the *manège*. As the King passed, His Highness bowed, and immediately turned and followed His Majesty to the goal, where trumpets and drums which were in readiness for that purpose, sounded in applause of the conqueror, which was the horse of Sir — Elliot.

DUKE COSMO OF TUSCANY, *Memoirs*

*Sixty years later, a second visitor strayed onto the Heath, the spy John Macky who wrote:*

THE VAST company of horsemen on the plain at a match contains all mankind on an equal footing from the Duke to the country peasant. Nobody wears swords but are clothed suitably for horse sports. Everybody strives to outjockey (as the phrase is) one another.

JOHN MACKY, *Journey through England*

*A third tourist of that era was Daniel Defoe who saw little in the pleasures of Newmarket.*

BEING come to Newmarket in the month of October, I had the opportunity to see the horse-races; and a great concourse of the nobility and gentry, as well from London as from all parts of England; but they were all so intent, so eager, so busy upon the sharping part of the sport, their wagers and bets, that to me they seem'd just as so many horse-coursers in Smithfield, descending (the greatest of them) from their high dignity and quality, to picking one another's pockets, and biting one another as much as possible, and that with such eagerness, as that it might be said they acted without respect to faith, honour, or good manners.

There was Mr Frampton, the oldest, and as some say, the cunningest jockey in England, one day he lost 1000 guineas, the next he won two thousand; and so alternately he made as light of throwing away five hundred or one thousand pounds at a time, as other men do of their pocket-money, and as perfectly calm, cheerful, and unconcern'd, when he had lost one thousand pounds, as when he had won it. On the other side, there was Sir R—— Fagg, of Sussex, of whom fame says he has the most in him and the least to shew for it, relating to jockeyship, of any man there; yet he often carry'd the prize; his horses, they said, were all cheats, how honest soever their master was; for he scarce ever produc'd a horse but he look'd like what he was not, and was what no body cou'd expect him to be: If he was as light as the wind, and could fly like a meteor, he was sure to look as clumsie, and as dirty, and as much like a cart-horse as all the cunning of his master and the grooms could make him; and just in this manner he bit some of the greatest gamesters in the field.

I was so sick of the jockeying part, that I left the crowd about the posts, and pleased my self with observing the horses; how the creatures yielded to all the arts and managements of their masters; how they took their airings in sport, and play'd with the daily heats which they ran over the course before the grand day; but how! as knowing the difference equally with their riders, would they exert their utmost strength at the time of the race itself; and that to such an extremity, that one or two of them died in the stable when they came to be rubb'd after the first heat.

Here I fansy'd myself in the Circus Maximus at Rome, seeing the antient games, and the racings of the chariots and horsemen; and in this warmth of my imagination I pleas'd and diverted myself more and in a more noble manner, than I could possibly do in the crowds of gentlemen at the weighing and starting posts, and at their coming in; or at their meetings at the coffee-houses and gaming-tables after the races were over, where there was little or nothing to be seen, but what was the subject of just reproach to them, and reproof from every wise man that look'd upon them. N.B. Pray take it with you as you go, you see no ladies at New-Market, except a few of the neighbouring gentlemen's families who come in their coaches on any particular day to see a race and so go home again directly.

As I was pleasing myself with what was to be seen here, I went in the intervals of the sport to see the fine seats of the gentlemen in the neighbouring county, for this part of Suffolk, being an open champain country, and a healthy air, is form'd for pleasure, and all kinds of country diversions; nature, as it were, inviting the gentlemen to visit her, where she was fully prepar'd to receive them; in conformity to which kind summons they came; for the country is, as it were, cover'd with fine palaces of the nobility, and pleasant seats of the gentlemen.

DANIEL DEFOE, *Tour Through the Eastern Counties*

*The Frampton mentioned was Tregonwell Frampton, keeper of the royal horses from the reign of Charles II until his death when Queen Anne was on the throne. His, as Defoe noted, was a betting stable and was involved in the great north to south match commemorated by the verse:*

> Four-and-twenty Yorkshire Knights
> Came out of the North Countree
> And they came down to Newmarket
> Mr Frampton's horses to see.

*Frampton lost a bundle on that race, a match marked by skulduggery on both sides. The popularity of riding and gambling was noted by the social commentators of the day who then, as now, saw little good in the world of the turf. Alexander Pope blamed it for a decline in England's prosperity, writing in his Fifth Satire:*

> Then peers grew proud in horsemanship to excel
> Newmarket's glory rose, as Britain's fell.

*But wringing hands never stopped anything and bets continued to be struck over the following centuries. Students at neighbouring Cambridge University became particularly keen on the races, to such an extent that some colleges required their undergraduates to report twice a day during race weeks. Though smart enough to enrol at one of England's great seats of learning, the students were not always wise to the ways of the Turf, as this spoof letter from the* Sporting Magazine *makes clear a century later.*

DEAR JACK,
I was in high hopes I should have met you at Newmarket races; but to say the truth, if your luck had turned out so bad as mine, you did better to stay away.

Dick Riot, Harry Scamper, and I, went together to Newmarket, the first day of the meeting. I was mounted on my little bay mare, that cost me thirty guineas in the north . . . I never crossed a better tit in my life; and if her eyes stand, as I dare say they will, she will turn out as tight a little thing as any in England. Then she is as fleet as the wind. Why, I raced with Dick and Harry all the way from Cambridge to Newmarke; Dick rode his roan gelding, and Harry his chestnut mare (which you know have both speed), but I beat them hollow. I cannot help telling you that I was dressed in my green riding frock, with plate buttons, with my cordovan boots, and my round hat, in the true sporting taste, so that altogether I don't believe there was a more knowing figure on the course. I was very flush too, Jack; for Ladyday happening damn'd luckily, just about the time of the races, I had received fifty guineas for my quarterage. As soon as I came upon the course I met with some jolly bucks from London; I never saw them before; however, we were soon acquainted, and I took up the odds, but I was damnably let in, for I lost thirty guineas slap the first day. The day or two after, I had no remarkable luck one way or another, but at last I laid all my cash I had left, upon Mr Cookson's Diamond, who lost, you know; but between you and me, I have a great notion the jockey rode booty.

However, I had a mind to push my luck as far as I could, so I sold my poor little mare for twelve pieces, went to the Coffee-house, and left them all behind me at the hazard-table; and I should not have been able to have got back to Cambridge that night, if Bob Whip, of Trinity, had not taken me up in his phaeton.

We have had a round of dinners at our rooms since; and I have been drunk every day, to drive away care. However, I hope to recruit again soon, Frank Classic, of Pembroke, has promised to make me out a long catalogue of Greek books; so I will write directly to old Squaretoes, send him the list, tell him I have taken them up, and draw on him for money to pay the bookseller's bill. Then I shall be rich again, Jack; and perhaps you may see me at the Bedford by the middle of next week; till when I am,

Dear Jack, yours,

H. HAREBRAIN.<br>
Sporting Magazine Vol. XIV

*H. Harebrain may have lost his fortune by allowing nature to follow name. Many, however, believed the population of nineteenth-century Newmarket to be sharks, waiting to strip the assets of visitors like so many Michael Milkens. R. S. Surtees' immortal Mr Jorrocks was deeply wary of a suggested visit to the town by a friend from Yorkshire.*

A MUFFIN – and the *Post*, sir,' said George to the Yorkshire-man, on one of the fine fresh mornings that gently usher in the returning spring, and draw from the town-pent cits sighs for the verdure of the fields – as he placed the above mentioned articles on his usual breakfast table in the coffe-room of the 'Piazza'. With the calm deliberation of a man whose whole day is unoccupied, the Yorkshireman sweetened his tea, drew the muffin and a select dish of prawns to his elbow and turning sideways to the table, crossed his legs and prepared to con the contents of the paper. The first page as usual was full of advertisements. Sales by auction – Favour of your vote and interest – If the next of kin – Reform your tailor's bills – Law – Articled clerk – An absolute reversion – Pony phaeton – Artificial teeth – Messrs. Tattersall – Brace of pointers – Dog lost – Boy found – Great sacrifice – No advance in coffee – Matrimony – A single gentleman – Board and lodging in an airy situation – To ominbus proprietors – Steam to Leith and Hull – Stationery – Desirable investment for a small capital – The fire reviver or lighter.

Then turning it over, his eye ranged over a whole meadow of type, consisting of the previous night's debate, followed on by City news, Police reports, Fashionable arrivals and departures, Dinners given, Sporting intelligence, Newmarket Craven meeting. 'That's more in my way,' said the Yorkshireman to himself as he laid down the paper and took a sip of his tea. 'I've a great mind to go, for I may just as well be at Newmarket as here, having nothing particular to do in either place. I came to stay a hundred pounds in London it's true, but if I stay ten of it at Newmarket, it'll be all the same, and I can go home from there just as well as from here'; so saying, he took another turn at the tea. The race list was a tempting one, Riddlesworth, Craven Stakes, Column Stakes, Oatlands, Port, Claret, Sherry, Madeira, and all other sorts. A good week's racing in fact, for the saintly sinners who frequent the Heath had not then discovered any greater impropriety in travelling on a Sunday, then in cheating each other on the Monday. The tea was good, as were the prawns and eggs, and George brought a second muffin, at the very moment that the York-shireman had finished the last piece of the first, so that by the time he had done his breakfast and drawn on his boots, which were dryer and pleasanter than the recent damp weather had allowed of their being, he felt completely at peace with himself and all the world, and putting on his hat, sallied forth with the self-satisfied air of a man who had eat a good breakfast, and yet not too much.

Newmarket was still uppermost in his mind, and as he sauntered along in the direction of the Strand, it occurred to him that perhaps Mr Jorrocks might have no objection to accompany him.

\* \* \*

'Newmarket!' exclaimed Jorrocks, throwing his arm in the air, while his paper cap fell from his head with the jerk – 'by Newmarket! why, what in the name of all that's impure, have you to do at Newmarket?'

'Why, nothing in particular; only, when there's neither hunting nor shooting going on, what is a man to do with himself? – I'm sure you'd despise me if I were to go fishing.' 'True,' observed Mr Jorrocks somewhat subdued, and jingling the silver in his breeches-pocket. 'Fox-'unting is indeed the prince of sports. The image of war, without its guilt, and only half its danger. I confess that I'm a martyr to it – a perfect wictim – no one knows wot I suffer from my ardour. If ever I'm wisited with the last infirmity of noble minds, it will be caused by my ingovernable passion for the chase. The sight of a saddle makes me sweat. An 'ound makes me perfectly wild. A red coat throws me into a scarlet fever. Never throughout life have I had a good night's rest before an ' unting morning. But werry little racing does for me; Sadler's Wells is well enough of a fine summer evening especially when they plump the clown over head in the New River cut, and the ponies don't misbehave in the Circus – but oh! Newmarket's a dreadful place, the werry name's a sickener. I used to hear a vast about it from poor Will Softly of Friday Street. It was the ruin of him – and wot a fine business his father left him, both wholesale and retail, in the tripe and cow-heel line – all went in two years, and he had nothing to show at the end of that time for upwards of twenty thousand golden sovereigns, but a hundredweight of children's lamb's-wool socks, and warrants for thirteen hogsheads of damaged sherry in the docks. No, take my adwice, and have nothing to say to them – stay where you are, or, if you're short of swag, come to Great Coram Street, where you shall have a bed, wear-and-tear for your teeth and all that sort of thing found you, and, if Saturday's a fine day, I'll treat you with a jaunt to Margate.'

'You are a regular old trump,' said the Yorkshireman, after listening attentively until Mr Jorrocks had exhausted himself, 'but, you see, you've never been at Newmarket, and the people have been hoaxing you about it. I can assure you from personal experience that the people there are quite as honest as those you meet every day on 'Change, besides which, there is nothing more invigorating to the human frame – nothing more cheering to the spirits, than the sight and air of Newmarket Heath on a fine fresh spring morning like the present. The wind seems to go by you at a racing pace, and the blood canters up and down the veins with the finest and freest action imaginable. A stranger to the racecourse would feel, and almost instinctively know, what turf he was treading, and the purpose for which that turf was intended. There's a magic in the web of it.'

'Oh, I knows you are a most persuasive cock,' observed Mr Jorrocks interrupting the Yorkshireman, 'and would conwince the devil himself that black is white, but you'll I never make me believe the Newmarket folks are honest, and as to the fine hair (air) you talk of, there's quite as good to get on Hampstead Heath, and if it doesn't make the blood canter up and down your weins, you can always amuse yourself by watching the donkeys cantering up and down with the sweet little childrcn – haw! haw! haw! But tell me what is there at Newmarket that should take a man there?' 'What is there?' rejoined the Yorkshireman, 'why, there's everything that makes life desirable and constitutes happiness, in this world, except hunting. First there is the beautiful, neat, clean town, with groups of booted professors, ready for the rapidest march of intellect; then there are the strings of clothed horses – the finest in the world – passing indolently at intervals to their exercise – the flower of the English aristocracy residing in the place. You leave

the town and stroll to the wide open heath, where all is brightness and space; the white rails stand forth against the clear blue
sky – the brushing gallop ever and anon startles the ear and eye;
crowds of stable urchins, full of silent importance, stud the heath;
you feel elated and long to bound over the well groomed turf and
to try the speed of the careering wind. All things at Newmarket
train the mind to racing. Life seems on the start, and dull indeed
were he who could rein in his feelings when such inspiring
objects meet together to madden them!'

'Bravo!' exclaimed Jorrocks, throwing his paper cap in the air
as the Yorkshireman concluded. – 'Bravo! – werry good indeed!
You speak like ten Lord Mayors – never heard nothing better. Dash
my vig, if I won't go. By Jove, you've done it. Tell me one thing
– is there a good place to feed at?'

'Capital!' replied the Yorkshireman, 'beef, mutton, cheese, ham,
all the delicacies of the season, as the sailor said'; and thereupon
the Yorkshireman and Jorrocks shook hands upon the bargain.

*On arrival Mr Jorrocks found the town below his expectations, though
the natives did run to form.*

He turned into the main street of Newmarket, where he was lost
in astonishment at the insignificance of the place. But wiser men
than Mr Jorrocks have been similarly disappointed, for it enters
into the philosophy of few to conceive the fame and grandeur
of Newmarket compressed into the limits of the petty, outlandish,
Icelandish place that bears the name. 'Dash my vig,' said Mr
Jorrocks, as he brought himself to bear upon Rogers's shop-
window, 'this is the werry meanest town I ever did see. Pray, sir,'
addressing himself to a groomish-looking man in a brown
cut-away coat, drab shorts and continuations, who had just emerged
from the shop with a race list in his hand, 'Pray, sir, be this your
principal street?' The man eyed him with a mixed look of incredulity
and contempt. At length, putting his thumbs into the armholes
of his waistcoat, he replied, 'I bet a crown you know as well as I
do.' 'Done,' said Mr Jorrocks holding out his hand. 'No – I won't
do that,' replied the man, 'but I'll tell you what I'll do with
you – I'll lay you two to one, in fives or fifties if you like, that
you knew before you axed, and that Thunderbolt don't win the

Riddlesworth.' 'Really,' said Mr Jorrocks, 'I'm not a betting man.' 'Then, wot the 'ell business have you at Newmarket?' was all the answer he got.

\* \* \*

*The business was the racing.*

The races were going forward on one of the distant courses, and a slight insignificant, black streak, swelling into a sort of oblong (for all the world like an overgrown tadpole), was all that denoted the spot, or interrupted the verdant aspect of the quiet extensive plain. Jorrocks was horrified having through life pictured Epsom as a mere drop in the ocean compared with the countless multitude of Newmarket, while the Baron, who was wholly indifferent to the matter, nearly had old Jorrocks pitched over the mare's head by applying the furze-bush (which he had got from the boy) to her tail while Mr Jorrocks was sitting loosely, contemplating the barrenness of the prospect. The sherry was still alive, and being all for fun, he shuffled back into the saddle as soon as the old mare gave over kicking; and giving a loud tally-ho, with some minor 'hunting noises' which were responded to by the Baron in notes not capable of being set to music, and aided by an equally indescribable accompaniment from the old mare at every application of the bush, she went off at score over the springy turf, and bore them triumphantly to the betting-post just as the ring was in course of formation, a fact which she announced by a loud neigh on viewing her companion of the plough, as well as by upsetting some half-dozen black-legs as she rushed through the crowd to greet her. Great was the hubbub, shouting, swearing, and laughing – for though the Newmarketites are familiar with most conveyances, from a pair of horses down to a pair of shoes, it had not then fallen to their lot to see two men ride into the ring on the same horse – certainly not with such a hat between them as the Baron's.

The gravest and weightiest matters will not long distract the attention of a black-leg, and the laughter having subsided without Jorrocks or the Baron being in the slightest degree disconcerted, the ring was again formed; horses' heads again turn towards the post, while carriages, gigs, and carts form an outer circle. A solemn silence ensues. The legs are scanning the list. At length one gives tongue. 'What starts? Does Lord Eldon start?' 'No, he don't,' replies the owner. 'Does Trick, by Catton?' 'Yes, and Conolly rides – but mind, three pounds over.' 'Does John Bull?' 'No John's struck out.' 'Polly Hopkins does, so does Talleyrand also O, Fy! out of Penitence; Beagle and Paradox also – and perhaps Pickpocket.'

Another pause, and the pencils are pulled from the betting-books. The legs and lords look at each other, but no one likes to lead off. At length a voice is heard offering to take nine to one he names the winner. 'It's short odds, doing it cautiously. I'll take eight then,' he adds – 'sivin!' but no one bites. 'What will anyone lay about Trick, by Catton?' inquires Jem Bland. 'I'll lay three to two again him.' 'I'll take two to one – two ponies to one, and give you a suv. for laying it.' 'Carn't' is the answer. 'I'll do it, Jem,' cries a voice. 'No, you won't,' from Bland, not liking his customer. Now they are all at it, and what a hubbub there is! 'I'll back the field – I'll lay – I'll take – I'll bet – ponies – fifties – hundreds – five hundred to two.' 'What do you want, my lord?' 'Three to one against Trick, by Catton.' 'Carn't afford it – the odds really arn't that in the ring.' 'Take two – two hundred to one.' 'No.' 'Crockford, you'll do it for me?' 'Yes, my lord. Twice over if you like. Done, done.' 'Do it again?' 'No, thank you.'

'Trick, by Catton, don't start!' cries a voice. 'Impossible!' exclaim his backers. 'Quite true, I'm just from the weighing-house, and told me so himself.' 'Shame! shame!' roar those who have backed him, and 'honour – rascals – rogues – thieves – robbery – swindle – turf-ruined' – fly from tongue to tongue, but they are all speakers with never a speaker to cry order. Meanwhile the lads have galloped by on their hacks with the horses' cloths to the rubbing-house, and the horses have actually started, and are now visible in the distance sweeping over the open heath, apparently without guide or beacon.

The majority of the ring rush to the white judge's box, and have just time to range themselves along the rude stakes and ropes that guard the run in, and the course-keeper in a shooting-jacket on a rough pony to crack his whip, and cry to half a dozen stable-lads to 'clear the course', before the horses come flying towards home. Now all is tremor; hope and fear vacillating in each breast. Silence

stands breathless with expectation – all eyes are riveted—the horses come within descrying distance – 'beautiful!' three close together,
two behind. 'Clear the course! clear the course! pray clear the course!'
'Polly Hopkins! Polly Hopkins!' roar a hundred voices as they near.
'O, Fy! O, Fy!' respond an equal number. 'The horse! the horse!'
bellow a hundred more, as though their yells would aid his speed,
as Polly Hopkins, O, Fy! and Talleyrand rush neck-and-neck along
the cords and pass the judge's box. A cry of 'dead heat!' is heard.
The bystanders see as suits their books, and immediately rush to
the judge's box, betting, bellowing, roaring, and yelling the whole
way. 'What's won? what's won? what's won?' is vociferated from
a hundred voices. 'Polly Hopkins! Polly Hopkins! Polly Hopkins!'
replies Mr Clark with judicial dignity. 'By how much? by how
much?' 'Half a head – half a head,' replies the same functionary.
'What's second?' 'O, Fy!' and so, amid the song of 'Pretty, pretty
Polly Hopkins', from the winners, and curses and execrations long,
loud, and deep, from the losers, the scene closes.

The admiring winners follow Polly to the rubbing-house, while
the losing horses are left in the care of their trainers and stable-boys,
who console themselves with hopes of 'better luck next time'.

After a storm comes a calm, and the next proceeding is the wheeling of the judge's box, and removal of the old stakes and ropes
to another course on a different part of the heath, which is accomplished by a few ragged rascals, as rude and uncouth as the
furniture they bear. In less than half an hour the same group of
anxious careworn countenances are again turned upon each other at the betting-post, as though they had never separated. But
see! the noble owner of Trick, by Catton, is in the crowd, and Jem
Bland eyeing him like a hawk. 'I say, Waggey,' cries he (singling
out a friend stationed by his lordship), 'had you ought on Trick,
by Catton?' 'No, Jem,' roars Wagstaff, shaking his head, 'I knew
my man too well.' 'Why now, Waggey, do you know I wouldn't
have done such a thing for the world! no, not even to have been
made a Markiss!' a horse-laugh follows this denunciation, at which
the newly created marquis bites his livid lips.

The Baron, who appears to have no taste for walking, still sticks
to the punch mare, which Mr Jorrocks steers to the newly formed
ring aided by the Baron and the furze-bush. Here they come upon
Sam Spring, whose boy has just brought his spring-cart to bear
upon the ring formed by the horsemen, and thinking it a pity

a nobleman of any county should be reduced to the necessity of riding double, very politely offers to take one into his carriage. Jorrocks accepts the offer, and forthwith proceeds to make himself quite at home in it. The chorus again commences, and Jorrocks interrogates Sam as to the names of the brawlers. 'Who be that?' said he, 'offering to bet a thousand to a hundred.' Spring, after eyeing him through his spectacles, with a grin and a look of suspicion replies, 'Come now – come – let's have no nonsense – you know as well as I.' 'Really,' replies Mr Jorrocks most earnestly, 'I don't.' 'Why, where have you lived all your life?' 'First part of it with my grandmother at Lisson Grove, afterwards at Camberwell, but now I resides in Great Coram Street, Russell Square – a werry fashionable neighbourhood.' 'Oh, I see,' replies Sam, 'you are one of the reg'lar city coves, then – now, what brings you here?' 'Just to say that I have been at Newmarket for I'm blowed if ever you catch me here again.' 'That's a pity,' replied Sam, 'for you look like a promising man – a handsome-bodied chap in the face – don't you sport any?' 'O a vast! – 'unt regularly – I'm a member of the Surrey 'unt – capital one it is too – best in England by far.' 'What do you hunt?' inquired Sam. 'Foxes to be sure.' 'And are they good eating?' 'Come,' replied Jorrocks, 'you know, as well as I do, we don't eat 'em.' The dialogue was interrupted by someone calling to Sam to know what he was backing.

'The Bedlamite colt, my lord,' with a forefinger to his hat. 'Who's that?' inquired Jorrocks. 'That's my Lord L——, a baron-lord – and a very nice one – best baron-lord I know – always bets with me – that's another baron-lord next him, and the man next him is a baron-knight, a stage below a baron-lord – something between a nobleman and a gentleman.' 'And who be that stout, good-looking man in a blue coat and velvet collar next him, just rubbing his chin with the race card – he'll be a lord too, I suppose?' 'No, – that's Mr Gully, as honest a man as ever came here, – that's Crockford before him. The man on the right is Mr C——, who they call the "cracksman", because formerly he was a professional housebreaker, but he has given up that trade, and turned gentleman, bets, and keeps a gaming-table. This little ugly black-faced chap, that looks for all the world like a bilious Scotch terrier, has lately come among us. He was a tramping pedlar – sold worsted stockings – attended country courses, and occasionally bet a pair. Now he bets thousands of pounds, and keeps racehorses.

The chaps about him all covered with chains and rings and brooches, were in the duffing line – sold brimstoned sparrows for canary-birds, Norwich shawls for real Cashmere, and dried cabbage-leaves for cigars. Now each has a first-rate house, horses and carriages, and a play-actress among them. Yon chap, with the extravagantly big mouth, is a cabinet-maker at Cambridge. He'll bet you a thousand pounds as soon as look at you.'

'The chap on the right of the post with the red tie, is the son of an ostler. He commenced betting thousands with a farthing capital. The man next him, all teeth and hair, like a rat-catcher's dog, is an Honourable by birth, but not very honourable in his nature.' 'But see,' cried Mr Jorrocks, 'Lord —— is talking to the Cracksman.' 'To be sure,' replies Sam, 'that's the beauty of the turf. The lord and the leg are reduced to an equality. Take my word for it, if you have a turn for good society, you should come upon the turf. I say, my Lord Duke!' with all five fingers up to his hat, 'I'll lay you three to two on the Bedlamite colt.' 'Done Mr Spring,' replies his Grace, 'three ponies to two.' 'There!' cried Mr Spring, turning to Jorrocks, 'didn't I tell you so?' The riot around the post increases. It is near the moment of starting, and the legs again become clamorous for what they want. Their vehemence increases. Each man is *in extremis*. 'They are off!' cries one. 'No, they are not,' replies another. 'False start,' roars a third. 'Now they come!' 'No they don't!' 'Back again.' They are off at last, however, and away they speed over the flat. The horses come within descrying distance. It's a beautiful race – run at score the whole way, and only two tailed off within the cords. Now they set to – whips and spurs go, legs leap, lords shout, and amid the same scene of confusion, betting, galloping, cursing, swearing, and bellowing, the horses rush past the judge's box.

But we have run our race, and will not fatigue our readers with repetition. Let us, however, spend the evening, and then the 'Day at Newmarket' will be done.

R. S. SURTEES, *Jorrocks' Jaunts and Jollities*

*Mr Jorrocks escaped Newmarket without being picked clean by its touts as he had feared. Of course, most people are capable of losing money at Newmarket without the assistance of crooks, badmashes, con artists and the like. All they need is horses.*

ONCE, after Newmarket, my father was missing for two days. My mother did not seem to be in the least worried. 'Newmarket,' she said, 'is always a special occasion for him. He was once away for eight days celebrating his losses.' It says something for my father's robust nature that he always 'indulged in festivities', as my aunt called it, whether he lost or won. This time he came back in a most boisterous mood. He had lost at the races, but had won at cards, and then lost again at billiards, and then won again at cards, and lost again at billiards, and won again at cards. He reckoned that he would have been 17s. up on the two days if he hadn't lost £2 at a final game of billiards. 'But it was a near thing,' he said. Then, patting my head, he said, 'We'll get the boy into Eton yet, if the luck holds.'

J. B. MORTON, *Best of Beachcomber*

# *Cheltenham*

*The age of matches and private racing died with the rise of Admiral Rous, a stern gentleman who brought order to the chaos of the British turf. From the primordial swamp he fashioned the racing calendar we know today, a summer of Newmarket, Epsom, Royal Ascot, Goodwood, Doncaster and Newmarket again and a winter, though this postdates the good admiral, of Cheltenham and Aintree. Everyone has their individual favourite festival – for many it is simply the next one – but Cheltenham draws the greatest support because of the famine of decent racing that precedes it. Jump racing has not always had the best press:*

TIME WAS: and not long ago either, when steeplechasing was synonymous with robbers, and with no recognised laws to protect it, and with the demoralising light-weight system in full force, got up for the most part as an instrument of fraud and barefaced swindling, it gradually but surely sunk into the lowest depths of degradation, and abuse was literally heaped upon it from all sides.

BELL'S LIFE NEWSPAPER

*A case, one would imagine, of a really bad Cheltenham, a Cheltenham bad enough to have the country's bank managers weeping. A good Cheltenham, however, was enjoyed by Hugh McIlvanney in 1986.*

THE REST of humanity had better be wary from now on of the 42,000 of us who were on Cheltenham racecourse last Thursday. We cannot begin to guarantee that our babblings of what we saw there will not be sufficiently relentless to clear bars, cause communication cords to be grabbed on trains or tempt fellow passengers on aeroplanes to head for the exit at 35,000 feet.

People who witness miracles, even small ones of the sporting kind, are liable to carry around forever afterwards a deadly parcel of reminiscence and anyone who wants to avoid my 1986 Gold Cup monologue should be ready with emergency measures whenever the names of Dawn Run, Jonjo O'Neill, Charmian Hill and Paddy Mullins are mentioned. In three decades of watching supreme performers in a wide range of contests, there have been few experiences that have precipitated a greater flood of excitement and pleasure than the sight of Jonjo and that incomparable mare battling out of what seemed the hopeless finality of third place at the last fence. Dawn Run galloped with unbreakable pride up the killing slope of Cheltenham's run-in to pass Forgive 'n' Forget and Wayward Lad and make history by becoming the first horse to add a Gold Cup to a Champion Hurdle victory. The melodrama belonged in the last reel of one those old Hollywood films in which someone like the young Roddy McDowall came from about two parishes back to land the big prize.

Jonjo, with no director to adjust the positions for him in the closing scene, and with a phenomenon under him who prefers to boss her rivals from the front, had never exposed himself to the slightest danger of having a lot of ground to make up. He had concentrated on setting a dominating, draining pace while coping patiently with the wearing company of Run and Skip, whose tough rider, Steve Smith-Eccles, was determined to maintain the nagging proximity that might have invited the blunders to be expected from an eight-year-old with only four previous outings over fences. In spite of making her task more difficult by dropping her hind legs in the water and suffering a noticeable loss of momentum and then committing a more significant error by clattering the fifth fence from home, Dawn Run had burned off Run and Skip by the second last but the superb veteran Wayward Lad (on which O'Neill took third place in the Gold Cup of 1983) and last year's winner, Forgive 'n' Forget, were swiftly, ominously overhauling her. And to everyone in the stands it looked as if she and Jonjo had been fatally engulfed at the final jump.

When the talent and heart of this inspired Irish partnership proved otherwise, the explosion of euphoria was such that some of the hats sent spiralling into the air might have had heads in them for all the owners cared. No result, not even the three Gold Cup wins in a row by the greatest of steeplechasers, Arkle, ever stirred a more emotional response than greeted Dawn Run's success, which had the unsurprising additional distinction of clipping 1.9 seconds off the record time for the three miles two furlongs and 22 fences of the ultimate test of the jumping code's elite.

The stampeding crowds in the winner's enclosure could have been extremely dangerous but good nature just held the line against hysteria and nothing happened to taint the happiness that suffused the entire occasion as thoroughly as it did the glowing face of Mrs Hill, who looked closer to 40 than 67 as she accepted the trophy from an almost equally delighted Queen Mother. With Dawn Run a noble, steaming presence off to the side, it was quite a day for heroines. But no one was likely to forget the heroes, especially when Jonjo O'Neill, rider of a race of flawless control and purity, produced another stroke of inspiration by taking an affectionate grip on Tony Mullins – son of Dawn Run's trainer Paddy and her regular jockey until being dislodged in more ways than one at Cheltenham in her fourth steeplechase in January – before hoisting the younger man on to his shoulders and carrying him up to the presentation dais.

It was a spontaneous, marvellously unforced gesture, utterly characteristic of the little Cork man, whose bravery, resilience, warmth and generosity of spirit so perfectly represent the irresistible qualities of a game which, at its best, is one of the most natural and attractive metaphors for life that sport has to offer. Maybe the natures that inhabit it tend to be so appealing because they learn early (and go on relearning) how to live not only with losing but with losing painfully, sometimes in the intensive care unit.

Jonjo himself has come through experiences severe enough to have put a more ordinary man in a wheelchair, if not in a hole in the ground. He remembers the time when his right leg was so hideously broken that it was 'like a sack of gravel', so devastated that an extensive metal plate and screws had to be inserted to help bind the bones, but he has readily put such ordeals behind him. When I asked during a long telephone conversation late on Friday night if the leg still bothered him, I got the riposte I deserved. 'Don't you think it was working all right yesterday?' he asked. Everything, of course, had worked beautifully, which was not something he was entitled to assume after schooling Dawn Run at Gowran Park in Ireland in January. Her behaviour that day was nightmarishly bad and after enduring two circuits on which she backed off from some fences, dived to the left at others and generally conducted herself like an eccentric menace, Jonjo was as near to despair as he ever sinks.

'At the end of that I didn't think she should be running in the Gold Cup, let alone be favourite to win it,' he said. 'She did jump the last fence of that schooling run well but one out of about 14 isn't exactly encouraging. Then on the Thursday before Cheltenham I went over to school her again at Punchestown and this time Tony Mullins rode another horse round with me and Dawn Run did everything I asked her to do, which I didn't think was possible after Gowran Park. So that raised our hopes, though there had to be worries about how she would go about her work on the day. Still, when people say they could see that I was a lot more nervous than usual before the Gold Cup, that I was obviously feeling the extra pressure, I think I've got to correct that a little bit. There's no point in denying that I had to be aware of how important Thursday was for me and everybody connected with the mare, but the responsibility that brought is not the kind to weigh me down.

'The way I look at it, I love the old game, it's my flippin' hobby as well as my livin' and above all I love riding really good horses. Going out there with something exceptional underneath you and getting the job right together is the greatest satisfaction. It is far better to be on a good horse than a moderate one and the responsibility involved can never reduce the thrill of that for me. But whether it's a favourite or 100–1 shot I go out to try to get the job right, I'm riding to fit the horse as much as I want the horse to fit me.'

He never considered charging off into the distance as Dawn Run has done while murdering opponents in the past. Cheltenham's hills and stiff obstacles would, he knew, have made such tactics madness. So we were privileged to see the ride of a lifetime, a monument to patience, nerve, courage and technical brilliance, the mature masterwork of a great jockey. 'Half-way through the run to the last fence she seemed beat,' he said on Friday night. 'But I let her get her own feet and she jumped it well. She's a moody old devil, and neither me nor anyone else could get her to do something if she didn't want to. She wasn't absolutely knackered. She was taking a breather, saying, "I'm going fast enough here". After Wayward Lad went two or three lengths up he began to hang across in front of me towards the rails. I realised he was tired and stopping and so did she. So we both got stuck in together.'

They did, even more dramatically than when winning the Champion Hurdle in 1984. At the line Jonjo, he admits, 'went crackers', which left him about twice as sane as a reception party that nearly made him the first rider to have a leg broken in the winners' enclosure. Through it all the bright face under the dump of reddish hair never lost its expression of delirious bliss.

Some man. Some horse. Some day.

HUGH McILVANNEY, The Observer

# Aintree

*If Cheltenham is for the jumping purists, Aintree is for the nation. The Grand National is the most popular race in the country with almost every household having its tuppence hapenny on its fancy. Remarkably it is also one of the few races Jeffrey Bernard's bank manager can look forward to with serenity.*

THE NATIONAL is one of my best races – after something like thirty-five of the wretched events I fancy myself something of an expert at it. As the great day approaches and every housewife in the country is blindfolding herself with a duster and poising a finger over the pinsticker's guide, I find myself thinking that it must be the easiest bet of all the big handicaps. Merryman II and Nicolaus Silver, for instance, stood out like sweet cherries. I even backed Russian Hero, Ayala and Maori Venture, none of which had much of a shout on paper. But the thing about the National is that you can always eliminate most of the horses on one of two grounds: inability to jump and inability to stay – both vital in the longest major steeplechase with those old-fashioned Aintree fences along the way.

The dodgy one to judge is staying power. Russian Hero – famous simply because it was tipped by what was then the *Daily Worker* – had never previously won over more than two and a half miles; Specify was another National winner that wasn't supposed to have the stamina. The complicating factor is that a good jockey can persuade a decent middle-distance horse to stay by getting it to *hack* round for the first circuit. It was Fred Winter who first drew my attention to this when he dismounted from one of his National winners and told the press in the most disarming way that the first circuit had been sweet as hunting.

Fred Winter once helped me back a winner at Aintree, but I never felt very good about this one. He was showing me his yard at Lambourn and took me round the stable lads' hostel. Being the middle of the day it was deserted, except for a solitary lad lying on his bunk with his head swathed in bandages. I asked what had happened. Apparently this was the lad who did Anglo and the brute had almost brained him with a kick to the skull which needed thirty-five stitches. I mumbled something feeble about how sorry I was. Fred looked at it rather differently. 'Actually,' he said as we left the hostel, 'I feel rather optimistic. It shows Anglo's really on his toes.' I thought this somewhat callous, but it didn't stop me backing Anglo come the National six weeks later.

At the time it was a rather horrific and embarrassing experience. I was very short of readies, unemployed and living with a paranoid girl of great wealth who quite rightly thought that everyone was after her money. We had a party on Grand National day and as I watched Anglo skip over the last few fences and draw farther and farther away as though he was having a little canter on the Lambourn Downs, I could have won an Oscar for my acting. I knew that if the lady in question tumbled the fact that I'd just backed a 50–1 winner, then I wouldn't see much of it since it would be levied as a love tax. But I managed to hold my head in my hands and moan and moan and utter phrases like 'stuffed again'. Inwardly I was jumping over the then unsullied moon.

I have suffered far worse at the Derby. I don't mean especially from the financial point of view, though I've bled as much on Epsom Downs as any man; no, it's just that it's not worth going to the Derby unless things are absolutely right for you on the day. By this I mean getting there in good time, getting there in a car (and not on that travelling lunatic asylum known as the Derby Day 'Special' train) but avoiding the ghastly traffic jams, and cadging an invitation to someone's box to escape being trampled on by a hundred thousand twice-a-year punters who don't know a betting slip from a Chinese laundry ticket. Also, I refuse to wear a morning suit as I already look daft enough in my usual clothes to raise laughs from the bookmakers.

Nijinsky's Derby was one of the worst. A great horse, but the price wasn't good enough for me, so I hunted around for a long shot and of course came away with a fractured pocket. At least it was a lovely day, and sunshine always alleviates impecunity. Mill Reef will always stick in my mind because I was absolutely convinced it wouldn't win, and had to run the last mile and a half uphill to the course because of the damned traffic, arriving just in time to see the bugger sail first past the post. I did have the sense to recoup my money by backing him for the Arc de Triomphe that October, the day I lost my job. After the race my Irish trainer friend Mick O'Toole, who had also won, bought the entire stock of Dom Perignon in the paddock bar.

In spite of my interest in – sorry, I mean obsession with racing it wasn't until Charlottown's Derby that I actually clapped eyes on the brutes in the flesh. I did my usual thing. I went down to Epsom with a hundred pounds, a gigantic sum in those days, as they say (and come to that I couldn't half do with another ton now), intending to shove the lot on Charlottown, so impressed had I been with its running in the Lingfield Derby Trial Stakes. I don't need to tell you that I changed my mind five minutes before the off and did my lot. After the last race I remember standing by a fish and chip stall crying. No one noticed since it was pouring with rain. In a trance I slowly put cold pieces of cod in my mouth and watched the Rolls Royce glide majestically by.

I don't believe I've told you yet which are the greatest race-horses of my time, and it's not an opinion I intend to keep to myself. They are Sea Bird II, Ribot and Dancing Brave; then Nijinsky and Mill Reef.

JEFFREY BERNARD, *Talking Horses*

# Epsom

*Aintree and Epsom, the Grand National and the Derby. Two very different races but two equally cherished by Britain. Fifty years ago crowds of 300,000 would wash over the Downs at Epsom to see the Derby. Parliament would rise for the day, a holiday that one Prime Minister, Lord Palmerston, made official when he proposed the motion that 'to adjourn over that day is part of the unwritten law of Parliament and that Her Majesty's Government do not wish to depart from so whole-some a custom'. The popularity of Epsom is dwindling, however. The crowds on Derby Day are but a quarter of the inter-war years and fewer of the top three-year-olds take on the gradients and contours of Epsom. Former jockey Jack Leach describes the course in its heyday.*

SOMEBODY, whose name I've forgotten and good riddance to him, said that from a grain of sand a man might deduce the universe. Well, here is a sample from which you may deduce the Derby madness.

Motoring back to London from Epsom in Midday Sun's year, we were held up in a traffic jam alongside the lunatic asylum. One of the inmates was leaning against the fence watching the traffic, and asked 'What price was the winner?' Our driver told him a hundred to seven. The lunatic replied, 'We got twenty-five to one in here.' So I don't suppose there is any place where they don't take an interest in the Derby. I know they listen to the broadcast, whatever time of day or night it is, in California, Melbourne, Sydney, and other far places, as I have friends who have done it, and a ship in distress would be unlucky if it had to send an SOS out while the race was being run.

Today, people wherever they are, know the winner as soon as the numbers go up at Epsom. Yet this is not much quicker than in 1901, when Volodyovski won and some of the American trainer's pals were drinking Huggins's punch in Saratoga ten minutes after the race – the then new Atlantic cable had been kept open for the result.

The English Derby is the greatest test for speed and stamina in the world. It is one and a half miles for three-year-olds on June 1, or near enough. The Kentucky Derby is run in May, but is only one and a quarter miles. Other Derbies – the French, Irish, German, and so on – take place later, and anyway they are not run on such a turbulent testing ground as Epsom.

This course has got everything, uphill to start with, round a turn, down a very steep hill to Tattenham Corner, the home turn, and then an uphill finish, and they go a cracking pace all the way. It is the running of those first few furlongs at perhaps a fifth of a second faster than any other one and a half mile race run on this course that finds out the non-stayers, even before they get into the straight.

From Tattenham Corner home, it's just sheer stamina and guts. There has never been the slightest doubt about the Derby winner being a great three-year-old on that day. Not since Running Rein anyway: a four-year-old called Maccabeus was rung in for Running Rein many years ago, but the swindle was found out, and the horse disqualified.

The tremendous excitement caused by the running of the Derby has often been added to by sensational incidents. When Hermit won it, he had broken a blood vessel in a gallop only a few days before; and this, incidentally, broke the Marquis of Hastings, who laid against the colt to lose a fortune. The owner, Mr. Chaplin, won a large sum as he couldn't lay off his bets, or, as he was a great sportsman, wouldn't take advantage when he obviously must have thought Hermit had practically destroyed his chance.

Then there was Aboyeur's year, full of sensations. As the field came herding round Tattenham Corner into the straight, a suffragette threw herself under King Edward VII's horse Anmer and brought him down. The suffragette was killed, and Herbert Jones the jockey badly injured. That was not all; in a bumping finish, Craganour, the hot favourite, savaged Aboyeur and was disqualified, although many people thought that Aboyeur was the cause of the trouble, and there was a lot of bad feeling all round. Craganour's owner, Mr Bower Ismay, immediately sold his horse to the Argentine, and I believe never raced in England again.

Nowadays, there are quite a few races with bigger stake money than the Derby, but any owner, trainer, breeder or jockey, and the boy who 'does' the horses too, would rather win the Derby than any other two races in the world.

Follow Steve if you want to win a Derby – those were my orders in 1922. I carried them out; Steve won it on Captain Cuttle. I carried them out again in 1923 when he won on Papyrus and was still following him in 1925 when he won on Manna. It got monotonous.

Donoghue certainly had the Indian sign on the Derby – he had won three before I started the follow-my-leader business. All his winners were quick beginners and handy horses and nobody could ride this type of animal quite as well as he could. He seemed to know how to use their terrific initial speed and yet always have a bit left up his sleeve. Of course, he picked his mounts to a certain extent, having a very persuasive manner, and he could get himself off a horse in his own stable if he thought he could get the ride on a better one in another.

Always a great rider, he was, if anything, a bit better on the big occasion: nothing upset him, nerves didn't interest him. He had a kind of genius on a horse, but off one he was like a child, though a child wouldn't be so vague as to book four sleepers to Scotland from King's Cross and then travel in the guard's van from St Pancras. In the early 1920s he was sitting on top of the world, except when the world was sitting on top of him, and of course nearly everybody thought he had found out the only way to ride at Epsom.

He somehow dominated the race. He was always wonderfully good at anticipating the start, he was never caught flat-footed, and he got his horse running quickly in the first three furlongs to ensure himself a very handy position with the leaders. At about the mile post he would give his animal an easer – not much, of course, but just enough to give it a chance to take a few deep breaths, and at the same time he would call to the jockeys alongside him: 'We're overdoing it a bit.' Knowing that Steve was such a good judge of pace they would most probably ease with him, and those behind would naturally be slowed up, or have to go round.

Of course it caused a lot of trouble; at this point the race always got rough. About sixteen jockeys wanted the same position, near the inside just behind the leaders, with the ones on the outside trying to get in and the boys on the inside pushing them off and the ones behind chopping each other's heels off. Then, about opposite the six-furlong gate, Steve would off for his life down the hill to Tattenham Corner, and he generally turned for home in front, or anyway in the first three. In this way he tried, and very often succeeded, in getting the race run to suit him and the type of horse he so often rode.

Most of the jockeys started to copy him, but they had not got the same judgement of pace or lacked something the old maestro had; anyway, they overdid it. In 1928 Gordon Richards on Sunny Trace and Charlie Elliott on Flamingo were both determined to make the running, but they forgot how Steve used to give his horse a breather between the mile post and the seven – they went mad and cut each other's throats. Harry Wragg was sitting about six or eight lengths behind on Felstead, and he was not to be kidded by anybody. He rode with a stopwatch in his head, and if he thought the pace was slow he was up in front or close to it from the start, but if in his opinion it was too fast he would wait till the cows came home or the others came back, which was most probably a little sooner. That was what happened in 1928, and Felstead won.

This mad race completely altered things. There was another master at Epsom. If the other jockeys went too fast, Wragg waited. Here was a different way to win the Derby. Wragg did it again on Blenheim in 1930 and nearly brought it off on Sandwich and Miracle in 1931 and 1932.

No jockey dominates the situation today like Steve did, and none of them has quite the patience of Harry Wragg. Rae Johnstone, who was blamed so much for the defeat of Colombo in 1934, has won twice since, in 1948 and 1950, by employing the Wragg method, or it may be just the Johnstone method – anyway, it's more or less the same.

So it looks as if the way to win the Derby is to get on the best horse and ride as if it was just another one and a half mile race at Epsom, provided the other jockeys will let you, which, of course, they won't. They won't because the Derby is the Derby and the difference can be felt in the dressing-room during the twenty-minute wait after weighing-out and going down to the paddock to mount. The tension is terrific. Race-riding is like any other profession, only more fun, but not before the Derby.

The jockeys would lose an arm to win this one. So that is why, unless you are very lucky, you can't ride your own race. At least half of them lose their heads. I can't remember how many times I rode in the Derby but I never rode when there wasn't trouble, a bit like a polo match, only with more horses.

Opposite the six-furlong gate, things have generally sorted themselves out a bit. The short runners have gone already, and the milers won't last much longer although they are getting in the way on the descent to Tattenham Corner, which, incidentally, is a perfect turn. It's extraordinary how many die out just after they turn for home. I know it so well, and in a way it's a kind of relief, you know you've had it and can do nothing about it. The thing is to relax and watch the finish if you've got good eyesight.

After the race, the jockeys' room is a very different place; first of all everybody congratulates the winner, and then it's like the Irish Parliament, everybody talking and nobody listening. There is no jealousy of the winning jockey – after all, he's a pal, you are drinking his champagne and it may be your turn next year.

JACK LEACH, *Sods I Have Cut on the Turf*

*Winston Churchill was another devotee of Epsom. A late convert to horse-racing, Churchill was Prime Minister in a more conscientious age than Lord Rosebery and Parliament no longer rose for Epsom. As can be seen from his letters to his wife, he faced an annual juggling match to combine politics and pleasure.*

I BEGAN dictating this going down to Kempton where Prince Arthur was running. He was said to have a very good chance and he certainly galloped ahead of all the others for three-quarters of the way. He then continued to go on at the same or even a faster pace, but the mass overtook him and he came in only fourth. He certainly looks beautiful and has a very long stride. It is thought now he may do better over two miles than over one and a half and he will run that distance in a race at Ascot. Audrey Pleydell-Bouverie turned up on the racecourse having come over from Paris to see her horse run. She was very confident of it. It ran second and as I backed it both ways I was no loser. Randolph and June also came and I think enjoyed themselves.

L'Avengro is still reported to be galloping well. I am going to the Derby on Wednesday; if we are able to finish Cabinet at about 12.45 p.m., there seems to be a general desire on the part of my colleagues to go, and Rab is making a feature of it.

*He made it with twenty-five minutes to spare.*

Cabinet till 12.20 p.m. Six or eight Ministers wanted to go to the Derby and I said they were 'under starter's orders'. I went and lunched with the Derbys.

SIR WINSTON CHURCHILL

# *Brighton*

*A similar course to Epsom, in gradients if not grandeur, is Brighton, a course which has provoked more nostalgie de boue in recent years than any other. Brighton's fortunes were at their height at the beginning of this century but the crowds who flocked to the seaside also attracted the razor gangs and crooks described by Graham Greene.*

THEY rolled the old car up into the park and got out. The Boy passed his arm through Spicer's. Life was good walking outside the white sun-drenched wall, past the loud-speaker vans, the man who believed in a second coming, towards the finest of all sensations, the infliction of pain. 'You're a fine fellow, Spicer,' the Boy said, squeezing his arm, and Spicer began to tell him in a low friendly confiding way all about the 'Blue Anchor'. 'It's not a tied house,' he said, 'they've a reputation. I've always thought when I'd made enough money I'd go in with my friend. He still wants me to. I nearly went when they killed Kite.'

'You get scared easy, don't you?' the Boy said. The loudspeakers on the vans advised them whom to put their money with, and gipsy children chased a rabbit with cries across the trampled chalk. They went down into the tunnel under the course and came up into the light and the short grey grass sloping down by the bungalow houses to the sea. Old bookies' tickets rotted into the chalk: 'Barker for the Odds', a smug smiling nonconformist face printed in yellow: 'Don't Worry I Pay', and old tote tickets among the stunted plantains. They went through the wire fence into the halfcrown enclosure. 'Have a glass of beer, Spicer,' the Boy said, pressing him on.

'Why, that's good of you, Pinkie. I wouldn't mind a glass,' and while Spicer drank it by the wooden trestles, the Boy looked down the line of bookies. There was Barker and Macpherson and George Beale ('The Old Firm') and Bob Tavell of Clapton, all the familiar faces, full of blarney and fake good humour. The first two races had been run: there were long queues at the tote windows. The sun lit the white Tattersall stand across the course, and a few horses cantered by to the start. 'There goes General Burgoyne,' a man said, 'he's restless,' starting off to Bob Tavell's stand to cover his bet. The bookies rubbed out and altered the odds as the horses went by, their hoofs padding like boxing gloves on the turf.

'You going to take a plunge?' Spicer asked, finishing his Bass, blowing a little gaseous malted breath towards the bookies.

'I don't bet,' the Boy said. 'It's the last chance for me,' Spicer said, 'in good old Brighton. I wouldn't mind risking a couple of nicker. Not more. I'm saving my cash for Nottingham.'

'Go on,' the Boy said, 'have a good time while you can.'

They walked down the row of bookies towards Brewer's stand: there were a lot of men about. 'He's doing good business,' Spicer said. 'Did you see the Merry Monarch? He's going up,' and while he spoke, all down the line the bookies rubbed out the old sixteen to one odds. 'Ten's,' Spicer said.

'Have a good time while you're here,' the Boy said. 'Might as well patronize the old firm,' Spicer said, detaching his arm and walking across to Tate's stand. The Boy smiled. It was as easy as shelling peas. 'Memento Mori,' Spicer said, coming away card in hand. 'That's a funny name to give a horse. Five to one, a place. What does Memento Mori mean?'

'It's foreign,' the Boy said. 'Black Boy's shortening.'

'I wish I'd covered myself on Black Boy,' Spicer said. 'There was a woman down there says she's backed Black Boy for a pony. It sounds crazy to me. But think if he wins,' Spicer said. 'My God, what wouldn't I do with two hundred and fifty pounds? I'd take a share in the "Blue Anchor" straight away. You wouldn't see me back here,' he added, staring round at the brilliant sky, the dust over the course, the torn betting cards and the short grass towards the dark sea beneath the down.

'Black Boy won't win,' the Boy said. 'Who was it put the pony on?'

'Some polony or other. She was over there at the bar. Why don't you have a fiver on Black Boy? Have a bet for once to celebrate?'

'Celebrate what?' the Boy asked quickly.

'I forgot,' Spicer said. 'This holiday's perked me up, so's I think everyone's got something to celebrate.'

'If I did want to celebrate,' the Boy said, 'it wouldn't be with Black Boy. Why, that used to be Fred's favourite. Said he'd be a Derby winner yet. I wouldn't call that a lucky horse,' but he couldn't help watching him canter up by the rails: a little too fresh, a little too restless. A man on top of the half-crown stand tic-tacked to Bob Tavell of Clapton and a tiny Jew, who was studying the ten shilling enclosure through binoculars, suddenly began to saw the air, to attract the attention of the Old Firm. 'There,' the Boy said, 'what did I tell you? Black Boy's going out again.'

'Hundred to eight, Black Boy, hundred to eight,' George Beale's representative called, and 'They're off,' somebody said. People pressed out from the refreshment booth towards the rails carrying glasses of Bass and currant buns. Barker, Macpherson, Bob Tavell, all wiped the odds from their boards, but the Old Firm remained game to the last: 'Hundred to six Black Boy': while the little Jew made masonic passes from the top of the stand. The horses came by in a bunch, with a sharp sound like splintering wood, and were gone. 'General Burgoyne,' somebody said, and somebody said: 'Merry Monarch.' The beer drinkers went back to the trestle boards and had another glass, and the bookies put up the runners in the four o'clock and began to chalk a few odds.

'There,' the Boy said, 'what did I tell you? Fred never knew a good horse from a bad one. That crazy polony's dropped a pony. It's not her lucky day. Why' – but the silence, the inaction after a race is run and before the results go up, had a daunting quality. The queues waited outside the totes. Everything on the course was suddenly still, waiting for a signal to begin again; in the silence you could hear a horse whinny all the way across from the weighing-in. A sense of uneasiness gripped the Boy in the quiet and the brightness. The soured false age, the concentrated and limited experience of the Brighton slum drained out of him. He wished he had Cubitt there and Dallow. There was too much to tackle by himself at seventeen. It wasn't only Spicer. He had started something on Whit Monday which had no end. Death wasn't an end; the censer swung and the priest raised the Host, and the loudspeaker intoned the winners: 'Black Boy. Memento Mori. General Burgoyne.'

'By God,' Spicer said, 'I've won. Memento Mori for a place,' and remembering what the Boy had said, 'And she's won too. A pony. What a break. Now what about Black Boy?' Pinkie was silent. He told himself: Fred's horse. If I was one of those crazy geezers who touch wood, throw salt, won't go under ladders, I might be scared to –

Spicer plucked at him. 'I've won, Pinkie. A tenner. What do you know about that?'

– to go on with what he'd planned with care. Somewhere from farther down the enclosure he heard a laugh, a female laugh, mellow and confident, perhaps the polony who'd put a pony on Fred's horse. He turned on Spicer with secret venom, cruelty straightening his body like lust.

'Yes,' he said, putting his arm round Spicer's shoulder, 'you'd better collect now.'

GRAHAM GREENE, *Brighton Rock*


*Money wasn't the only thing Spicer collected that afternoon. But the gangs have long since gone and David Ashforth paints a kinder picture of the course.*


To GET the best out of a day at Brighton races, you have to arrive early. Drive straight down to the sea, stop before you get there, and turn left. Half a mile along the seafront there is a lovely pitch-and-putt golf course with a café where they do a nice line in breakfasts and pretty waitresses. I've always been very successful with the breakfasts.

If you are too late for golf at least make sure you have time to stop off at a little country pub on the Sussex Downs. Order a pint of dry cider and a ploughman's lunch, and sit down to work out what is going to win the selling race. The first time you work your way through the form, you'll be convinced that none of them can win it. They're not good enough. Have another look. One of them's got to win. It won't be the one you choose, but that isn't the point. It is better to have bet and lost than never to have bet at all.

When you've found the sea, turn round and head straight up the steep hill. Near the top is a Ladbrokes shop for punters who have spent so long in betting shops that they think that's where racing happens. Besides, by saving the price of admission, they can have another losing treble. When you can't climb any higher you have reached Brighton racecourse. This is the place that Graham Greene wrote about in *Brighton Rock*, with its race-gangs and small-time crooks. The gangs have long gone, and so has one of the grandstands. Luckily, there is a spare one and when you climb up it, the view is wonderful unless there happens to be a sea fret, in which case there is a wonderful view of the fret.

Fret permitting, across to the right you can see the sea and across to the left a racetrack like no other. The one-and-a-half-mile start lies way up high on the edge of the Downs, and half a mile out the runners turn sharp left and pour helter-skelter downhill into a deep hollow before scooting uphill to the finish. The steep hill was introduced in order to give the slower horses a chance to build up a bit of speed, because the standard of racing here is what is politely called 'moderate'. It doesn't matter. If you took the runners from a Brighton seller, changed their names, switched the race to Epsom and called it the Derby, most people wouldn't notice the difference.

When the runners eventually pass the post you will want to know what to do while other people are collecting their winnings. If you like a challenge, you could try to get a drink. In Tattersalls, one of the bars has all the pipes and pumps stuck up on the wall, like intestines worn on the outside. Downstairs, opposite the racecourse betting shop, you can get jellied eels.

A man in a wheelchair used to spend the whole afternoon wheeling himself backwards and forwards in front of the betting shop screens, crushing people's toes. Personally, I prefer to stay in the stand and watch other people. If you like men with huge beer bellies, this is the racecourse for you. We have competitions to see who can spot the biggest belly on parade. Believe me, madam, you wouldn't want to be lying under the winner. Brighton bellies. Big ones, huge ones, ones hanging over waistbands in the afternoon sun. Bellies carried in front of their backward-leaning owners.

A bottle of champagne on one of the white tables out in the sun between the parade ring and the course, just mulling things over, chatting idly. It's bliss.

Don't forget to keep a record of your losers. When you have had six, the racing is over. Don't go home, though. Go into Brighton, instead. Easy-going Brighton. There are some great pubs and restaurants, but you have to be a bit careful. I once strolled into a pub and ordered two beers. The looks seemed a bit out of the ordinary, and then I glanced up at the walls. They were covered with pictures of men's bottoms. I didn't want mine on the wall, so we moved on to the Chequers, an old haunt near Regency Square. They have a sign there that reads 'No Shirt. No Shoes. No Serve.' Two women were kissing at the bar. A man was dancing to a Billy Fury record. Brighton's like that. No one cares.

DAVID ASHFORTH, *Hitting the Turf: A Punter's Life*

*For Jamie Reid, Brighton basks in the never-never world twixt past and present, a land where the threat of Graham Greene lurks beneath the decay of David Ashforth.*

B UT THE other fascinating thing about a run down to Brighton is that as well as bringing back memories of some of the great old respectable names of Turf history it also brings on thoughts of one of the darker and less palatable periods in racing and bookmaking's past, when low-life characters walked tall around Brighton racecourse and not always in the shadows, an era vividly evoked in *Brighton Rock*, the best and most famous of all novels about the town and particularly by its unforgettable opening line: 'Hale knew, before he had been in Brighton three hours, that they meant to murder him.' Of course Graham Greene's story isn't solely about the race gangs, but images of gangsterism (and in particular of pre-war betting-oriented protection rackets) form a constant backdrop to the riveting saga of the teenage hoodlum, Pinkie Brown, and of his gradual descent into hell.

Greene didn't invent this seemingly melodramatic background. At the end of the First World War a number of top London villains relocated their rackets on the south coast, especially in Brighton. Rich pickings were to be had there from running night clubs, amusement arcades and dance halls and, in those far-off days long before legalised off-course cash gambling, from extorting protection money from both the illicit street bookies and the legitimate on-course layers.

Even after the rumble on Lewes racecourse in 1936, the subsequent trials and draconian prison sentences, a detectable sense of danger, now embodied in the national folklore, continued to cling to the places where bookies and punters gathered to do business. And that element of danger and risk, along with its natural accomplice, the indulgent spend-now-pay-later mentality, which Brighton has traditionally catered to for more than a century, continues to play a seductive and by no means negligible part in persuading people to go to a racetrack and gamble on horses. It is also connected with that intoxicating but usually harmless boost to the virility that comes from being a winner, a bragging, self-afffirmative statement, particularly attractive to men, that says, 'Look at me. I'm Jack the Lad with cash to burn. I'll have three monkeys on the 5–1 shot, bubbly all round; and a new suit, a suite at the Grand and a new and fabulously glamorous lover before tea.' Not the least entertaining aspect of a jaunt up onto the Downs is that, even after the passage of more than forty cleaned-up years including thirty of legitimate off-course gambling, some real sense of spivvery and guile, if not of physical danger, still remains.

'Hale knew, before he had been in Brighton three hours, that they meant to murder him.' As our taxi swung out of the station forecourt and pulled away down Queens Road we glanced back over our shoulders at the Victorian station façade. But unlike those superbly atmospheric opening scenes in the 1948 black-and-white film version of *Brighton Rock* we could see no chipper William Hartnell spying watchfully from beneath the clock. Neither was there any sign of his fellow actor, Nigel Stock, lounging indolently in a pub doorway or about to jump on one of the special buses up to the course. At that point we felt that our lives were in greater danger from the weather than from a razor blade or a cosh. Greene's

Brighton raceweek opened against a background of sundrenched blue-sky summer with short brown grass, dust dry chalk on the Downs and old yellowing Tote tickets lying abandoned in the sun amid the plantains of the south coast bungalow gardens. This June morning there was no sun and no blue sky, only horrendous fog-like cloud and exhausting humidity. I had asked the cab driver not to take the usual shortcut up to the track but to follow Hale's route down to the front. As we trickled along slowly in the trafffic, past 'Sergeant Yorke's Casino', the offices of 'Casa Sorrento: Apartments To Let' and past all the little chip fryers, pubs and cafés between the station and the clock tower, drops of warm rain started to spit down from the grey sky. Even with the cab windows open we all felt as if someone was wrapping a hot thick towel very tightly around our heads.

Greene described a band playing on the pavement by the Old Steyne and 'a negro wearing a bright striped tie', sitting on a bench in the Pavilion garden smoking a cigar. We saw only a pair of gaunt-looking charity collectors standing either side of a large bill-board proclaiming grim details of AIDS deaths worldwide accompanied with a warning to Brighton's epidemic population of hard drug-users never to inject with a dirty needle and never to share a fellow addict's syringe.

It is a steep climb from the Pavilion up through Kemptown past the cheerless American Express headquarters and on to the racecourse above Whitehawk Bottom. No overcrowded trams surged up the hill in our wake, no Packards or Morrises or little scarlet racing models with brasses perched fetchingly on the driver's knee. At the top of Freshfield Road we paid off the monosyllabic cab driver and as the hot showers continued to drip down from the grey-green sky, Moynahan flashed his metal press badge, Kincaid and I bought the usual Members' Enclosure passes and then we all ducked in through the panelled doorway that leads on to the course. 'In the first race the runners are as on your racecard,' declaimed a blocked-nosed loudspeaker announcement in the background. We were on home territory once again.

The back of the main stand at Brighton, which was erected in 1965, looks like a hideous grey pebble-dash and breeze-block National Car Park blot on the landscape, the kind of thing that would drive The Prince of Wales to talk to a whole flowerbed of geraniums. It's not much better on the inside. Amazingly, the firm that designed and built it, Sir Alfred McAlpine Ltd, are shameless enough to allow their identity to be displayed for all the race-going world to see via a plaque commemorating their 'achievements' in the foyer leading to the Tote betting hall on the ground floor.

If the view from the back of the stand is bleak then the view from the front, from the terracing and Members' Lawn, is of an apparently absurd and implausible racecourse where you would think that any chance of consistently turning up a profit ought to be 100–1 at least. Brighton is constructed on the Epsom principle, which roughly translates into 'Let's all scramble around the rim of the Downs and the first one to reach the winning post without falling over is the winner.' The track is a dead ringer for Epsom and once upon a more adventurous time they ran an influential Derby trial there each May. Not any more: these days the municipally owned course, with its sliding turns and perilous descent – a jockey was killed there in a fall in 1981– is firmly in the fourth division of the quality league. But, for all that, its regular summertime cards of selling races, claiming races and low-grade handicaps, few of them offering much in the way of prize money and most attracting the poorest level of competition, provide splendidly entertaining opportunities for jobs, touches and general raffish no-goodery. The biggest problem is trying to guess which of the supposed batch of non-triers in the two-year-old race or the six-furlong three-year-old handicap are really 'not off' and which one has been prepared by his crafty trainer to hoodwink the rest. If it is already something of a challenge for the mug punter to make money, if they insist on backing horses who may or may not be trying and who are in any case racing around a switchback circuit it's harder still to distinguish the lean from the overwrought, and the seriously committed from those carrying an off-games note, when the racetrack is partly shrouded, as it still was this early Monday afternoon, in a shifting blanket of sea mist and fog.

While Moynahan went off to get the latest information from the weighing room, which he insisted would be of a different calibre from the whispered champagne-bar advices now being canvassed by A. J. Kincaid, I climbed right up to the top of the terracing beneath the roof of the stand. It was 1.50 p.m. on a June Monday and the lights were all on in the Palace Pier. Even so I could only make out the Channel as a block of flat, wet, clammy-looking greyness with no clearly delineated horizon. I could just see a red-and-cream double-decker bus trailing through the murk down the road from Rottingdean away beyond the mile-and-a-quarter start. Closer to hand the mist had cleared briefly to reveal the blocks of mini high-rise flats and the little rows of post-war housing beneath the edge of the Downs and the rows of caravans parked along the infield rail. But the colour of the turf between the seven- and the two-furlong marker was a mystery.

Not that everything was quiet on the gambling front. Far from it. Down in the ring the scattering of on-course bookies appeared to be doing some lively business as the runners cantered down before the first. Which you could say underlines the point that most punters are even more dumb than they look and will still go on betting even when they can make out little more than the ears and tails of the objects of their speculation. Thoughtful gamblers, even if they have already placed their bets ante-post or by phone, will invariably want to study their selection in the paddock before a race. There are certain tell-tale signs to look out for, well known to the habitual racegoer. Everybody wants to back a calm, relaxed and unflustered horse who is not so completely asleep that he seems unprepared for the challenge ahead but who is not playing up unduly or fretting and sweating his chance away before the start. If it's a particularly chilly afternoon in mid-April a three-year-old thoroughbred filly may not yet have come into her summer coat and may not quite be ready to do herself justice. Conversely if the race is taking place in late October, the same filly may have already 'gone' in her coat or grown her woolly, winter covering, a sign that she might be over the top for the season. You don't have to have been racing very often to be able to spot these differences, or to be able to distinguish between a sleek and rippling athlete ready to race and a skinny little ferret with its ribs peeping through or a lumbering and overweight plodder. But the one thing you absolutely have to have if you are going to make a proper assessment is a close-up view of the horses. Betting blind at a fourth-rate venue like Brighton is not a guaranteed way of make money.

But part of the crack about a day down at Brighton, and there is plenty of crack to be had for all the concrete and pebble-dash and sea-fret gloom is the crowd, the company, the players. Brighton racecourse, like Epsom is still as it always has been (and here an atmospheric connection with Greene's era, if not with the razor blades, still persists), a home from home for the Good Fellas of the betting and racing community – for Cheltenham Tony, for Barry and Tel, for double-glazing barons and kings of the motor trade, for south London and south coast Del Boys and Trevs, who just might, no disrespect, be not entirely on the up. Even the equine participants seem to reflect some of the characteristics of the onlookers in the stand and in the ring: fly, wide, rough, hard, perhaps not entirely to be trusted. Their names, too, are usually more suggestive of Catford or Hackney dog stadium than of Ascot Heath: on this very programme we would be watching such blue-blooded athletes as Sharlie's Wimpy, Calvanne Miss, Hightown Executive and Chin the Ref.

'Willie'll win this,' opined one tasty-looking punter about the first race, his grazed knuckles and broken nose suggesting that he might have done a bit of ref-chinning himself in his time – possibly quite recently.

'Trevor says he's nailed on,' agreed a friend, as he chomped his way stoically through a dry-looking white-bread sandwich.

Willie, Carson naturally, may not always feel flattered to be so heavily identified with by the ordinary non-Timeform punters but they are his most devoted admirers and they make up the majority of racegoers at every Brighton meeting. They perceive Carson, not entirely accurately, to be their kind of jockey. A hard-riding unpretentious 'little man'. A cheeky Scots chappie who may be one of the highest-paid riders in the world but still gives his all every time. And who probably reads the same paper they do. 'Go on, Willie. Go on, my son.'

As it was, Willie didn't win the first, a five-furlong two-year-old dash worth two grand to the winner. He was on a striking-looking chestnut debutante, saddled by the Newmarket-based trainer Mick Ryan, who resembles a cross between Rupert Murdoch and Bill Sykes. This popular combination, sent off the 11–4 second favourite by the crowd, were turned over by a skinny little wired-up beast from the Epsom stables of the crafty seventy-two-year-old handler, Ron Smyth. Tasty, the ref-chinner, was not at all pleased and even removed his unflattering short-sleeved shirt in disgust.

'Trevor,' he bellowed to his mate down below, 'you abomination.' Trevor, who had been attempting to lurk interestingly by the winning post, turned round with a start. When he saw Tasty he broke into a sheepish grin. Tasty waved a muscular arm back again, his naked and pungent armpits taking no prisoners among those punters unfortunate enough to be standing nearest to him.

Remembering Moynahan's wise advice about the favourite I had decided to pass on the first race altogether. Kincaid, the true gambler, had also passed on the favourite and placed instead a couple of expensive forecast bets on two of the other runners, who unfortunately finished third and fourth. Sidling down along the rails afterwards in our swanky dark glasses, a rather pointless accessory in the prevailing hot cloud, Kincaid and I tried to take a leaf out of Trevor's book by lounging nonchalantly next to the Victor Chandler pitch. What, I wondered, did the other punters make of us? Did we look like big-time faces? Did we have sufficient cool? I didn't like to ask Kincaid how much he'd just lost but he certainly looked the part of a high-roller especially as he chose this moment to light up an enormous Monte Cristo cigar. So is effrontery all? Were the bookies taken in? And if the bluff is big enough will you always be treated as a four-figure winner even if you are nothing of the sort?

The second race and the next challenge to our own and John Moynahan's judgement was a mile-and-a-quarter maiden event for three-year-olds and up. Now, the gospel according to the professional gambler is that, if you want to win at racing, you must know not only when to bet but also when not to bet. As this maiden race was such a mediocre contest and as the bookmakers were offering only very cramped prices about the two possible winners, our form and value expert insisted that we should not bet on this competition at all. Tasty and Trevor were altogether bolder. They were convinced that Willie would definitely be their man this time and they and their brothers in the ring plied his mount with enough handfuls of cash to send it off as the 6–5 favourite in a field of ten with only one serious rival to beat. And in beating it our Willie applied to his mount some of his own distinctive brand of physical assistance, especially when the rival refused to give in with a furlong to run. 'Go on, Willie. Give it some,' roared the lads in the stands and little Willie most certainly did give it some, seeming to turn round in the saddle and select his spot before applying half a dozen four-square whip-cracking smacks to the three-year-old's velveteen quarters. 'He runs for the whip,' Moynahan sagely informed us afterwards, whereas it may have been equally true that the horse ran as gamely as it did to get away from the wretched thing and from the midget sadist perched on its back. But whatever the horse's pain barrier he stayed on to such effect that he managed to get his nose over the line a split second ahead of his rival. The cheering broke out, the hugging and thumping took over and fresh drinks were ordered in the cheap seats for an on-course gamble triumphantly brought off. Kincaid was cheering. He had backed the winner so at least he had something to celebrate, even though there was not a lot of profit to come as he'd also gone in hard with another losing forecast bet. Moynahan and myself, J. P. McManus's little known second and third cousins twice removed, had nothing to come. We were both much too smart to bet on anything.

Next on the card was a seven-furlong seller, but Moynahan, now flushed with non-playing superiority, like someone who takes you out to lunch and orders two salads after watching you choose lobster, filet béarnaise and crème brûlée, was adamant that we should pass on this too. 'How can you expect to make a profit backing fourth-rate horses in a selling race in semi-fog at Brighton?' he reasoned, making something of a mockery of his supposed preference for egg-and-spoon races at the gaff tracks. 'Follow the money,' would be the traditional small-time punter's response but we were supposed to be above such clichéd truisms. Let the common folk believe it if they wished, but we were no suckers. Of course, we were no winners either because the money very much followed the eventual victor, MCA Below The Line (owned, according to the racecard, by an all-class outfit by the name of Mike Clyne Associates) who was backed in from sixes to 3–1 and who pissed up by three lengths with Chin The Ref trailing in sixth, leaving Moynahan still triumphantly and uncommonly smug, even with no apparent reason, and leaving Kincaid and me, three races down, no richer and beginning to feel like peabrains and prunes. This was not the sort of afternoon we had bargained for.

A modest portion of the crowd, some backers of the winner, some losers, some disinterested parties like ourselves, trooped around the corner to watch the subsequent auction in the unsaddling enclosure. The auctioneer, a suave rather foxy-looking type in senior-partner country-solicitor gear, opened the proceedings on an inadvisably smug note. 'Fifteen hundred guineas, ladies and gentlemen. Fifteen hundred guineas for this decent-looking prospective sprint handicapper. Already a winner. Fifteen hundred guineas. At fifteen hundred guineas, ladies and gentlemen. Who's coming in with me at fifteen hundred guineas?' Pause. Silence. 'Who's coming in? Are you all coming in? Who's coming in? Who's coming in with me to have a chance of this attractive south coast specialist. At fifteen hundred guineas; ladies and gentlemen. At fifteen hundred. Who's coming in?' Pause. Silence. 'Who's coming in with me at fifteen hundred guineas? Well?' Pause. Silence. No one was coming in by the look of it. Not a single solitary professional or amateur, regular or casual, trainer's or knacker's arm was raised in response. Perhaps some prospective bidders were puzzled by the auctioneer's rather arch manner and phraseology. 'Who's coming in with *me*?' Did that mean that he had already bought two legs and the tail himself and would be at least a joint partner in the venture? A matey chum to share the training bills with and someone who could be relied upon to buy the champagne next time out? Anyone would have thought that he'd already arranged for the gelding (yes, it was only a gelding and a pretty manky-looking one at that) to be transferred from Hambleton trainer Will Pearce to Luca Cumani or Michael Stoute. Perhaps he had only just had Lester on the phone or had booked Pat Eddery for the Stewards Cup. Perhaps . . . but not very likely and the crowd, not so unsophisticated for once, weren't having any of it. They may not all have been bloodstock agents but they could definitely tell the difference between Mill Reef and this slice of potential hamburger meat. 'Who's coming in?' continued the auctioneer. 'Who's coming in with me at fifteen hundred guineas? Who's coming in?' Pause. Silence. 'Is there anyone coming in? Is there any bid at all?' People started to turn their heads away in embarrassment, to stare intently at their shoes or at their racecards or at the runners' and riders' board for the next. But the auctioneer's humiliation was not yet complete. 'Well . . . is there any bid?' He ploughed on, trying to make us feel suitably ashamed as if in our craven lack of enterprise we had personally let him down. 'Any bid?' He turned to a plump and blushingly red-faced official standing nearby. 'Why won't they bid?' The official grinned at him stupidly. 'We won't bid my cocker,' explained a *basso profondo* Millwall voice from the front of the crowd, 'because the race was a piece of piss, the horse is probably a dog and you are definitely a plonker.' Cruel, ribald laughter ran around the edges of the ring. The auctioneer blanched and a pained expression crossed his face as if he had just sat on the wrong end of a shooting stick. *His* gamble had come entirely unstuck.

Craning our necks with the rest to try to discover the identity of the speaker we discovered him to be none other than Tasty the ref-chinner who had assumed an authoritative pose by the rail with Trevor and the sandwich eater on either side. Tasty's intervention brought the 'sale' to an inglorious end. The auctioneer's mumbled finale of, 'Unsold,' was barely heard over the continuing laughter. His brief moment of authority, his temporary command of the stage had been blown away and as the horse was led out Moynahan, Kincaid and myself, in common with assorted other sniggering and mainly proletarian onlookers, turned our backs on the scene and headed once more for the ring.

The fourth race, a mile-and-a-half handicap and the most valuable event on the card, finally presented us with the kind of opening we'd been looking for, a modest opportunity for value betting. Our selection was a three times Brighton-course winner who had been comprehensively beaten last time out on soft ground at Epsom, but who was now back running over his favoured fast surface and who would have William Hunter Carson's assistance in the saddle. He had been allotted the welter burden, as the form scribes like to call it, of ten stone, four pounds more than any winning weight he had ever carried before. But this was only a three-horse race and we reckoned that he only had one other horse to beat, a light and hard-trained-looking three-year-old, who on his previous outing had won a more valuable Newbury handicap, heavily gambled on, by four lengths. The three-year-old was expected to start favourite but with not a lot to choose between the pair. Moynahan estimated that evens would not be an unattractive price about ours and that even a single percent-age point better than that would be value all the way.

Kincaid and I duly got on at 11–10 on the rails and then saw office money push the price right through evens to 10–11 (11–10 on) at which point there was still some demand. And who on earth at that daft but exhilarating moment of triumph could possibly have preferred to bet with a Tote monopoly where you don't know the exact odds of your runner until after the race and where you cannot shop around for a price?

The race, though brimming with tension for those of us with an interest, was about as nail-biting as an average edition of *A Question of Sport*. The three-year-old, who was sweating in front of as well as behind the saddle, went straight to the head of things with Willie tucked in on the rails a few lengths behind him and the outsider or 'rag' three lengths in arrears. And that's the way they stayed for the first two-thirds of the contest. Three minute, semiluminous shapes, blurs in the still not completely cleared mist, edging along the rails beside the ice-cream vans, school buses and semi-detached houses beneath what might as well have been the edge of the world. Then, just below the distance, which means with just over a furlong to run, Carson drew alongside the long-time leader.

'No danger, Willie. No danger,' yelled a heavyweight profes-sional punter in front of us.

'Yeah. No danger, Willie. You little Scots git,' enjoined an un-complimentary associate. They were both right, though. With less than half a furlong still to go the 'little Scots git' just shook the reins up and down a few times and without the slightest recourse to the whip stylishly and cleverly nudged his mount over the line by what looked like a margin of three-quarters of a length (but which the judge, who must have been prematurely celebrating his own winning bet, instantly declared to be a clear two lengths).

We cheered. Commonly, vulgarly and not all like suave, un-emotional high-rollers. In fact it would be no exaggeration to say that we cheered our heads off. 'Go on, Willie. Go on, my son. Go on, my beauty.' Then with one quick, grateful look up at the heav-ens above, illuminated by sunshine for the first time all day, we bounded back down the concrete terracing, collecting Moynahan on the way who informed us very smugly that he had 'invested at twos' and then raced over the tarmac and grass and swung in through the doors of the Winning Post bar. We'd had enough of Moynahan's rules and self-discipline and were emphatic that this occasion should be devoted to the observance of a slightly different, less ascetic rule. The maxim of the rarely winning, usually imprudent but determinedly high-spirited punter: 'Don't ever pay the bank manager until you've slaked your thirst.'

JAMIE REID, *A Licence to Print Money*

*Festivals are as much about fun. The sport of good racing is interrupted by the camaraderie of evenings of consolation or celebration. One day spills into a second with nary a thought of the end of the week or the summons of the bank manager. No one does this better than the Irish, especially the Irish at Cheltenham. On home soil they are pretty good too. Across the Irish sea there is a host of festivals each summer. Horseracing is combined with horse trading, dances and craic. Fun is everything and W. B. Yeats believed there was more fun to be had amongst horsemen than anyone else.*

## *At Galway Races*

THERE where the course is, Delight makes all of
the one mind,
The riders upon the galloping horses,
The crowd that closes in behind:
We, too, had good attendance once,
Hearers and hearteners of the work;
Aye, horsemen for companions,
Before the merchant and the clerk
Breathed on the world with timid breath.
Sing on: somewhere at some new moon,
We'll learn that sleeping is not death,
Hearing the whole earth change its tune,
Its flesh being wild, and it again
Crying aloud as the racecourse is,
And we find hearteners among men
That ride upon horses.

W. B. YEATS

# Longchamp

*Nana, Emile Zola's nineteenth-century courtesan, also believed there was fun to be had amongst racing folk. She, however, managed to have fun just about everywhere and her day out at Longchamp for the Grand Prix de Paris was, if anything, tamer than her nights at the theatre where she made her name or in the boudoirs of the great and not-so-good. As with everything else, Nana threw herself into the races with brio.*

THAT Sunday the race for the Grand Prix de Paris was being run in the Bois de Boulogne under a sky heavy with the first heat of June. The sun, that morning, had risen in a reddish mist, but towards eleven o'clock, just as the carriages were arriving at the Longchamp course, a southerly wind had swept away the clouds; long streamers of grey vapour drifted away and gaps of intense blue began spreading from one end of the horizon to the other. In the bright bursts of sunlight which alternated with the clouds the whole scene lit up, from the public enclosure, which was gradually filling with a crowd of carriages, riders and pedestrians, to the still vacant course, with the judge's box, the winning-post, and the poles of the telegraph, and thence on to the five symmetrical stands, rising in galleries of brickwork and timber in the middle of the weighing-enclosure opposite. Farther on, bathed in the noonday sunshine, lay the vast level plain, bordered with little trees, and shut in to the west by the wooded heights of Saint-Cloud and Suresnes, which, in their turn, were dominated by the grim silhouette of Mont-Valérien.

Nana was as excited as if the Grand Prix were going to determine her fortune, and decided to take up a position by the rail next to the winning-post. She had been one of the first to arrive, driving up in a landau with silver fittings, a present from the Comte Muffat, drawn *à la Daumont* by four splendid white horses. When she had made her appearance at the entrance to the public enclosures, with two postilions jogging along on the left-hand horses, and two footmen standing motionless behind the carriage, people had rushed to see her, as if a queen were passing. She was wearing the blue and white colours of the Vandeuvres stable in a remarkable outfit. This consisted of a little blue silk bodice and tunic, which fitted closely to her body and bulged out enormously over the small of her back, outlining her thighs in a very bold fashion for this period of ballooning skirts. Then there was a white satin dress with white satin sleeves, and a white satin sash worn cross-wise, the whole decorated with silver point-lace which shone in the sun. In addition to this, in order to be still more like a jockey, she had jauntily stuck a blue toque with a white feather on her chignon, from which her golden locks flowed down to the middle of her back like a huge russet horse's tail.

Twelve o'clock struck. The public had over three hours to wait for the Grand Prix to be run. When the landau had drawn up beside the rail, Nana settled down comfortably as if she were at home. She had taken it into her head to bring Bijou and little Louis with her, and the dog nestled among her skirts, shivering with cold in spite of the heat, while in his trappings of ribbon and laces, the child's poor little waxen face was pale and silent in the open air. Meanwhile the young woman, paying no attention to the people near her, talked at the top of her voice with Georges and Philippe Hugon, who were sitting in front of her on the other side in such a pile of bouquets of white roses and blue myosotis that they were buried up to their shoulders.

*One of the attractions for Nana was the presence in the big race field of a namesake, a filly called Nana, a supposedly unfancied 50–1 shot and outsider of the Vandeuvres stable whose other runner is the favourite Lusignan. Shortly before the off, there was a late plunge on Nana: from 50–1 in to 10–1. Nana the courtesan's crowd are trying to find out whose money was going down on their friend Vandeuvres's horse when the race starts.*

The sound of a quarrel brought them to their feet. It was Georges defending Vandeuvres against the vague rumours which were circulating among the various groups.

'Why should you say that he's dropping his own horse?' the young man was shouting. 'Yesterday, at the Salon des Courses, he bet a thousand louis on Lusignan.'

'Yes, I was there,' said Philippe. 'And he didn't put a single louis on Nana. . . . If the betting's ten to one against Nana, he's got nothing to do with it. It's ridiculous to imagine people are so calculating. Where would he stand to gain?'

Labordette was listening calmly. Shrugging his shoulders he said:

'Oh, drop it; people are bound to talk. . . . The Count has just bet at least another hundred louis on Lusignan, and if he's laid a hundred louis on Nana, that's because an owner has always got to look as if he believes in his horses.'

'Oh, what the hell does it matter to us?' yelled la Faloise, waving his arms. 'It's Spirit that's going to win. . . .Down with France! Up with England!'

A long tremor ran through the crowd, while a fresh peal from the bell announced the arrival of the horses on the racecourse. At this Nana climbed up on the seat of her landau to get a better view, trampling on the bouquets of roses and myosotis. With a sweeping glance she took in the whole vast horizon. At this last feverish moment the first thing she saw was the empty course, shut in by its grey rails, with a policeman standing at every other post; and the strip of grass, which was muddy in front of her, grew greener as it stretched away, and turned into a soft velvet carpet farther off. In the middle distance, as she lowered her eyes, she saw the public enclosure swarming with people, some on tiptoe, others hanging on to carriages. Horses were neighing and tent-canvases flaping, while riders urged their horses forward among the pedestrians rushing to get places along the rails. When Nana turned in the direction of the stands on the other side, the faces seemed to have shrunk, and the dense masses of heads were only a motley array, filling the gangways, the tiers of seats and the terraces on which ranks of dark profiles were outlined against the sky. Then she looked even farther, over the plain around the Hippodrome. Behind the ivy-covered windmill on the right, meadows inter spersed with shady woods stretched away into the distance; in front of her, as far as the Seine flowing at the foot of the hill, parkland avenues intersected one another, lined just now with motionless files of waiting carriages; and in the direction of Boulogne, on the left, the landscape widened again, opening out towards the bluish shadows of Meudon through an avenue of paulonias, whose rosy, leafless tops formed a sheet of bright lake. People were still arriving, a trail of human ants kept coming across the distant fields along the narrow ribbon of road, while far away, in the direction of Paris, the non-paying public, like a flock of sheep in the woods, moved in a line of dark spots under the trees on the edge of the Bois.

Suddenly the hundred thousand souls covering this part of the plain, like insects swarming madly under the vast skies, had their spirits raised as the sun, which had been hidden for a quarter of an hour, reappeared, spreading out in a sea of light. And everything caught fire again, the women's parasols looking like countless golden bucklers above the heads of the crowd. The sun was greeted with cheers and bursts of laughter, and people stretched out their arms as if to brush aside the clouds.

Meanwhile a police officer advanced alone down the middle of the empty racecourse, while higher up, on the left, a man appeared with a red flag in his hand.

'That's the starter, the Baron de Mauriac,' said Labordette in reply to a question from Nana.

Around the young woman exclamations came from the men who were clustered about her carriage and even standing on the footboards. They kept up a disconnected conversation, tossing off words on the spur of the moment. Indeed Philippe and Georges, Bordenave and la Faloise found it impossible to keep quiet.

'Don't push . . . Let me see! . . . Ah, the judge is going into his box. . . . Did you say it was Monsieur de Souvigny? . . . He must have good eyesight if he can decide a close finish from a contraption like that! . . . Do be quiet – the flag's going up. . . . Look! Here they are! . . . It's Cosinus in front.'

A red and yellow banner was flapping in the air at the top of the mast. The horses came on to the course one by one, led by stable-boys, with the jockeys sitting in the saddle with their arms at rest, the sunlight making them look like bright patches of colours. After Cosinus came Hasard and Boum. Then a murmur of voices greeted Spirit, a magnificent big brown bay, whose harsh colours, lemon and black, had a melancholy British quality. Valerio II scored a success as he came in; he was small and very lively in pale green bordered with pink. The two Vandeuvres horses were a long time coming, but at last the blue and white colours appeared behind Frangipane. However, Lusignan, a very dark bay, of irreproachable build, was almost forgotten in the astonishment caused by Nana. Nobody had seen her looking like this before, for the sudden sunlight lent the chestnut filly the golden sheen of a redhead's hair. She shone in the light like a new louis; her breast was deep, and her head and neck rose lightly from the delicate, sinewy line of her long back.

'Look, she's got my hair!' Nana shouted in delight. 'You know, I feel quite proud of her!'

As more people clambered on to the landau, Bordenave almost stepped on little Louis, whom his mother had forgotten. He picked him up with a fatherly growl and hoisted him on his shoulders, murmuring:

'The poor kid deserves to get a look-in too. . . . Wait a minute and I'll show you Mama. . . . Look at the gee-gee over there.'

As Bijou had started scratching his legs, he took charge of him too; while Nana, delighted by the animal bearing her name, glanced round at the other women to see how they were taking it. They were all fuming with rage. At that moment La Tricon, who till then had been sitting motionless on the top of her cab, began waving her hands about, giving a bookmaker instructions over the heads of the crowd. Her instinct had just spoken to her; she was backing Nana.

Meanwhile la Faloise was making an insufferable noise. He had taken a fancy to Frangipane.

'I've had an inspiration,' he kept shouting. 'Just look at Frangipane. What action, eh? . . . I'll bet eight to one on Frangipane. Any takers?'

'Oh, pipe down,' Labordette said at last. 'You'll be sorry if you do.'

'Frangipane's a screw,' declared Philippe. 'He's sweating already. . . . You just watch the canter.'

The horses had gone up to the right, and now they set off for the preliminary canter, passing the stands in loose order. Immediately there was a passionate new burst of talk, with everybody speaking at once.

'Lusignan's too long in the back, but very fit. . . . Not a penny, I tell you, on Valerio II; he's skittish and galloping with his head up – that's a bad sign. . . . Hey, it's Burne who's riding Spirit. . . . I tell you he's got no shoulders. Well-made shoulders, that's the important thing. . . . No, Spirit's definitely too quiet. . . . Listen, I saw Nana after the Grand Poule des Produits; she was dripping with sweat, her coat was deadly dull, and she was panting like

mad. I'll bet you twenty louis she isn't placed! . . . Oh, why does-
n't he shut up? He's getting on our nerves with his precious Frangipane. It's too late – they're heading for the off.'

This was a reference to la Faloise, who was almost in tears and
frantically trying to find a bookmaker. The others had to talk him
out of it. Everybody was craning forward, but there was a false
start, for the starter, who looked like a thin black line in the distance, had not lowered his flag. The horses came back to their places
after galloping a little way. There were two more false starts, but
at last the starter got the horses together and sent them off with
a skill which elicited shouts of applause.

'Magnificent! . . . No, he was just lucky! . . . Never mind, they're
off!'

The shouts died down, smothered by the anxiety filling every
breast. The betting dropped now, as the battle was joined on the
vast course. Silence reigned at first as if everybody were holding
his breath. White faces were raised and bodies trembled. At first
Hasard and Cosinus made the running, taking the lead; Valerio
II came hard on their heels and the field followed in a confused
mass. When they passed the stands, thundering over the ground
like a sudden storm-wind, they were already strung out over some
fourteen lengths. Frangipane was last, and Nana was slightly
behind Lusignan and Spirit.

'By God!' muttered Labordette. 'That English horse is moving
fast out there!'

The whole company in the landau started talking and shouting again. Everybody stood on tiptoe to follow the bright splash-
es of colour which were the jockeys as they sped along in the
sunshine. At the rise Valerio II took the lead and Cosinus and Hasard
lost ground, while Lusignan and Spirit, running neck and neck,
still had Nana behind them.

'Dammit, the English horse has won, that's obvious,' said Bordenave. 'Lusignan's tiring and Valerio II can't stay the course.'

'Well, it'll be a fine thing if the English horse wins!' exclaimed
Philippe, in a burst of patriotic grief.

A feeling of anguish was beginning to take hold of the whole
vast multitude. Another defeat! And an extraordinary prayer, almost religious in its intensity, went up for Lusignan, while people cursed Spirit and his funereal jockey. Among the crowd scattered

over the grass, excitement sent groups of people running hell for leather. Horsemen crossed the grass at a furious gallop. And Nana, turning slowly, saw at her feet a surging mass of animals and men, a sea of heads swept round the course by the whirlwind of the race, which was streaking the horizon with the bright flash of the jockeys. She had followed the horses from behind, as their cruppers retreated and their legs gathered speed, diminishing in size until they looked like thin strands of hair. Now, at the far end of the course, they were speeding along in profile, tiny delicate creatures silhouetted against the distant green of the Bois. Then all of a sudden they disappeared behind a big clump of trees in the middle of the Hippodrome.

'Don't worry!' cried Georges, who was still full of hope. 'It isn't over yet. . . . The English horse is falling back.'

But la Faloise, seized again with contempt for his country, started cheering on Spirit in a quite outrageous fashion. Bravo! It served them right! France needed to be beaten! Spirit first and Frangipane second – that would teach his fellow countrymen! Labordette, exasperated beyond endurance, seriously threatened to throw him off the carriage.

'Let's see how many minutes they take,' said Bordenave calmly pulling out his watch while still holding up little Louis.

One after another the horses reappeared from behind the clump of trees. There was a long murmur of amazement from the crowd. Valerio II was still in the lead, but Spirit was gaining on him: and behind him, Lusignan had dropped back, while another horse was taking his place. The crowd could not make out what was happening straight away, for they mixed up the colours. Then there was a chorus of amazement.

'Why, it's Nana! . . . Nana! . . . Get along with you! I tell you Lusignan hasn't budged. . . . Yes, it's Nana all right. You can recognize her by her golden colour. . . . Can you see her now? She looks as if she's on fire. . . . Bravo, Nana ! What a minx she is. . . . Nonsense, it doesn't make any difference. She's making the running for Lusignan.'

For a few seconds that was everybody's opinion. But little by little the filly went on steadily gaining. At that a wave of feeling swept the crowd. The line of horses bringing up the rear ceased to interest anybody as a supreme struggle began between Spirit,

Nana, Lusignan and Valerio II. People pointed them out, commenting on their performance as they gained ground or fell back in stammering, disconnected phrases. And Nana, who had just climbed up onto her coachman's seat, as if borne upwards by some unseen force, stood there white-faced and trembling, so deeply moved that she said nothing. Beside her, Labordette was smiling again.

'The English horse is in trouble,' said Philippe joyously. 'He's not doing well at all.'

'In any case it's all up with Lusignan,' shouted la Faloise. 'That's Valerio II coming up. . . . Look, there are the four of them bunched together.'

The same word was on every tongue.

'What a pace! . . . What a hell of a pace!'

The main body of horses was now arriving opposite them like a flash of lightning. You could feel it coming, the breath of it like a distant rumbling which grew louder every second. The whole crowd had thrown themselves impetuously against the rails, and preceding the horses a deep roar came from countless breasts, drawing nearer and nearer like the sound of breakers on the shore. It was the brutal climax of a colossal game, with a hundred thousand spectators possessed by a single passion, burning with the same gambling fever, as they watched these animals whose galloping hooves were carrying off millions with them. The crowd jostled and pushed, fists clenched and mouths gaping, every man for himself, and every man whipping on the horse of his choice with voice and gesture. And the cry of the multitude, the cry of a wild beast reappearing in a frock-coat, grew more and more distinct:

'Here they come! Here they come! Here they come!'

Nana was still gaining ground, and as Valerio II fell back, she went into the lead, with Spirit two or three necks behind. The thunder of voices had increased. They were coming nearer and nearer, and a storm of oaths greeted them from the landau.

'Gee up, Lusignan, you great coward, you dirty screw! . . . Come on, Spirit! Come on, old boy! . . . That Valerio's disgusting! . . . What a nag! . . . That's the end of my ten louis! . . . There's only Nana now! Bravo, Nana! Bravo, you bitch!'

And on the seat, without realizing what she was doing, Nana

had started swaying her thighs and hips as if she were running the race herself. She kept jerking her belly forward, imagining that this was a help to the filly. With each jerk she gave a sigh of fatigue, saying in a low, anguished voice:

'Go on . . . go on . . . go on . . .'

Then the crowd witnessed a splendid sight. Price, riding in the stirrups and brandishing his whip, flogged Nana with an arm of iron. The dried-up old child with his long, hard, dead face seemed to be breathing fire. And in a burst of furious audacity and triumphant will-power, he poured his heart into the filly, picked her up and carried her forward, drenched in foam, her eyes all bloodshot. The whole field went by with a roar of thunder, taking people's breath away and sweeping the air with it, while the judge sat waiting coldly, his eye fixed on his sighting-mark. Then there was a huge burst of cheering. With a supreme effort Price had just flung Nana past the post, beating Spirit by a head.

There came a sound like the roar of a rising tide: 'Nana! Nana! Nana!' the cry rolled along, swelling with the violence of a storm, and gradually filling the horizon, from the depths of the Bois to Mont Valérien, and from the meadows of Longchamp to the plain of Boulogne. All over the public enclosure wild enthusiasm reigned, with cries of 'Long live Nana! Long live France! Down with England!' The women waved their parasols; men leapt and spun around, shouting and cheering; while others, with shouts of nervous laughter, threw their hats in the air. And from the other side of the course, the weighing-in enclosure responded, as emotion swept through the stands, although nothing was really visible but a trembling of the air, like the invisible flame of a brazier above that living mass of little disjointed figures, with waving arms and black dots which were eyes and open mouths. Far from dying down the noise swelled, beginning again at the end of the distant avenues, among the common people camping under the trees, and spreading until it reached its climax in the emotion of the imperial stand, where the Empress herself had applauded. 'Nana! Nana! Nana!' the cry rose in the glorious sunshine, whose golden rain beat down on the dizzy heads of the crowd.

At that, Nana, standing tall and erect on the seat of her landau, imagined that it was she whom they were applauding. For a moment she had stood motionless, stupefied by her triumph, gazing at the course as it was invaded by such a dense flood of people that the grass was hidden from sight beneath a sea of black hats. Then when all these people had come to a halt, leaving a lane as far as the exit, and applauding Nana again as she went off with Price lying exhausted and drained of energy on her neck, she slapped her thighs hard, forgetting herself completely, and triumphing in a succession of crude phrases.

'God, it's me, you know! . . . God, what marvellous luck!'

And not knowing how to give expression to her overwhelming joy, she hugged and kissed little Louis, whom she had just discovered high in the air on Bordenave's shoulder.

EMILE ZOLA, *Nana*

*Nana's presence at the races would appear to confirm Ovid's first rule of racecourse attendance, 'Nec te nobilium fugiat certamen equorum' – never miss a good race meeting. His reason? The 'Ars Amatoria': it was the best place to pick up a lover. Twenty centuries later and Jeffrey Bernard is complaining there are no longer beautiful women at the races, and this from a man who has practised the Ars Amatoria in the ditch of the Pond fence at Sandown. What satisfied Ovid, Nana and Bernard infuriated a second Roman author, Dio Chrysostom who, in the third century AD, noted his fellow racegoers were:*

'. . . constantly leaping and raving and beating one another and using abominable language and often reviling even the gods themselves, flinging their clothing at the charioteers and sometimes even departing naked from the arena. One need only throw bread and give a spectacle of horses, since they have no interest in anything else. When they enter a stadium they lose all consciousness of their former state and are not ashamed to do anything that occurs to them.'

*May it never change.*

# ACKNOWLEDGEMENTS

The publishers would like to thank the following:

The National Horseracing Museum for the jacket illustration, 'The Life of a Thoroughbred' by John Alfred Wheeler (1821-1877) – Timeform for *St Paddy*. This essay is taken from the Timeform 'Racehorses' annual which, for half a century, has provided a definitive record of the flat-racing year, dealing individually with every horse seen out in Britain, plus the best horses from overseas. The 'Racehorses' annual is published each March by Portway Press Ltd., Halifax, West Yorkshire HX1 1XE to whom grateful acknowledgement is made for permission to reproduce this extract – Constable Publishers for the extract from *It Comes Up Mud* and *All Horse Players Die Broke* from *On Broadway Collection* by Damon Runyon – *At Grass* by Philip Larkin is reprinted from *The Less Deceived* by permission of The Marvell Press, England and Australia – Reed Books for the extract from *The Brigadier* by John Hislop – J. A. Allen & Co. Ltd for extracts from *Men and Horses I Have Known* by George Lambton and *The Druids Lodge Confederacy* by Paul Matthieu – The Duke of Devonshire for the extract from *Park Top* – Headline Book Publishing Ltd for the extracts from *Hitting The Turf: A Punter's Life* by David Ashforth – Lady Rosebery for the poems by Lord Arthur Rosebery – The extracts from *Talking Horses* by Jeffrey Bernard © 1987 are reprinted by permission of Fourth Estate Ltd – William Heinemann and Simon Barnes for the extract from *Horse Sweat and Tears* by Simon Barnes – Susan Gallier and Stanley Paul (Random House) for the extract from *One of the Lads* – John Murray for the poem *Upper Lambourne* by John Betjeman from *Collected Poems* – Penguin Books Ltd and Dick Francis for the extract from *Break In* by Dick Francis (Michael Joseph 1985) – To George T Sassoon for the poem *What The Captain Said At The Point-To-Point* by Siegfried Sassoon – To A. P. Watt Ltd on behalf of The National Trust for *The Broken Link Handicap* by Rudyard Kipling – Random House UK Ltd for the story *My Old Man* from *The First 49 Stories* by Ernest Hemingway – The extract from *Money* by Martin Amis is reprinted by permission of the Peters Fraser & Dunlop Group Ltd – *Punch* for the extract from *Boswell the Optimist* by E. P. White – Faber and Faber Ltd and Guy Griffith and Michael Oakeshott for the extract from *A Guide to the Classics* – The extract from *The Best of Beachcomber* is reprinted by permission of the Peters & Dunlop Group Ltd on behalf of The Estate of J. B. Morton – The Observer for *Jonjo and the Run of a Lifetime* by H. McIlvanney – The Churchill Estate for extracts from letters and diary entries of Winston Churchill – David Higham Associates for the extract from *Brighton Rock* by Graham Greene (Heinemann) – Macmillan General Books for the extract from *A Licence to Print Money* by Jamie Reid – A. P. Watt Ltd on behalf of Michael Yeats for the poem *At Galway Races* from *The Collected Poems of W. B. Yeats* – Winston S. Churchill for permission to quote from *The Letters of Sir Winston Churchill* – The extract from *Vile Bodies* by Evelyn Waugh is reprinted by kind permission of The Peters Fraser & Dunlop Group Ltd – Elizabeth Campbell Golding and Richard Marsh for the extract from *Racing With The Gods* by Marcus Marsh.

While every effort has been made to trace author and copyright holders of material, it was not possible in all cases to do so.